D1617511

An Admiral for America

New Perspectives on Maritime History and Nautical Archaeology

Florida A&M University, Tallahassee
Florida Atlantic University, Boca Raton
Florida Gulf Coast University, Ft. Myers
Florida International University, Miami
Florida State University, Tallahassee
University of Central Florida, Orlando
University of Florida, Gainesville
University of North Florida, Jacksonville
University of South Florida, Tampa
University of West Florida, Pensacola

New Perspectives on Maritime History and Nautical Archaeology
James C. Bradford and Gene A. Smith, Series Editors

An Admiral for America

Sir Peter Warren, Vice Admiral of the Red, 1703–1752

∽

Julian Gwyn

Foreword by James C. Bradford and
Gene A. Smith, Series Editors

University Press of Florida
Gainesville · Tallahassee · Tampa · Boca Raton
Pensacola · Orlando · Miami · Jacksonville · Ft. Myers

Copyright 2004 by Julian Gwyn
Printed in the United States of America on recycled, acid-free paper
All rights reserved

09 08 07 06 05 04   6 5 4 3 2 1

Library of Congress Cataloging-in-Publication Data
Gwyn, Julian.
An admiral for America : Sir Peter Warren, Vice Admiral of the Red,
1703–1752 / Julian Gwyn ; foreword by James C. Bradford and Gene A. Smith.
p. cm. – (New perspectives on maritime history and nautical archaeology)
Includes bibliographical references and index.
ISBN 0-8130-2709-8 (alk. paper)
1. Warren, Peter, Sir, 1703–1752. 2. Great Britain–History, Naval–18th
century. 3. Admirals–Great Britain–Biography. 4. United States–History–
King George's War, 1744–1748. 5. Louisbourg (N.S.)–History–Siege, 1745.
I. Title. II. Series.
DA87.1.W35G89   2004
973.2'6–dc22
[B]   2003066572

The University Press of Florida is the scholarly publishing agency
for the State University System of Florida, comprising Florida A&M
University, Florida Atlantic University, Florida Gulf Coast University, Florida
International University, Florida State University, University of Central
Florida, University of Florida, University of North Florida, University
of South Florida, and University of West Florida.

University Press of Florida
15 Northwest 15th Street
Gainesville, FL 32611-2079
http://www.upf.com

Contents

For Clare,

and to the memory of our beloved son,

John Joseph (1967–1969)

〜

Foreword

Water is unquestionably the most important natural feature on earth. By volume, the world's oceans compose 99 percent of the planet's living space; in fact, the surface of the Pacific Ocean alone is larger than that of the total land bodies. Water is as vital to life as air. Indeed, to test whether the moon or other planets can sustain life, NASA looks for signs of water. As such, the story of human development is inextricably linked to the oceans, seas, lakes, and rivers that dominate the earth's surface. The University Press of Florida series "New Perspectives on Maritime History and Nautical Archaeology" is devoted to exploring the impact of the earth's water while providing lively and important books that cover the spectrum of maritime history and nautical archaeology broadly defined. The series includes works that focus on the role of canals, rivers, lakes, and oceans in history; on the economic, military, and political use of those waters; and upon the people, communities, and industries that support maritime endeavors. Limited by neither geography nor time, volumes in the series contribute to the overall understanding of maritime history and can be read with profit by both general readers and specialists.

Julian Gwyn's study of British Admiral Peter Warren provides a wonderful infusion of biography to this series, as he reminds us that the sea has long provided a means for individuals to achieve status and wealth. Expanding on his earlier studies, including *The Enterprising Admiral: The Personal Fortune of Admiral Sir Peter Warren* (1974) and *The Royal Navy and North America: The Warren Papers, 1736–1752* (1975), Gwyn's biography aptly describes a quintessential mid-eighteenth-century British naval hero who used his fame, position, and connections to emerge as one of the wealthiest and most powerful members of the British navy.

Born the youngest son of an indebted and declining Irish Catholic family, Peter Warren converted to the Church of England, reversed his family's financial fortunes, and influenced policymakers in London. He achieved status as a wealthy English gentleman and ultimately as a member of parliament in the most democratically elected constituency in England. Joining the navy at an early age and rising remarkably fast through the ranks, the popular and well-connected Warren secured considerable property in both England and in North America. Deeply involved in the politics of colonial New York and New England, he influenced decisions made by these colonies with both his actions and his advice. In fact, by the time he died prematurely in 1752, Warren was recognized as one of the most important officers in the British navy, holding the rank of Vice Admiral of the Red and status as one of the most influential property owners in colonial America. Despite his importance in life, with death he quickly faded from memory, becoming little more than a footnote to British naval operations in colonial North American waters.

Gwyn's biography of Warren is more than the account of an officer who effectively used his naval and political connections to climb through the ranks of the British naval hierarchy. It is a skillful analysis of the character and ambitions of a man of wide vision, who seized the opportunities that luck frequently put in his way and used them not only to realize his own goals but to further those of the American colonies. Simply stated, Warren was at the right place at the right time when he commanded naval operations in North American waters, just as the region became increasingly important to British policymakers. In fact, this study uses both the Royal Navy and Peter Warren as a lens through which to view the interconnectedness of the British North Atlantic world.

Warren served as the first commander of the British North American squadron during King George's War (the War of Austrian Succession) and was given credit for the 1745 capture of the French bastion on Cape Breton Island, Fortress Louisbourg. Warren's leadership and heroics during the British victory against the Spanish off Cape Finisterre earned him a knighthood and election to Parliament. Admiral Warren's marriage to the New York–born Susannah DeLancey and his substantial real estate investments in New York, on Manhattan Island and in the Mohawk River valley reflect the social and economic ties that bound transatlantic Anglo-Americans. His career ultimately paralleled a period in which Britain, France, and, to a lesser degree, Spain vied for hegemony over the North American continent.

Drawing on some forty years of research in Canadian, American, British, and French manuscript repositories, Gwyn demonstrates why he is qualified to write this biography. He deftly illuminates Peter Warren, interspersing his account with vignettes of Warren's life and using the experiences of Warren's career as an officer to elucidate the Royal Navy's role in the defense and expansion of British power in the North Atlantic during the middle of the eighteenth century. Through the rich detail expressed in Warren's large correspondence, Gwyn reveals and defines the influence of the North American colonies in the British decision-making process. As we follow Warren from one theater of conflict to the next, up and down America's eastern coast, Gwyn interprets both British naval history and the late American colonial period in the crucial era before the "Great War for Empire." Prior to the Seven Years' War—or, as it is better known to Americans and Canadians, the French and Indian War—the North American colonies began playing a crucial role within the British Atlantic imperial system and Warren advocated significantly on their behalf.

During his naval career Warren witnessed and, indeed, was very familiar with the issues that would serve to foment a spirit of independence in the minds of influential colonial figures, from impressment to trade regulation and the imperial Navigation Acts. In recounting Warren's story, throughout much of which runs a current of frustrated American political ambition, Gwyn astutely cultivates the soil in which the seeds of American and British discontent were beginning to take root, allowing us to catch a glimpse of the bitter harvest that would divide them within a quarter century.

James C. Bradford
Gene A. Smith
Series Editors

Preface

I first encountered Peter Warren in the summer of 1963, when I benefited from a small contract with the Fortress Louisbourg Restoration Project. My task was to uncover all the British materials available in the Public Archives of Canada in Ottawa of value to the project. Although I had a sixteen-week contract, I completed the work and rather naively submitted my report in half the time and was of course paid for eight weeks' work! It was enough time, nevertheless, to conclude that there was then little in the way of manuscripts in Ottawa—originals, transcribed, or microfilmed—of use to the project. There was much more promise, I suggested, in systematically searching for relevant manuscripts available in various United Kingdom archives, especially the Public Record Office, then still at Chancery Lane, WC1. Such manuscripts needed first to be located, then studied, microfilmed or photocopied, and sent to Canada for analysis if the restoration project and the historical interpretation were to have credibility with both scholars and the public.

It was in this context that Peter Warren began to assume some significance, for he had been the British commodore at the 1745 siege of Louisbourg and the first to command the newly formed North American squadron.

A few months later, I was invited to head a research team to be based in London for a year, in order to pursue the very suggestions outlined in my brief report of the previous summer. With permission to take an unpaid leave of absence from the Department of History at the University of Ottawa, I accepted. Armed with Crick and Almon's recently published *Guide to Manuscripts Relating to America in Great Britain and Ireland* and with weeks of work in the National Registry of Archives,[1] I discovered many collections in record offices outside London of interest to the project. Among these was a cache of Warren papers in Viscount Gage's manuscripts deposited in the Sussex Archaeological Society and at the East Sussex Record Office, both in Lewes. I inspected them carefully, but I was unable to begin work on them until I next returned to England on my first sabbatical leave in 1968–69. By then I had also learned that an earlier Viscount Gage had sold other Gage family papers to the William L. Clements Library in Ann Arbor, Michigan. Among them were four boxes of Warren family papers. At that stage I made the decision to write something substantial about Warren and a naval biography at first seemed the most obvious approach.

By November 1968 a 155-page draft manuscript had sketched his story to the end of 1746, stopping at the juncture of the aborted attack on Canada and Warren's sudden return to England without orders. As I considered the notes I had collected and the photocopies of documents surrounding me, I was drawn instead to attempt something more original: an analysis of his private fortune. One black mid-November night in Wiltshire, where I had lodged my wife and five little children, I made the decision to set aside the uncompleted naval biography and begin afresh a study of the admiral's private wealth, a completed first draft of which was ready by July 1969. The book which emerged from this study, *The Enterprising Admiral*, was published in 1974.[2] A year later, many of Warren's naval letters touching upon North America, especially for 1745–46, on which I had partly drawn for the naval biography, were used in compiling a volume for the Navy Records Society.[3]

As both of these books have long been out of print (though the Navy Records Society has reprinted its volume), I have returned to the original project conceived forty years ago: to write a biography of one of the most interesting and creative minds in the British navy in the first half of the eighteenth century. One of my motives to complete the task begun so long ago arose from two earlier attempts to chronicle his life that had been abandoned.[4] As I still retained all the necessary research materials, I now sought to avoid a third failure.

To British historians, Vice Admiral Warren, like so many other eighteenth-century naval figures, is more or less forgotten. He is never mentioned in the standard one-volume general histories of eighteenth-century Britain. Only in those general surveys that concentrated on the early Hanoverians did Warren find his way, however briefly, into the narrative.[5] He hardly fared better in naval histories and is remembered only for his connection with the 1745 siege of Louisbourg and the battle off Cape Ortegal two years later, but Louisbourg is not included among the navy's battle honors.[6] The first nearly contemporary account gave Warren full credit for his behavior at the 1747 battle.[7] In 1796 Charnock included Warren in his *Biographia Navalis;* these details were later copied in a biographical memoir, published in the *Naval Chronicle,*[8] and in John Campbell's *Naval History of Great Britain* in 1818.[9]

Warren was included in the 1899 *Dictionary of National Biography* and has entries in the *History of Parliament: House of Commons* and in the *New Oxford Dictionary of National Biography,* but notably it was historians in North America who sustained an interest in him.[10] In the nineteenth century, two individuals actually began to collect materials for a biography, but left only their notes and incomplete drafts, one to Houghton Library at Harvard,[11] and the other to the New York Public Library, where they still may be examined.[12] New York historians have remembered Warren as a prominent Manhattan landowner of what became Greenwich Village, or as the uncle of one of the most remarkable figures to emerge on the New York frontier before the revolutionary war, namely Sir William Johnson.[13] The first balanced article about him appeared in the *Dictionary of American Biography.*[14] In the 1960s Warren's political associations with the DeLancey family of New York began to be noticed.[15] New England historians never ceased singing the praises of their ancestors who besieged Louisbourg in 1745 and their numerous publications on the subject have always had something to say about Commodore Warren, yet not all of it flattering.[16] Most of these critics absurdly accuse him of having tried to steal the glory that was rightly due the colonists, when actually New England probably never had a better friend in England.

Historians of Cape Breton have always given Warren some scope.[17] Until the 1960s the singular, most detailed treatment from this perspective was penned by Sen. J. S. McLennan.[18] Through the historical research underpinning the reconstruction of part of the fortifications and town of Louisbourg, Warren, now no longer a mere shapeless historical curiosity, acquired as much flesh and bone as sources allowed.

Irish historians have wholly ignored him and his equally celebrated cousin Richard Warren, who remained a Catholic, entered French service, became a marshal of France, and ultimately in the 1760s and 1770s, as governor of Belle Isle, had much to do with some of the very Acadiens whom Peter Warren had recommended for deportation in the 1740s.[19]

My debts in preparing this book are many. It is to B. Carman Bickerton and Frederick Thorpe that I owe my first debt of thanks. By contracting with me in the summer of 1963 to work on the Fortress Louisbourg Restoration

Project they stimulated my interest in British and French colonial history. More particularly, they introduced me to Peter Warren and later allowed my curiosity to mature when they sent me to London in 1964–65. My thanks are also due to Viscount Gage, who allowed me to use the extensive Warren material that his family had deposited with the Sussex Archaeological Society and the East Sussex Record Office. I wish to thank as well the staffs of the various archives mentioned in the bibliography. Their helpful suggestions, professionalism, and kindnesses were greatly appreciated.

In helping to bring this manuscript to the light of day, I was especially dependent on the help of Carol Tobin, who typed the 1968 manuscript to disk. She also helped by proofreading the entire manuscript when completed. Her aid made my efforts a far better book than otherwise would have been the case. I cannot conclude without expressing my gratitude both to the editorial staff of the University Press of Florida for their fine professionalism and to the co-editor of the series in which this volume appears, James Bradford, for his interest and encouragement.

Abbreviations

AN   Archives Nationales, Paris
BL   British Library, London
cwt.   hundredweight = 112 lbs.
ESRO   East Sussex Record Office, Lewes
f.   folio
MHS   Massachusetts Historical Society, Boston
NB   Navy Board, London
NMM   National Maritime Museum, Greenwich
NYHS   New-York Historical Society, New York
PRO   Public Record Office, Kew
WLCL   William L. Clements Library, Ann Arbor, Mich.
$ peso or piece of eight = 5s. or £0.25 sterling
£   pound sterling = 20s. or £1
M£   Massachusetts currency par from 1749, M£133 to £100
NY£   New York currency exchanged at a rate of NY£160 to £100
NJ£   New Jersey currency in 1751 exchanged at NJ£185 to £100
SC£   South Carolina currency par from 1731, SC£700 to £100

Note: The name of a naval warship the first time she is mentioned, followed by a number in parentheses—as an example, *Vigilant* (64)—indicates the number of carriage guns she mounts.

1

Early Life and Connections, 1703–1730

Peter Warren, the future vice admiral, was born in Ireland, probably in 1703. On both parents' sides he could claim a respectable Anglo-Irish lineage. On his father's side, the earliest certain forebear was Oliver Warren of Warrenstown, County Meath, who had married Anne Lynch and whose son Peter, in July 1566, was assigned "a tower and a hall thereunto adjoining in Waringstown and 180 acres arable land, with a sufficient pasture in Waringstown and Corbaillie."[1] This first Peter Warren had a son, John, who married Mary Barnaby and inherited the family estate before he died in 1638. Among his sons was Oliver Warren, husband of Catherine Roe, who suffered confiscation of all his land when Oliver Cromwell conquered Ireland in 1651 to end a decade of Irish independence. The Warren land was recovered only in 1663 when Charles II's special court of claims, convened to hear those innocent of having being involved in the Irish rebellion of 1641, listened sympathetically to his plea and that of his mother.[2]

It was this estate, described in the 1663 judgment as containing "320 acres, three roods and eight perches," that Oliver Warren left to his son, Michael, the father of the vice admiral. In 1674 Oliver had raised the sum of £500 by giving a mortgage to Thomas Hussey, a gentleman of Culmullen, County Meath. The estate was then described as "the town and lands of Warringstown, Corbane, Ballinglassen and Moortown."[3]

Little is known of Michael Warren. A Jacobite, he held James II's commission as captain in the Royal Regiment of Infantry. He fought on behalf of his king and surrendered under the terms of the capitulation of Limerick in 1691. By these terms he was restored to his estate, which had been confiscated two years earlier through a bill of attainder against Irish Jacobites and passed by the Westminster Parliament.[4] He was attainted in 1692 and only in 1708 was he granted, upon terms that are unknown, a decree of "innocency." Around 1695 Michael Warren married Catherine, the widow of Sir Nicholas Plunkett, a brother of the Earl of Fingal. There were five surviving children, of whom Peter was the youngest.

Catherine Warren's maiden name was Aylmer, an old gentry family considerably more distinguished than the Warrens.[5] She was descended from Bartholomew Aylmer and Margaret Chevers, the parents of Sir Gerald Aylmer of Dullardstown, the chief justice of Ireland who married Alison Fitzgerald. Their son, Bartholomew, married Elinor Warren, daughter of Thomas Warren of Navan, County Meath. One of Bartholomew's sons married Margaret Plunkett. Their son, Christopher Aylmer of Balrath, in turn had a son, Gerald, a barrister who became the father of Sir Christopher Aylmer, the first Baronet of Balrath, whose wife, Margaret Plunkett, was a cousin. They were Catherine Warren's parents. Catherine had two elder brothers, Sir Gerald the second baronet, and Matthew, then one of England's most distinguished admirals and from 1718 onwards the first Baron Aylmer.

Of Peter Warren's siblings little can be said. His eldest brother, Oliver, joined the navy shortly after his father's death and was promoted lieutenant in 1719 by Adm. Sir John Norris.[6] His career came to an early end, as he died while on half-pay in 1724 living on the Warrenstown estate.[7] The next brother, Christopher, was referred to in a 1748 document as "long since dead without issue."[8] The historian of the Warren family believed that he was the Very Reverend Christopher Warren, who in 1729 had been appointed guardian of the Franciscan convent of Kildare.[9] There were two sisters, Mary and Anne, both of whom were married by 1717 when their husbands are first mentioned as parties to an agreement relating to the mortgage on Warrenstown, then still in effect. Mary married James Tyrrell, a Dublin merchant. One of their two sons, Richard, entered the navy and died with the rank of rear admiral. The younger sister married Christopher Johnson, a tenant farmer on the estate of the Earl of Fingal who lived at Smithstown, the ancient home of the Johnson family and no great distance from Warrenstown. Of their many children, the eldest— William—was born in 1717.[10] The other Johnson children were Peter Warren, John, and six daughters, the eldest of whom, Ann, married Richard Dease, the grandparent of Peter Warren Dease, the Hudson's Bay Company officer and Arctic explorer.[11]

Peter Warren's parents were Catholics and "died in that persuasion."[12] Unquestionably Warren himself had been baptized a Catholic, though the parish records are believed to have been destroyed during the 1798 uprising. Yet when he entered the British navy, like his brother before him, he conformed to the established church. In doing this, he and his eldest brother followed a course blazed by their uncle, Admiral Aylmer, who perhaps as early as 1665 had cast his lot with the established church. In 1708 two cousins, Robert and Patrick Aylmer, made a public renunciation of their old faith in order to make professional careers. Peter's father's brother, Patrick Warren, who like his father had held a commission from James II and who subsequently had been made a prisoner and attainted, recovered his position by taking the oath of conformity in 1709.[13] For his part, Peter Warren remained an active supporter of the Church of England throughout his life, endowing new churches in the colonial towns of Boston and New York and subscribing funds for the education of Protestant children in Ireland and Native American children in America. On another occasion, he attempted unsuccessfully to convince one of his nephews, John Johnson, to follow his example and that of his brother William and abandon Catholicism for the established Church of Ireland.

By the time Warren joined the navy in 1716, the family's land at Warrenstown had expanded to 433 acres. In County Meath, some twenty miles northeast of Dublin, it lay between the hamlets of Summerhill and Dunshaughlin and the ancient town of Trim. One of its boundaries ran along the banks of the Skane, a rivulet that meandered its way to the River Boyne nearby. The estate lay on the southeast slope of a shallow valley looking across to Castle Killeen, the principal seat of the earls of Fingal. A description in 1700 referred to a very good farmhouse, with barn, malt house, and stable, all thatched-roofed and mud-walled.[14] It boasted two orchards and a large walled kitchen garden, with 150 mature ash trees forming an avenue to the house and yard. All the land was arable, and then mostly under tillage, with the rest in meadow. Nearby, on the estate, was "perhaps the most remarkable of all the holy 'wells' in Meath" noted for its miraculous cure.[15] Known as St. John's Well in Warren's childhood as today, it is a scene of pilgrimage on the Feast of St. John the Baptist, when the faithful and the curious gather to drink the waters and to pray. In 1708 this well, and all others like it, became an object of concern by the Irish House of Commons. Parliament used as an excuse the impossibility of keeping the peace and public safety and prohibited pilgrimages to Warrenstown.

Peter Warren entered the navy at Dublin in April 1716 when he was not yet thirteen.[16] As with so many younger sons of the English and Irish gentry who entered the eighteenth-century British navy, nothing is known of his early formal education. As a member of a Catholic family of the gentry, he probably was tutored at home. Equally he could have been sent to the nearest school supported by the Protestant gentry for his instruction in reading, writing, and arithmetic—skills he clearly needed when he entered the navy. There was nothing found in his surviving correspondence to indicate an exceptional education or even a particularly good one. His style was repetitious and his letters largely unplanned. He had little interest in the paragraph and allowed his sentences to escape his control frequently. He carried the abbreviations of his logs and accounts into his letters. He had far less interest in spelling than most of his fellow sea officers whose official letters survive, and he tended to spell phonetically. Nor did any of his secretaries excel as stylists or grammarians. In some ways his education perhaps began with his entry in the navy. Though many ships then had schoolmasters on board, none were mustered on the first ships that Warren joined. Whatever instruction he received came from ships' officers, gunners, boatswains, and their mates. From them he learned the arts of sailing and navigation, essential to his promotion to the quarterdeck.

His active life at sea lasted thirty-two years, from 1716 to 1748, during which time he was almost continuously employed. If the last decade was one of constant danger, with Britain at war first with Spain and later with France—its two most formidable rivals on the world's oceans, the two decades before 1739 were hardly ones of profound peace, as they have been so often characterized by historians. It would thus be erroneous to think of Warren making his way for many years in an untroubled peacetime navy.

Warren first went to sea (1715) the year Britain concluded an alliance with France, the year following the Jacobite menace that had threatened the 1702 Protestant succession and which had brought, in 1714, the Elector of Hanover to the British throne as George I. Indeed, the fear, after 1715, of further internationally supported attempts on behalf of the heirs of James II was the dominant feature of British foreign policy until the defeat of Bonnie Prince Charles in 1746 at Culloden. It was not only the Jacobite threat that worried successive British administrations, but the reverberations occasioned by the new king's active political interest in northern Europe. In 1715 the Admiralty first dispatched a fleet to the Baltic. Initially directed against Sweden and then later against Russia, successive squadrons remained in the Baltic until 1727. The death of George I that year and the accession of his son as George II, whom the Walpole ministry managed to control more ably than his father, eased the tension, although the first Anglo-Russian trade treaty was not concluded until 1734.

At all times more important than the politics of the Baltic was Britain's relationship with its principal antagonist, Spain, once France had become an ally in 1716. Hardly a year passed between 1713 and 1739 that did not witness some sharp dispute between Britain and Spain. Twice diplomatic relations were severed and hostilities ensued, first in 1718–19 then again in 1726–28. Both times the navy played a decisive part. In the first, Adm. Sir George Byng destroyed an unsuspecting Spanish fleet off Cape Passero, on the coast of Sicily, and another squadron aided the French army to invade northern Spain. In the second, a squadron under Adm. Francis Hosier blockaded the Spanish treasure fleets at Portobelo and Cartagena, while another under Adm. John Jennings cruised menacingly off the Spanish coast and gave aid to Gibraltar when the Spanish opened trenches in an abortive attempt to besiege the fortress. Even in the years of peace, the Spanish use of *guardacostas* to check English and American commercial rapacity obliged the Admiralty to maintain a strong naval squadron at Jamaica to convoy trade as in wartime. Furthermore, with the outbreak of war in Europe in 1734 over the Polish succession quarrel, Prime Minister Robert Walpole was in time forced to sanction the equipping of a fleet that was sent to Lisbon the following year to keep a watchful eye upon Spain and to act, if necessary, against the nation. In 1737 a rumor raced along the American coast of an impending attack by Spanish troops from Havana on the new colony of Georgia. Though the rumor proved false, it is against this background of international tension that Warren's career must be set.

Warren entered the navy, as his eldest brother had before him, under the protection of his maternal uncle, Admiral Aylmer. Aylmer held a lucrative appointment as governor of the Royal Hospital at Greenwich and occupied the Queen's House in the Park—his was more or less a pleasant retirement after a long and distinguished career.[17] It is likely that Peter Warren visited him there.

Warren's first ship was *Rye*, a fifth rate built in 1696.[18] When he joined her at Dublin in April 1716, Arthur Field, a captain since 1709, was in command.[19] Warren's brother, Oliver, who had served in her in 1715 as a midshipman, rejoined *Rye* at the same time. Warren found himself part of a small squadron of four frigates and a sloop patrolling the Irish Sea from Greenock to Kinsale. It was at Kinsale that *Rye* and *Tartar*, both twenty-eight guns, spent much of their time. At best, it must have been monotonous for the old hands, as the cruising proved wholly uneventful, yet perhaps exciting for the new volunteer. It was as gentle a way as possible for a young lad to be inaugurated into the routine of naval life. Most of the time was spent in port or refitting at either Plymouth or Portsmouth. At length, in August 1717, Captain Field received new orders to sail for Sheerness, refit, take on fresh provisions, and prepare to convoy the trade of the East-land Company to the Baltic. With the possibility of attack from Swedish warships—or even Russian—the task was not routine, as life off Ireland had been. Indeed, when the convoy passed through the Danish Sound, *Rye* came close to action, as Field explained in his log: "[we] saw two sail one bearing SSE the other East standing towards us; the weathermost tack'd and stood from us, we bore down to the other, who after firing two guns under Sweeds colours put afore the wind, we stood after her on glass, and then haul'd upon a wind."[20] Warren had his first experience of the tense feeling pervading a ship cleared for action. *Rye* and her convoy did not stop at Elsinore Castle nor enter Copenhagen Roads, where the fleet under Sir George Byng lay at anchor, but pressed on for Danzig, her destination. During the three weeks' stay, the weather turned bitterly cold, bringing the first snows. Only when fresh provisions of beef and pork, bread, butter, cheese, beer, and water had been taken on board did *Rye* venture forth with her return convoy into the gale-driven seas. Beyond the Danish Sound, with storms still battering the convoy, *Rye* was blown within a few ships' lengths of some breakers, barely avoiding a fate that befell far many more of His Majesty's warships than were lost by enemy action in the eighteenth century. The convoy was scattered of course, but all eventually made port, with *Rye* reaching the Nore only in the first week of January 1718. Peter Warren came ashore with the rest of the ship's company.

Warren was discharged from *Rye* and appointed four weeks later to *Rose* as a volunteer *per order,* that is, appointed by warrant of the lords commissioners of Admiralty, thus destining him for eventual promotion to commissioned rank.[21] The interval had given him time to stay with his elderly uncle, Lord Aylmer, at the Queen's House in Greenwich Park. *Rose*, a 20-gun light frigate, had returned the autumn before from two years on the New England station and was now ordered to the West Indies.

The voyage was to prove of singular importance to the young volunteer. Not only did he receive promotion to midshipman before his return home, but he formed an incurable taste for the New World, where he was destined to spend so much of his life at sea and where so many of his ambitions came to be centered.

Rose was part of a small squadron under the command of Sir Peter Chamberlen and ordered to cruise against pirates whose exploits since the end of hostilities in 1713 had become open and very bold. Chamberlen commanded *Milford,* while Capt. Thomas Whitney commanded *Rose.* The rest of the squadron consisted of the sloops *Buck* and *Shark.* When the squadron sailed in May, two transports carrying troops to the Bahamas accompanied it. Chamberlen's orders took him first to Madeira, where wine was taken on board (the beer having run out), then to Barbados, Providence Island, and the port of Nassau in the Bahamas. The newly appointed governor of the islands, Woodes Rogers, went as a passenger. Rogers had undertaken a round-the-world voyage between 1708 and 1711 and had published a celebrated account of his adventures, from which he had gained considerable wealth.[22]

The squadron arrived at its destination at a most opportune moment, for the island was in the hands of pirates who had occupied it for some time. *Rose* was the first to reach Nassau and found at anchor a 26–gun pirate ship flying the Union flag. Instead of boldly attacking the pirate ship, which had opened fire, Captain Whitney stood off until the rest of the squadron came upon the scene. That night the pirate captain set his ship afire; with the tide and wind right, it drifted toward *Rose,* forcing Whitney to cut his cables and put to sea. Under cover of night, the pirates made good their escape in another vessel. When Commodore Chamberlen came upon the scene the next morning, he ordered *Rose* to seize all the vessels in the harbor and sent his two sloops to pursue the pirate ship. Five of the vessels were found to be carrying sugar, which, when the matter came before the Vice Admiralty Court, the masters claimed the pirate captain, Charles Vane, had forced them to carry, after having had their original cargoes placed on shore.[23] The vessels had been taken in the first week of July and brought by Vane to Nassau, which Vane virtually ruled as his own possession until the unexpected arrival of *Rose* on 26 July. The masters' testimony was accepted, and they and their vessels set free, although the sugar was condemned and later sold at auction. Warren received his first share of the one-eighth salvage money awarded in these cases. Vane, for his part, was eventually apprehended in April 1721, tried, condemned, and hanged in chains.[24]

After a seven-weeks stay at Nassau, during which illness struck the squadron and left many dead, *Rose* was ordered to carry out a long cruise in search of pirates. She was to sail as far south as Hispaniola and Cuba and then swing northward along the Florida, Carolina, and Virginia coasts to New York, where Chamberlen ordered her to refit. Later, the Admiralty accused Chamberlen of making for New York purely for his own commercial interest, but this he denied, pointing out that there was nowhere in the West Indies or the Bahamas suitable for refitting his squadron and that his orders left him free to refit anywhere in the colonies he thought best. This was true in the strict sense. Port Royal, Jamaica, afforded as good facilities as were found anywhere on the North American coast. Yet New York boasted a private careening wharf at Turtle Bay on Manhattan Island. The Admiralty did not press the matter, but New York was certainly a great distance from Chamberlen's appointed cruising area and the Admiralty's suspicions were understandable. How the commodore passed his time while his ships were refitting is unknown, but the layover introduced Midshipman Warren to a colony with which he was to be closely associated.

The laborious task of refitting the squadron took until December to complete. *Rose* was heaved down in mid-November 1718, but there was so much snow and sleet the ship had to be righted for fear of capsizing. When the frigate was heaved down on her other side the spar deck exploded under the pressure, and five feet of water got into the hold. The carpenters had to fashion another, much stronger, deck before the careening process could be completed and the guns and stores again brought on board. It was unlikely that Warren got ashore and made any contacts with the burghers of New York, as Turtle Bay was quite some distance up the East River north of the then built-up town of New York.[25]

By the time Chamberlen gave the orders to unmoor and weigh anchor it was 8 December. Winter cruising in such northern latitudes, even when making for the Caribbean, always proved hard on shipping. As soon as the little squadron put to sea, it was met by a violent storm that scattered it at once, although eventually all vessels made their ports of destination safely.

Rose's passage was not without interest, for on 20 December 1718 Whitney thought he had captured a pirate. His log describes the incident: "at 4 p.m. [I] saw a sail standing to the Northward. I gave chase at 6 p.m. I came up with and told him to send his boat aboard upon which he wore and made all the sail he cou'd from me. I wore and stood after him, hailed him again, and told him we was the King's ship, being night did not believe us, I fired 2 or 3 broadsides into him, which he answer'd, I kept all the night on his weather quarter. In the morning I ran along side and told him if he did not immediately bring to, I wou'd sink him."[26] It proved to be a merchant ship from Brest bound for Cap François, precisely as she had originally identified herself. The incident illustrated the intense fear caused by pirates, for both ships believed the other to be a pirate vessel. As at that time neither English nor French seamen or sea officers wore distinctive uniforms and many a pirate vessel resembled a British frigate, it is not surprising that the ships of England and France, though allied, should fire

upon each other. Moreover, the early dusk of a winter evening made iden-
tification even more difficult. Whitney must have been somewhat chas-
tened by his error, for throughout the rest of his tour of duty he never
again acted with such boldness.

Before reaching Jamaica in mid-January 1719, Whitney took *Rose* into
Petit Goâve Bay off the French part of Hispaniola. It was one of those rare
moments in the eighteenth century when an English warship could, without anxiety, put into a French base. There he learned of the worsening
relations between England and Spain and of the threat of war. A fortnight
later at Port Royal, Jamaica, news of the outbreak of war was confirmed.
Though Chamberlen's squadron, reinforced by the frigates *Diamond* and
Ludlow Castle, was well placed to raid Spanish shipping, few prizes fell to
it. In none of these did *Rose* have a share. Chamberlen, while receiving the
usual orders to attack Spanish shipping should he come across it, was given
no encouragement to mount a raid on any Spanish possession, and he took
no initiative of this kind. On the contrary, he, together with the governor
and council of Jamaica, felt that the island was open to attack by the Spanish. The Spanish, had they planned such a maneuver, might not have found
their task too difficult, for the commodore utterly failed to work harmoni-
ously with Gov. Nicholas Lawes. Despite the fact that Chamberlen's orders required him to consult with the governor and council, he used a variety of excuses to avoid giving them any ideas of his plans or the disposition
of his ships, for, as he explained to the Admiralty when sending copies of
his correspondence with the governor, "notices of that kind gather so
much air as to be very early communicated to the prejudices of the cruises,
especially if design'd upon pirates there being (I fear) too many friends
to them at Port Royal and other parts of Jamaica."[27] Though the governor and council made very specific suggestions about the disposition of the
squadron, Chamberlen remained uncooperative. Relations improved only
late in 1719 when the Admiralty sent Capt. Edward Vernon in the 60–gun
Mary to take command of the Jamaica squadron. *Milford,* on her passage
to England with Chamberlen still in command, was lost at sea with all her
crew.

In the meantime, *Rose* was occupied in escorting merchant vessels between Jamaica and the Bahamas. In the summer of 1719 one such convoy
was briefly becalmed off the Cuban coast, and two of the merchant ships
were taken by Spanish galleys. *Rose* was powerless to intervene. The wind
then came up, and the rest of the convoy made the safety of Nassau. There
Rose made a lengthy if unrewarding cruise against Spanish shipping along

the Florida coast and into the Gulf of Mexico before returning to Jamaica. With the arrival of Vernon in *Mary,* Captain Whitney received orders from the Admiralty to leave the Jamaica station for Antigua, taking with him the sloop *Shark,* commanded by George Pomeroy. Here too his responsibilities were largely those of convoying merchantmen. On one such voyage to Boston, *Rose* encountered a furious storm that sank several merchantmen and wreaked havoc among the rest. It was a rough introduction to a part of the coast with which Warren would later become so very familiar.

Upon Captain Whitney's return to English Harbour, Antigua, he learned of an unsuccessful attempt by the Spanish to seize New Providence. Twice in 1721 Captain Whitney followed up reports of the presence of pirates in the Leeward Islands, but none were found. Whitney only remarked to the Admiralty that the English islands were "much pestered with French traders who want our provisions, the southern parts of France being locked from them by reason of the plague."[28]

At length, he received orders to return to England with the trade in August. Though he called in at several islands, no ships were ready for England, so he sailed home alone.[29] After an unremarkable passage—except for enduring the tail end of a hurricane that shredded the mizzen shrouds, carrying away the mizzen mast and breaking the main yard—*Rose* reached Spithead in mid-October 1721.

Warren had by this time been at sea for more than six years. Since 1703 regulations had required that a midshipman spend at least four years at sea before attempting his examination for promotion to lieutenant. On 5 December 1721, Warren was examined before three sea officers. The journals he had kept in *Rye* and *Rose* were read by the examiners, and the eighteen-year-old was judged fit for promotion, having displayed his ability "to splice, knot, reef a sail, work a ship in sailing—keep reckoning of a ship by plain sailing and Mercator, observe by sun or star, find the variation of the compass, [and] shift his tides . . ."[30] As promotion was not automatic on passing the examination, Warren had to await appointment to a new ship.

While anticipating such a vacancy, he spent part of the winter with his widowed mother and his relations in Ireland and the remainder with the family of Adm. Sir John Norris, whose home was at Hempstead Park near Rye.[31] Norris now assumed the role of Warren's patron, after the death of Matthew Lord Aylmer in August 1720. Norris, probably of Irish heritage, entered the navy in 1680 as a captain's servant. Seven years later he became a midshipman; two years after that a lieutenant; the next year, in

1690, a post captain. Appointed a rear admiral in 1707, he became admiral two years later. He was first elected to Parliament in 1708 and continued to serve as a member until his death. Married to the daughter of the late Lord Aylmer, admiral of the fleet, Norris did not lack appointments. He commanded the Baltic squadron at a time of acute tension there in 1715–16, 1719–21, and again in 1727. Beginning in 1718 and for twelve years thereafter he served on the Admiralty Board.

Parliament voted money supplies for fewer seamen in 1722 than at any time in living memory, yet Norris found young Warren a ship that spring. She was *Guernsey*, a 50–gun ship of the line, and the smallest ship to bear that title. She had orders to prepare for a cruise on the western coast of Africa, both to protect the trade against pirate attacks and to maintain the British naval presence in rivalry with the French and Dutch. Since at least 1673 the navy had patrolled the west coast of Africa with some regularity. At the request of merchants, single vessels were usually sent there for a few months almost every year from the River Gambia to the then northern borders of Angola. During the years of war, two ships were usually sent, though in 1707–9 none could be spared.[32] With peace restored in 1713, the patrols were discontinued and were not revived until 1720. The appeals of the merchants trading in Africa for protection against pirates obliged the Admiralty to fit out a ship. The first successes against the pirates came in 1721, when Capt. Chaloner Ogle and Capt. Mungo Herdman captured three pirate vessels, bringing Ogle the reward of a knighthood of the Bath.[33]

In 1722 it was *Guernsey*'s turn. Her captain, Francis Percy, had spent several months on the West African station in 1712 when commanding *Tiger* (48). His first lieutenant, Thomas Willcocks, also had experienced the then much-feared West African climate two years earlier in *Lynn*. Percy's orders forbade him to trade, but he was permitted to accept "such gold & elephant teeth as shall be offer'd you" by masters of merchant vessels that he escorted.[34]

Guernsey sailed from Spithead late in August and reached Gambia in two months, after a stop at Madeira to take on wine. Percy conferred with the governor of the company fort at the River Gambia, but received no reports of pirates.[35] With provisions of fresh meat and water on board, *Guernsey* sailed southwards to Frenchman's Bay on the coast of Sierra Leone and called in at the company factory in a further attempt to get information about pirates. None was reported, and so it continued throughout *Guernsey*'s tour of duty, which lasted until March 1723.

As it turned out, danger came not from pirates but from the Africans. At

Cape Mesurado, on what was known as the Grain Coast at the mouth of the Saint Paul River, the next stop south of Sierra Leone, *Guernsey* was involved in a serious incident, the cause of which became a matter of controversy. Cape Mesurado was then known only as a place for mariners to secure fresh water and firewood although slaves were occasionally taken. As it afforded poor anchorage, it never became a center of trade, while contacts between Africans and Europeans were few. The Dutch maintained a temporary post only at Cape Mount up the coast toward Sierra Leone, but "no permanent station is recorded upon the entire length of the Grain Coast."[36] Contemporary published accounts rarely refer to the coast,[37] yet Captain Percy and his two senior lieutenants maintained that the Africans had attacked some of the crew without provocation on the fourth day while the seamen were cutting and collecting firewood.

Percy's log merely noted:

> as my barge, yawl, & longboat was coming out of Mesurado River, were attack'd by the negroes with a fire of small arms from the bushes on both sides of the river; wounded two men in my yawl, killed three, and wounded seven in the longboat, boarded & took her. My Lord James Hay 3rd lieut. went back in the yawl to demand my people & boat, to know the reason of such treatment, He no sooner came within their fire but they shot him in the breast & through the thigh, boarded the yawl took her and all the people. The next day they sent a canoe off with my surgeon's 2nd mate with an exorbitant demand for their ransom which tho' I complete with; yet did not send me one man; but a demand three times as great, which to save the poor peoples lives, I was forced to comply with so far as in my power.[38]

Twenty-eight of the crew had been made prisoner; Percy ransomed them over the next two days for twenty-one barrels of powder and one hundred muskets. Lord James Hay died of his wounds, and in his place Peter Warren was promoted lieutenant. No court martial was held to look into the matter when *Guernsey* eventually returned to England. Despite his lengthy protests, Percy's pay was reduced by £68 5s. to cover the cost of the powder and small arms used for ransom.[39] Percy informed the Admiralty that in 1712 he had taken on firewood and fresh water there "without any molestation, tho' our men lay on shore nine or ten nights successfully cutting wood."[40] He blamed the change in the Africans on "our Bristol and Liverpool ships, carrying their people away, when they go on board to trade." Percy's career was ruined. From 1724 until he died in reduced circumstances in 1741 he was given command on only three occasions and then for just a few weeks each time.[41]

The Admiralty limited its concern to accounting for the stores used as ransom, for which it was accountable to the Board of Ordnance. There the matter would have ended except that upon Percy's death a quite different account was provided by one of Lord Hay's servants, Edward Dixon. A very detailed signed statement, it must have been prepared years earlier and only sent to the Hay family when news of Percy's approaching death was made known. Dixon's statement agreed with many of the details provided by Percy, but it was far fuller; none of it out of character with Percy's own account, which of course Dixon had never seen. It was in its interpretation that Dixon's account so greatly differed from Percy's. Whereas Percy blamed English traders for slaving and so igniting the hostility of the Africans, Dixon claimed that not only was Percy deeply involved in trading, contrary to Admiralty orders, but also that the real cause of the incident arose from Percy's failure to secure permission to cut wood along the river's banks before he sent in his party. Dixon asserted that Percy temporarily lost control of himself and blundered badly. Percy's log and those of his lieutenants claim the incident took place on the first day off the river's mouth, yet Percy's later letters refer to the fourth day, not the first. Dixon's account states that matters came to a boil on the second day of trading. Before that, Dixon stated that Lord Hay while ashore had been the center of attention from the African king, who made him a present of a young boy. While Dixon, a former guardsman, agreed with Percy's description of Lieutenant Hay's wounds, Dixon claimed that his master died within three days of being returned to *Guernsey*. By contrast, Percy stated that Lord Hay died some six weeks after he sustained his wounds. Even so, it is somewhat difficult to understand how in the heat of tropical West Africa a man could survive more than a few days from the grievous wounds he received: a ball through his right arm, another through his left thigh bone near the groin, and a third striking his left leg. There is no accounting for this serious discrepancy, for both Percy and Dixon were eyewitnesses to most of the events each described, while other details must have been provided to them separately by Lieutenant Hay, after his release, and by the recovered seamen. There is not enough evidence to prove either man false, though Percy's need to protect his reputation against the charge of illegal trading or incompetence gave him every reason to doctor his log, to require conformity from his lieutenants, and to act as if such an incident was not unexpected upon such an inhospitable coast.[42]

By Dixon's account, Percy traded some small arms for gold dust and had dined ashore with the two chiefs representing the coastal area. Dixon, on the third day, erected two tents on shore, and on the next day food and drink were sent from the ship, upon Percy's invitation to the chiefs to dine with him. Afterwards, while Percy continued to trade, one of the chiefs invited Lord Hay to accompany him in a canoe. Upon his return he brought with him a black child, a present from the chief. Hay later told Dixon that the chief had also offered him the services of one of his wives, which he had declined, whereupon a working party broke up the camp. The next day Percy ordered the working party together with some passengers, including one as interpreter, to man the longboat upriver to cut and fetch firewood. The ship's barge was again used to land the captain and Lord Hay, with Dixon on board. Presents were exchanged by Hay and one of the chiefs. Yet the other chief scowled at Percy on several occasions. The cause of the enmity was obscure though the chiefs subsequently called Percy a "pickerrine" or great rogue, and it set Percy "swearing and cursing . . . like a mad man."

Shortly thereafter a large number of Africans unexpectedly emerged from the forest and ran along the beach to cut off the party from their boat. Lord Hay ordered the seamen and Dixon, who were all carrying arms, to form line and fire at them. The Africans then retreated but were soon joined by a much larger body of warriors, yet only after the party under Hay had made its escape. The Africans then turned toward the riverbank to fire at the longboat, which was making its way back to the ship. The long-boat's crew were made prisoners, stripped naked, and carried into the woods out of sight of the ship.

When the landing party arrived and regrouped on board *Guernsey*, Lord Hay manned the yawl and returned with a crew of only six men to show the Africans that they came in truce. Having rested on their oars just out of range of the muskets, Hay began to negotiate with those on shore. As soon as the vessel ran onto the beach, the Africans fired into the boat, grievously wounding and overpowering the rest of the crew, who were dragged ashore and secured with the survivors of the longboat's crew. With night fast approaching, the ship's crew voiced grievances against the cap-tain, on whose shoulders they placed the full blame for the disaster.

Early the next morning a coasting vessel happened on the scene, and its master assured Percy that one of the chiefs had a powerful enemy farther down the coast whom he believed could be induced to help Percy out of his predicament. Weighing anchor and unbending the sails, the ship slowly got under way. The Africans on shore reacted by lighting a bonfire as a signal to parley and sent off two canoes, in one of which was the surgeon's mate, who was left to rejoin his ship. He brought with him proposals, drawn up by the interpreter on behalf of the Africans, for the return of the surviving prisoners. The proposals were effected later that day with Hay the last to be released. Because Warren's name was never mentioned throughout the week, we may presume that he remained on board *Guernsey*.

From Mesurado, *Guernsey* made all sail for Dixcove, the Brandenburg fort then ruled by the Ashanti chief, John Couny. Percy was granted leave to take on fresh water after paying Couny an ounce of gold. At the Dutch fortress of Elmina and at Cape Coast Castle, Percy told the tale of his angry reception at Mesurado. What advice he received is not recorded. From the governor of the English fort he was able to purchase a longboat to replace the one the Africans had cleverly seized.

Percy avoided possible trouble at Cabo Lopez de Gonsalvez, the next place he tried to get water, by sailing off when the Africans demanded £50 for the privilege. Percy made for São Tomé, the most important of the Portuguese islands in the Gulf of Benin, where, after a visit on board *Guernsey* by the governor and the Catholic bishop, both water and firewood were purchased.[43] When he returned to the mainland, Percy again received a rebuff from the Africans, this time at the Sassandra River. Percy complained in his log that they had been "very rude to my officer."[44] For water Percy had to have recourse again to Cape Coast Castle.

Percy's orders had instructed him to return to England by way of the West Indies, the usual route for ships on the Guinea coast. It was from Cape Coast Castle in March 1723 that *Guernsey* began her passage to Barbados. By then her crew was very sickly; thirty-four had died from disease on the African coast and another twenty passed away before Barbados was reached. Of the rest, only one in three was fit for duty, so that by the time the ship reached Jamaica in early June the ship was hardly capable of being sailed.

Peter Warren did not accompany *Guernsey* when she left for England. At Jamaica he transferred to the 50–gun *Falkland*, as third lieutenant, under Commodore Barrow Harris, who commanded the Jamaica squadron based at Port Royal. The rest of the squadron consisted of *Adventure* (40) commanded by Thomas Davers, *Winchelsea* (20) under Ellis Brand's command, and the sloop *Spence*, commanded by Sir Yelverton Peyton. *Guern-*

sey had been on this station since 1721, when she had conveyed the new governor of the Leeward Islands, John Hart, Esquire, with his servants and equipage.

Off Jamaica the squadron had to deal not only with the menace of pirates but with Spanish armed vessels that repeatedly attacked British and colonial shipping. Harris had appealed to London for permission to attack these raiders, but was granted leave by limited rules of engagement to act only in a manner that would give the Spanish no just cause for complaint.[45]

Harris had been specifically instructed not to meddle in trade, as there had been frequent complaints laid before the Admiralty of naval ships that had "taken on board merchants' goods and proceeded therewith in trading manner from one port to another . . . for the sake of their private interest."[46] In a period of increased tension with Spain, Harris also had been directed not to provoke the Spanish but to try and catch the piratical Spanish *guardacostas*.[47]

Warren had not seen Port Royal since the summer of 1720, and great changes had come over the town. It had been heavily battered by a hurricane the previous August and most of the houses and other buildings had been destroyed. The plantations had also suffered greatly, and even after many months the damage had not been repaired.[48]

This tour, his second in the West Indies, lasted two and a half years. As before, Warren's time was largely spent in cruising among the islands: off Jamaica, Cuba, Hispaniola, the Leeward Islands, and Barbados. Though it was at all times a period of considerable tension with Spain, war did not actually break out until after *Falkland* had returned to England in the spring of 1726. Despite the numerous reports of pirates and of raids by the Spanish *guardacostas,* the squadron had few encounters and *Falkland* none at all.

Relations between the sea officers and the governor and council of Jamaica had not been good when Warren was first in the West Indies with Commodore Chamberlen in command; they were no better between the new governor, the Duke of Portland, and Commodore Harris. The duke complained to Secretary of State Lord Carteret that the sea captains meddled in trade, contrary to their orders and to the great discouragement of the merchants. Though the captains had stopped the practice of using the ships under their own command to carry merchandise, they had apparently begun hiring or purchasing sloops in their own names. Portland accused them of then using their own seamen, without cost to themselves, to man the trading vessels and "go from place to place with the sloops that are their own a-tradeing, and when they have done come into harbor again, 'till they supply themselves with fresh goods."[49] Moreover, although Harris was expressly instructed to consult the governor and council of Jamaica in laying plans to deal with pirates and the threat of Spanish depredations, like Chamberlen before him, he was exceedingly reluctant to take civilians into his confidence. An interesting aspect to this episode begs the question of the purity of Portland's motives in exposing the conflict of interest of the sea officers engaging in trade when his own interest in governorship in the islands was purported to be to recoup losses he incurred in the South Seas Bubble investment fiasco.[50]

Harris did not survive the homeward passage when, in March 1726, *Falkland* was replaced by *Dragon*. Harris died on Lady Day and was buried at sea.[51] Command fell to Peter Warren, who had been promoted second lieutenant in December 1724 and then first lieutenant in March 1725.[52] Despite much sickness on board and several more deaths, Warren managed to bring the ship to a safe anchorage off Spithead late in April. It had been his first brief command; he was then twenty-two.

After the ship was paid off and laid up, Warren went home to Ireland on half-pay and remained unemployed for more than a year. His time was spent on domestic concerns. His eldest brother, Oliver, who had also set out on a naval career, had died in August 1724, while on half-pay in Ireland. Because he had died unmarried, the family estate passed to the next brother, Christopher. While Peter Warren was home on leave, his mother died. She had made her will in August 1725, died a year later, and was buried next to her husband in the parish of Knockmark, near Warrenstown.[53]

Warren's next naval appointment was to the fireship *Griffin,* on 28 May 1727, as she lay at Copenhagen.[54] She was the smallest vessel in a squadron sent to the Baltic under the command of Sir John Norris. Warren had accompanied the fleet as a passenger on board the flagship *Cornwall.* When the commander of the fireship, the Hon. James Cornwallis, suddenly took ill and died, Norris appointed Warren in his place, with the prospect of a more suitable command in the near future. Advancement came almost at once. On 17 June 1727, news reached the fleet that George I had died at Osnabruck on his way to Hanover from England, six days before. Norris at once selected Captain Vernon, commander of the 70–gun *Grafton,* to leave for London to carry an address of loyalty from the entire

Baltic fleet to the new king.[55] To succeed Vernon, Norris appointed Warren, who took command on 19 June.

To mark the death of the king and the accession of his son as George II, the fleet, following Admiral Norris's lead, struck all colors and pennants in the evening and hoisted them to half-mast the next day. Then the admiral, in *Cornwall*, began to fire his great guns at half-minute intervals. This was taken up by Vice Admiral Sir George Walton in *Captain*, by Rear Admiral Richard Hughes in *Hampton*, and then by the entire fleet until noon. Then, again following *Cornwall*, the fleet spread its colors and fired volleys of small arms. The next day, all officers went aboard *Cornwall* to swear allegiance to the new king.

The fleet, which had sailed from the Nore on the last day of April, had been resting at anchor off Copenhagen since the middle of May. It had been designed against Russia, though no state of war between Russia and Britain existed. George I's ambitions in northern Europe appeared to be threatened by Tsar Peter as the power and ambition of Russia grew. Britain had first sent a fleet to the Baltic in 1715, ostensibly to protect its trade against Sweden, but as the Swedish war with Russia moved against Sweden, Britain's policy vacillated and at length sought to contain the new giant—the Russia of Peter the Great. Since the tsar's widow and successor, Catherine I, continued his policy and maintained the newly built Russian fleet in a fair state of preparedness after Tsar Peter's death in 1724, the tension with Britain had not greatly diminished. By the summer of 1727, Catherine too was dead and her successor, the boy-tsar Peter II, presented no menace to Baltic trade. All the news that reached Norris confirmed the view that there was no plan to outfit the Russian fleet that season and thus the need to penetrate further into the Baltic had evaporated. Before the end of July, Norris sailed past Elsinore Castle, through the Danish Sound, and returned home.

It had not been a summer of naval glory, but for Warren it marked a new and important phase in his career. Patronage had carried him to the rank of post captain at an early age and patronage would thereafter find him employment in the lean years, yet only his own ability and the accumulation of seniority would bring him an admiral's flag. Until then, as captain he wielded "powers almost of life and death over his whole company."[56]

From the Baltic, after the squadron's brief refit at Portsmouth, Warren found himself dispatched with several of Norris's fleet to the Mediterranean. In February 1727 the Spanish fleet had begun to besiege Gibraltar, while the British had dispatched a squadron under Admiral Hosier to intercept the treasure fleet and trade in the West Indies and another squadron to prey on Spanish shipping on the coasts of Spain.

Peace preliminaries were concluded in April 1728, and Warren was chosen to carry the news to the squadron under Commodore Edward St. Lo at Jamaica.[57] He gave up command of *Grafton* on 4 April and transferred to the frigate *Solebay*. After three weeks' preparation the frigate put to sea on 24 April under cloudy skies and a fresh southwesterly wind.[58] Five weeks later Warren sighted Antigua, but because his orders took him to Jamaica he bore away without coming into St. John's harbor. After six more days at sea *Solebay* reached Port Royal; here the ship saluted the commodore with fifteen guns. After conferring with St. Lo, Warren continued his passage to Vera Cruz with a packet for the Viceroy of Mexico. It took him three weeks to make the thousand-mile voyage. Off the harbor Warren sent his lieutenant ashore in the pinnace for a pilot. When safely at anchor, *Solebay* greeted the governor with a nine-gun salute when he came aboard to consult with Warren.

Warren's task was to see to the release of English officers and crew as well as two South Sea ships, *Prince Frederick* and *Princess Austina.* His stay at Vera Cruz lasted six weeks and was memorable not only for the hospitable manner in which the governor treated him, but by the fact that his crew began to sicken. His orders took him then took him to Havana; fifteen of his men had died by the time he made that port. Warren dared not set foot on shore for fear of contracting further disease but corresponded instead with the island's governor by means of the pinnace. In Havana he took on board several English seamen who had been made prisoner after being shipwrecked off the Florida coast. He next made for Charleston but was battered by a mighty hurricane before reaching the security of that port late in September. The mainsail split and blew away, then the mizzen mast had to be cut away, followed by the main and foretopmast, with the topsail yards and sails, the topgallant masts, and studding sails before the wind abated. Warren then had only to face a "great sea." At last on 26 September, *Solebay* came to anchor off the South Carolina coast and sent into Charleston for a pilot before sailing into Cooper River.

A lengthy stop in South Carolina was needed to repair *Solebay*'s masts and rigging. At Charleston Warren found the two commanders of the station ships *Guarland* and *Fox,* Capt. George Anson and Capt. Thomas Arnold, who occupied themselves by cruising off the coast and in preparing a detailed plan of Port Royal in the Bahamas.[59] It introduced Warren to Anson, a man whom he would in time call his friend and upon whose patronage much would later depend. Moreover he encountered a colony where he would spend more than a few months on another occasion.

Only in January 1729, after four months at anchor, with fresh provisions on board and dispatches to the Admiralty and the Lords of Trade from the sea officers and governor, did Warren again put to sea.[60] The rough winter weather soon took its toll on *Solebay*'s rigging, which once again was "pretty much shattered" by the time she reached Spithead in mid-February.[61] There Warren received orders to sail for Deptford and pay off the ship.

After only a fortnight's leave Warren was named to the command of the 50–gun *Leopard,* then completing her refit at Woolwich. Warren was not well and many of his crew were also sickly. In May he felt obliged to ask the Admiralty for ten or twelve days' leave to go into the country to recover his health.[62] He left his officers with orders to complete the ship's company by impressment, and they promptly pounced on the crews of two Levant Company ships just out of quarantine. On 10 June *Leopard* was ordered to sail from the Nore with *Portland, Burford,* and *Winchester* to join Sir Charles Wager's squadron at Spithead.[63] There *Leopard* lay for the rest of the year, except for a few weeks' cruise in September to the Dutch coast to escort the king safely back to England from Hanover.[64] Late in December Warren's ship was ordered to be paid off.[65]

Peter Warren's career to this point conformed to the developing pattern of a professional corps of sea officers.[66] He came of gentry stock. His promotion to lieutenant's rank depended both on adequate sea time and his ability to pass an examination. He enjoyed patronage among flag officers, which brought him early promotion to post captain's rank and almost regular employment in peacetime. Yet with prolonged peace further promotion was almost as unlikely as employment. The making of a fortune, a possibility in wartime only, was certainly out of reach. Thus, by the end of 1729 at the age of twenty-six, Warren perhaps counted himself blessed for the experiences he had undergone thus far in the navy and the skills he had thereby acquired. Yet, like all his brother officers below flag rank, so long as peace continued his future as a sea officer seemed anything but secure.

North America

First Taste of War, 1730–1740

To his surprise and delight, instead of lingering on four shillings a day on half-pay, Warren was almost immediately employed. After three weeks' leave, Warren was appointed to command the station ship at New York, the small frigate *Solebay* on which he had previously served. To many captains, this would not have been a desirable proposition; they would have chosen to live on half-pay in England rather than be exiled to the barbarous wilderness of the new world for the eight shillings daily pay of a sixth rate. Before leaving England, Warren had come to an agreement with his elder brother, Christopher, about the family estate. By deeds of lease and release, dated 19–20 February 1730, Peter Warren acquired Warrenstown with a rent roll of about £150 sterling per annum, for the sum of five shillings.[1]

Warren joined the ship at Deptford. Having signed on the 120 seamen volunteers, he put them to work stowing fifty-one tons of iron ballast and bringing on board the officers' stores. Then were loaded the provisions: bread, beef, pork, beer, peas, oatmeal, groats, butter, cheese, oil, and water. Next came the anchors and cables. Meanwhile part of the crew was employed in rigging the ship, blackening the topsail yards, mastheads, and lower yards. He then ordered *Solebay* to Galleon's Reach, where lighters brought the twenty great guns and twelve swivel with their carriages, while a hoy brought the gunpowder. Here part of the crew took up the task of scraping the masts and the ship's sides, paying the masts with rosin and tallow, and coating the sides with tar. When the ship sailed to Portsmouth, *Solebay* took on the usual allowance of fishing gear and vinegar for a foreign voyage, in each case two casks.[2]

Solebay sailed from Spithead accompanied by *Lowestoffe,* commanded by Warren's cousin, Capt. Matthew Norris, who was appointed to replace

Anson in Charleston. Warren was forced off course almost at once and found himself off the Isle of Guernsey, but off Plymouth *Solebay* was able to rejoin her sister ship. Later, in the mid-Atlantic, the ship was battered by hard gales forcing her onto the Virginia coast, where Warren put in for water and to repair the rigging.[3] With the aid of a pilot, *Solebay* was safely guided into the James River and there Warren found the frigates *Bideford* and *Greyhound* riding at anchor. Staying only long enough to take on fresh water, Warren eventually reached New York early in July, firing fifteen guns as he brought his ship to its moorings in the South River off the town. He found the frigate *Shoreham* riding near the fort.

Warren's time at New York was very idle if measured by his time at sea; *Solebay* spent the entire winter at Turtle Bay, unrigged and with all her stores and guns ashore, locked in by the ice, although it was generally not a bitter winter. Not until the end of March 1731 did Warren give orders to refit the ship and make ready for sea. After five weeks of hectic work, *Solebay* slipped her moorings off Turtle Bay and returned to her station in the South River.

The summer was interrupted by only one brief cruise to Providence, Rhode Island, where Warren heard the news of John Montgomery's death. Montgomery, a Scot, had been a soldier and member of Parliament and at one time had been a groom of the bedchamber of the Prince of Wales, then George II, who rewarded him with the government of New York. Upon Montgomery's death, the senior councilor, Rip Van Dam, automatically took up the reins of government until a successor arrived thirteen months later.

This event was of particular interest to Captain Warren, for since his arrival in New York he had become closely linked with the DeLancey family, whom the late governor had greatly favored. Through the DeLancey interest, Warren had been given the freedom of the City of New York in February 1731.[4] In July he completed a marriage contract for the hand of Stephen DeLancey's eldest daughter, Susannah; the marriage was solemnized in Trinity Church a few days later.[5] His father-in-law, a Huguenot, had come to New York in 1686 as a young man of twenty-three, having fled France. With capital raised by pawning the family jewels and plate in London, DeLancey had set himself up in business in which the fur trade came to play a large part. In 1700 he had married Anne, daughter of Stephanus van Courtland and Gertrude Schuyler, thus allying himself with two well-established Dutch families who had successfully adjusted to English rule. DeLancey had early on interested himself in politics, first as an alderman for the town of New York and then as a member of the assembly. He educated his sons at Cambridge, and they followed his lead in blending business with politics. By the time Warren entered the clan, the De Lanceys had become one of the leading families in the city.

Warren spent the winter of 1731–32 at Charleston, exchanging stations with Captain Norris on Admiralty orders. Warren may well have been accompanied by his bride when he sailed south in December. Also on board, but as part of his crew, were his New York brother-in-law, Peter DeLancey, and his Irish nephew Richard Tyrrell, both able seamen. Peter DeLancey was then twenty-six and on board solely for business; Tyrrell was perhaps fourteen and beginning what would become a long and distinguished naval career. Warren contrived to return to New York in the spring, conveniently meeting "with a hard southerly wind which loosen'd my rudder and oblig'd me to put into this port," on his first cruise from Charleston.[6] There he was delayed a month. On returning to Charleston, Warren was surprised to receive orders from the Admiralty to return home at once, in company with *Fox* and *Greyhound,* to be paid off.

Before leaving the colonies, Warren acquired his first property. From Jeremiah van Ranselaer he purchased a house on the Broadway for his wife. From Anthony Duane he bought a small farm. In South Carolina he received a grant of one thousand acres of unsettled land in Colleton County from the governor, Robert Johnson.

From the time of his discharge from *Solebay* on 19 August 1732, Warren remained unemployed for eighteen months. Only eight thousand seamen were employed in 1732 and again in 1733, the smallest number since 1722 and until 1751, when the number sank below the usual peacetime level of ten thousand seamen for the last time.[7] The difficulty of finding a ship had increased as his patron, Admiral Norris, had been dismissed by the king from the Admiralty Board in 1730 on the advice of Robert Walpole, and Warren could hope for no help from that quarter. He divided his time between his relations in Ireland and his lodgings in London.

Only in February 1734 did he receive a new commission. He was again to captain *Leopard.* He found her at Portsmouth where he had left her in 1729. When her fitting was completed, Warren took her out to Spithead, where she lay at anchor for months, venturing only once on a ten-day cruise in the Channel. The commissioning of *Leopard* with many other ships of the line was part of the sudden activity that swept English yards at the outbreak of hostilities, known to historians as the Polish War of Succession. It was one of the few eighteenth-century wars in which Great Britain managed to avoid becoming a combatant. For this Prime Minister Walpole was both roundly praised and sharply criticized in the realm as well as on the continent.

Not until the spring of 1735 did the Admiralty give orders for a fleet to be sent to sea, under the reinstated Admiral Norris. The fleet spent the entire summer and autumn off Lisbon in the Tagus River keeping an eye on the French and Spanish warships in the harbor of San Sebastian. There was some threat of war, and Warren was obliged to exercise his crew in gunnery and small arms; the chief incident was the visit of the King of Portugal to the fleet in July, when he was given a 21–gun salute by the entire fleet on boarding the flagship *Britannia.*

In October 1735 Admiral Norris relieved Warren of the command of *Leopard* and sent him back to England. On orders from the Admiralty Warren took command of the frigate *Squirrel,* which was to be sent to New England as the station ship. Many of Warren's fellow captains would have felt it an indignity to be offered a frigate after commanding a ship of the line, but Warren saw it as his opportunity to return to his wife with whom he had lived but five months since his marriage. In addition, it gave him once again an independent command, in contrast to the anonymity of a captain in a great but idle fleet. Warren used his six years in *Squirrel* to advance the career of his nephew, Richard Tyrrell, who signed on as a master's mate and ended as lieutenant within five years.

With two months' pay in their possession, Warren and his crew left Spithead for Madeira on 2 April 1736. From Madeira, where *Squirrel* took on five pipes of wine, Warren made first not for Boston but for New York. During the passage on the afternoon of 22 May, "a violent clap of thunder struck us, which split our mizzen mast & yard and struck twelve men down," his log noted.[8]

Upon his arrival at New York, he found the colony in the midst of a serious political crisis.[9] The governor, Col. William Cosby, had died in March, leaving the divided colony to be led by the senior member of council, George Clarke. Clarke's position was disputed by the adherents of the former chief justice, Lewis Morris, whom Cosby had removed from office in 1733 for refusing to hear the governor's suit against Rip Van Dam. The suit was over the half-salary paid to the senior councilor during the months after Governor Montgomery's death, before Cosby's arrival in the colony. Morris's suspension created a political crisis that lasted four years and included the trial for seditious libel of the young publicist, John Peter

Zenger, and his defense by Andrew Hamilton. It convinced Morris that he must plead his own case in England, where he arrived in the spring of 1735 and left eighteen months later, without being reinstated. Instead, in 1738 he was made governor of New Jersey, when the Board of Trade decided to separate that government from New York's jurisdiction. After Morris had been suspended, Cosby had appointed James DeLancey—until then second justice in the New York supreme court—to be chief justice. DeLancey and Clarke, who became senior councilor in November 1735 when Cosby suspended Rip Van Dam, were Cosby's chief adherents, together with Frederick Philipse, the third justice of the supreme court; Richard Bradley, the attorney general; Francis Harrison, the recorder of the city of New York; Archibald Kennedy, the receiver general; and Adolph Philipse, the leader of the assembly. Among the adherents of Lewis Morris, Warren was embarrassed to find the commander of the New York station ship, Matthew Norris, who had married one of Lewis Morris's daughters, and Capt. Vincent Pearse, who had done the same. Lewis Morris was also able to enlist the support of Adm. Charles Wager. These three sea officers became very much involved in the dispute. Warren, however, managed to remain detached, but his sympathies clearly rested with the DeLanceys. George Clarke asked Warren to convey the governor's widow to Boston, where she would board the homeward-bound *Scarborough*, the ship *Squirrel* had come to replace.

It was on this brief voyage to Boston that Warren made a very important purchase. From Grace Cosby, the governor's widow, he purchased a thirteen-thousand-acre tract on the south side of the Mohawk River, lying to the east of Fort Hunter and to the west of Chuctenunda Creek. The tract had been "patented for her husband by Charles Williams and company," and Warren bought it for a mere £110 sterling.[10] His coup aroused some jealousy in New York, where news of the transaction was soon known. Daniel Horsmanden, a barrister from England and recent arrival in New York, wrote Surveyor General Cadwallader Colden: "How she became so infatuated I know not, sure it could be so trifling a sum ready money that bewitched her but so it is which being done I suppose the Captn. will have no thought at present about getting any other tract, & I understood as much from the chief justice the other day talking upon this subject."[11] In fact, this success merely whetted Warren's appetite for further investments.

The routine that Warren had experienced as a commander of a station ship earlier at Charleston and New York soon established itself at Boston.

Warren brought his wife with him and for the first time since his marriage in 1731, he enjoyed a settled family life. It was at Boston that their first two children were born, Elizabeth in 1737 and Ann in 1738. With lodgings ashore, they entered fully into the social rhythm of the bustling city of twelve thousand souls. They dined from time to time with Governor Belcher and became good friends of the Boydells. John Boydell, who since 1732 had published the *Boston Gazette*, owned a bookshop that was something of a meeting place in the town, and as deputy postmaster of Massachusetts, sea officer for the port of Boston, and registrar of the court of probate of wills, he knew everyone and heard all the news.[12]

This pleasant life came to an abrupt halt in March when Warren received orders from his cousin, Captain Norris at New York, to fit out his ship with all speed.[13] News had come of a planned attack on Georgia and South Carolina by the Spanish at Havana. Norris had been asked for help and had the Admiralty's authority to take the New England station ship under his command. The news threw Warren into feverish activity as he struggled against the weather to get *Squirrel* to sea.[14] Carpenters and caulkers swarmed about the ship in one of the worst storms of the winter, while the crew heaved in ballast from four lighters lashed alongside. They were then put to repairing the sails and completing the rigging, taking on board the cables and anchor, guns and powder, and provisions for six months. On the last day of March all was ready; before Warren sailed he took the time to prepare as full a statement of his accounts as he could manage for his wife's reference, should he be killed in action.[15] By the time he reached New York in mid-April, the news he had received even before leaving Boston—that the reports of Spanish intentions were "false and groundless"—was confirmed.[16] He at once conferred with Norris and the council, presided over by Lieutenant Governor Clarke, and the alarm was over.

Warren delayed two months at New York on private business. He was brought up-to-date on the state of his capital put out to interest by his brother-in-law, the chief justice, and he took part in decisions to disburse further monies. Of more importance, he petitioned the New York council, jointly with his purser William Tatum and his surgeon Alexander Ramsey, for a grant of a tract of land in Albany county "as yet unpurchased of the native Indian proprietors" and amounting to six thousand acres.[17] The council eventually rejected the petition.

On his return to Boston Warren resumed his life ashore, not bothering to take *Squirrel* to sea again that year. *Squirrel* spent the winter months stripped and moored in Charles Ferry, first against White's wharf and then at Minot's. Warren only undertook one brief cruise in 1738, lasting less than three weeks, that took him along the New England coast, calling in at Marblehead and Kittery, where the merchant, William Pepperrell, based his enterprise, and sailing on to Casco Bay, where he took on wood and fresh water.[18] He returned to Boston in mid-August, and there he celebrated the birth of the Prince of Wales's heir and the future George III, his Royal Highness George William Frederick Augustus, with a 21–gun salute.[19]

In 1739 Warren received orders from the Admiralty to submit a report on the fishery at Canso on Chedabucto Bay, at the very northeastern tip of peninsular Nova Scotia, and supply what information he could about the French fishery off Cape Breton.[20] When New England fishermen established small stations along the Nova Scotia coasts after 1713, they were repeatedly attacked by the Mi'kmaq for some years thereafter. The Mi'kmaq by 1713 had become closely aligned with the French. A migratory people within their extensive region of Cape Breton, Nova Scotia, Île St.-Jean, and the south shore of the St. Lawrence to the Gaspé, they numbered perhaps 600 warriors by the 1740s. For all their skills as hunters on land and sea they played no traceable role in commercial fishery. Converted to Catholicism, they remained until 1760 greatly feared by English settler and soldier alike. The New England fishermen suffered the seizure of their boats, which the Mi'kmaq, as a display of their navigational skills, then briefly sailed before abandoning or destroying them.[21]

The British navy became involved first in 1716, when *Rose*, the station ship at Boston, had sailed to Louisbourg harbor to confer with the French governor of Cape Breton. Two years later, the captain of the frigate *Squirrel*, after visiting Louisbourg, ignited an international incident when he ordered the destruction of all French property found at Canso, the most important New England fishing station in Nova Scotia.[22]

Nova Scotia was still not deemed important enough to have its own station ship; however, beginning in 1721, the frigate stationed at New England was occasionally ordered to cruise along the coast to Canso. In 1723, for instance, *Solebay* cruised between Cape Sable and Canso, while in 1724 *Ludlow Castle*, fearing Mi'kmaq attack, sailed to Canso from her Newfoundland station at Placentia.[23] Guarded by a small British military detachment and visited occasionally by a British naval frigate, the fishery was not administered by those inhabiting peninsular Nova Scotia.[24] Of the 819 fishing boats noted in six seasons there between 1721 and 1730, the first years for which there is statistical evidence, some 89 percent were New England–owned. Another 2 percent came from Nova Scotia, Newfoundland, Pennsylvania, and New York.[25] The rest were from ports in the British Isles.

The only other manifestation of naval interest in Nova Scotia was the survey of the colony's Atlantic coast between Canso and Chebucto harbor. This was undertaken by Capt. Thomas Durell between 1732 and 1736, when in command of the New England station ship and apparently at his own initiative.[26] Canso was not dignified by the presence of a lieutenant governor: technically, it came under the jurisdiction of the government of Nova Scotia at Annapolis Royal at the mouth of the Annapolis River, several days distant by sea. Without a government vessel at its disposal, the Annapolis Royal authorities had to depend on very occasional coasters to maintain contact with the fishing station.

Warren's report is by far the most complete of any the Admiralty had received up to that point.[27] His information must have been gathered as much from those Massachusetts men who fished off Canso and traded with Louisbourg as from those few souls he found living at Canso. He found the garrison at Canso "in a most miserable condition not one gun mounted, not a barrack fit for a soldier to live in, there are now there four companys of thirty men each . . . had we a rupture with France it would not be supportable a week." So barren did he find the site that he suggested instead that the ministry consider establishing a new settlement at either La Have [later Bridgewater] or Chebucto harbor, which in 1749 was selected for the new town of Halifax. He found the Canso fishery much decayed in contrast to the French fishery off Cape Breton. He estimated that twenty-five hundred Frenchmen were employed in five hundred shallops during the summer months, with an average catch of three hundred quintals a boat. Moreover, the French also fished in the winter, whereas the English never went out in that season—and although fewer men were involved and the catch much smaller, both the French merchants and fishers appeared to consider it worthwhile. The French had developed a system of sorting their catch for different markets in Europe, which again contrasted with the English who made no such attempt. The result, Warren claimed, was that the French got much better prices for their catch than the English. Warren emphasized that twenty years earlier the French fishery had not been significant but that through careful management it had grown prodigiously. This provocative statement made no impact on the Board of Trade.

For some time Peter Warren had been seeking an opportunity to visit his Mohawk River tract. As soon as he purchased it in 1736, he wrote to his nephews in Ireland, William Johnson and Michael Tyrrell, and invited them to come to America, clear the land, help settle it, and generally assume charge of its management. Warren would supply the capital. The offer had been accepted, and the pair arrived in New York in the winter of 1737–38, heading up the Hudson River at the spring thaw. They worked hard, with the help of slaves sent there by Warren, to clear the land and begin tilling the soil; Warren imported linen from Ireland and general goods from England for them to begin trading. Johnson took to this strange new environment with great enthusiasm and was full of projects after his first weeks on the land. By May 1739 he had purchased land on his own account, discounting his uncle's doubts about the price and title. He wrote: "Your coming here is much longed for by us & several others who are inclined to come and settle on the land, but wait your coming, which I wish may be soon . . . They are all people in good circumstance."[28] Warren never saw the Mohawk, for his nephew's wish that so mirrored his own was made impossible by the gods of war.

On 9 August 1739, the frigate *Tartar,* commanded by Capt. George Townshend, sailed into Boston harbor with orders from the Admiralty "to commit all manner of hostilities upon the Spaniards."[29] The so-called War of Jenkins' Ear had begun, if it had not yet been declared.

Townshend, Warren, and Governor Belcher at once went into conference and decided that the safest and speediest means to forward the news to the other continental governments and station ships was by land.[30] Warren wrote to the Admiralty asking that if more than one ship were to be assigned to New England, he hoped to be given command of the larger vessel.[31] *Squirrel* and *Tartar* then sailed within a week for Georgia.

Warren practiced his crew daily in gunnery and small arms. Upon a report from South Carolina that a number of strange vessels had been sighted off Charleston bar, Warren altered his course for that port. The news proved false but added to the anxiety Warren felt as he sailed on his southerly course.

At Charleston, where he brought the first news of the rupture in diplomatic relations with Spain, he found *Phoenix* and *Seaford* unrigged, the sloop *Hawk* hauled up to begin fitting out, and only the sloop *Spence* ready for sea. As all their captains were junior to him, he immediately took command, ordering the ships to be made ready for sea with all haste. He communicated his orders to Gov. William Bull and asked for an audience that very evening. The governor was pleased with the ministry's decision to concentrate the station ships for the protection of the two southernmost colonies. He told Warren that he believed that the 1737 alarm had been real; it was the Spaniards who had changed their plans. He also told him that two months earlier that summer, a Spanish launch had been seen taking soundings in several inlets on the coast. Of much more importance was a recent proclamation issued by the governor of St. Augustine in Florida that called on the slaves of Georgia and South Carolina to flee to the Spanish, who would grant them their freedom. This had occasioned a brief and bloody revolt by some slaves and the escape of others to Florida. (At the time there were perhaps forty thousand African slaves in South Carolina, more than twice the number of whites.)[32] Wealth derived principally from the export of rice, the cultivation of which represented the most advanced horticulture in colonial America. Introduced by West African slaves and carried on by them, rice found its principal market in the Iberian Peninsula.

Warren told the governor of his intention to put to sea in company with *Spence* and to sail along the Florida coast to secure intelligence of the enemy.[33] He held a council of war with his captains, where it was agreed that Sir Yelverton Peyton, commanding *Hector* at Virginia, and Capt. Vincent Pearse, commanding *Flamborough* at New York, should immediately be informed of the request of the governor and the South Carolina council for the protection of all the ships stationed on the North American coast.[34] On the morning of 16 September, leaving Capt. Charles Fanshawe in command, Warren sailed over Charleston bar in company with *Spence*, and at once set sail for St. Augustine.

St. Augustine, the principal Spanish settlement on the Atlantic coast of America since 1565, had been attacked three times by the English: once by Drake in 1586, by Capt. John Davis in 1665, and by James Moore, governor of South Carolina, in 1702. None had succeeded. The town stood on a narrow sandy peninsula, formed by the Matanzas and San Sebastian rivers. It was separated from the ocean by Anastasia Island, at the north end of which lay the only channel by which ships could reach the town. St. Augustine was protected by a fortress built of congealed shells, dug out in the shape of stones from a quarry on Anastasia Island, and more or less formed a square, with bastions at each corner. Each curtain wall was almost 180– feet long, the parapets were 9 feet thick, and the ramparts 20 feet high. In

1739 the covertway was incomplete. The castle mounted almost fifty guns; sixteen of the heaviest were brass 24–pounders, superior to any carried in the British ships then on the North American coast. The garrison was thought to consist of a company of artillery of about one hundred officers and men, a troop of horse of about the same number, and at least six hundred others, in addition to the fifteen hundred souls in the town.[35]

Warren was particularly concerned to discover the water depth over St. Augustine's bar. It was only nine feet, too shallow for anything larger than a schooner. Beyond the bar toward the town Warren saw several small vessels, and when one ventured out he made a prize of it. The prisoners told him that the town was unaware of hostilities between Spain and Britain. Warren remained on his station until relieved by *Phoenix*, whereupon he returned to Charleston to report his findings to the governor and council.

The possibility of an attack on St. Augustine was now immediately raised. The idea had struck the ministry at home at the same time as the colonists in Georgia and South Carolina. To seize St. Augustine, it was argued, would remove all direct threat to these two southern English colonies. On 9 October 1739, Gen. James Oglethorpe, who in 1737 had been given a regiment and had brought it to Georgia in 1738, was sent orders to make an attempt on the fortress if the governor and council of South Carolina approved. Ordnance stores were sent to him, and all the ships at North American stations were ordered by the Admiralty "to join and assist in this enterprize; and to prevent, if possible, the Spaniards . . . from being supplied with men, provisions, or ammunition from Havana."[36] Oglethorpe did not receive these orders until April, nor did several sea officers, as was evidenced by the state of unreadiness that Warren encountered late in the summer in Charleston.

In the meantime, the possibility of just such an expedition had captured Oglethorpe's imagination, and by mid-November he was convinced the attempt should be made:

> We have no cannon from the King, nor any others but some small iron guns bought by the trust. We have very little powder, we have no horse for marching & very few boats and no fund for paying the men, but of one boat. The Spaniards have a number of launches, also horse, and a fine train of artillery well-provided with all stores. The best expedient I can think of, is to strike first, & as our strength consists in men, and that the people of the colony as well as the Soldiers handle

their Arms well and are desirous of action, I think the best way is to make use of our strength & beat them out of the field & destroy their plantations and out settlements . . . and to form the siege of August- ine If I can get the artillery.[37]

Warren spent five hours with Oglethorpe at Savannah on board *Squir- rel* on the last day of November. There he learned of the general's plans to raid Florida overland, to create as much alarm as possible, and to familiar- ize himself with the terrain. The raid was a success, though the Spanish were not provoked to action except when Oglethorpe attacked a new fort built on the Georgia side of the St. Johns River. This success produced sev- eral prisoners, two cannon, one mortar, three swivel guns, shells, powder, and a great variety of provisions. The news was greeted with excitement in Charleston, where Oglethorpe sent a full description with an invitation to South Carolina to join in an expedition against St. Augustine. In a matter of days, the South Carolina council had committed itself to a six-month expenditure of SC£120,000 (about £17,100) to equip a regiment of foot of almost five hundred officers and men, a troop of rangers numbering about fifty, a thousand natives each with a musket, hatchet, and blanket, an artil- lery train of a dozen 18–pounders with eighteen hundred shot, together with all the necessary supplies.[38]

In April 1740 Oglethorpe wrote formally to ask the naval vessels to assist in the expedition. The letter went not to Warren, but to Capt. Vin- cent Pearse, who had reached Charleston in February from New York and superceded Warren as senior captain. Then almost sixty, Pearse had joined the navy in 1696 and served throughout the years of war with France. He was commissioned post captain in 1715, but Pearse did not seize this oppor- tunity and he lacked all ambition for war glory. Instead, he now displayed great caution bordering on trepidation, general pessimism, and an inflex- ibility that made success doubtful. He wrote to the Admiralty: "as we think that this undertaking (if it succeeds) will be highly for his Majesty's ser- vice, and a great benefit to the whole continent of America. And, that if it was not put in execution, the whole blame might be laid upon us. We have consented to it and hope it will meet with their lordships approbation."[39]

Pearse sent Warren to St. Augustine to cut off its supply from the sea and ordered Capt. William Laws north to Providence for mortars. The Spanish realized their danger and sent six galleys to attack Warren, who was becalmed off the bar. Warren was saved only by a sudden breeze, but

before he beat off his assailants the ship's rigging had been greatly damaged and one able seaman killed.[40] The gun battle had lasted for six hours.
The galleys were to prove the most effective weapon in the enemy's arse-
nal. Warren had his revenge before the end of April. At dusk on 29 April,
Warren spied through his telescope a sail coming out of the harbor and
stretching close under the shore. He too stood to southward, showing only
as much sail as a sloop would use. All night he cruised on the same course,
and the next morning the sail was in sight. Warren at once gave chase,
came under fire, tacked, cut the enemy off from the shore, and closed on
her. By eight o'clock in the morning, the sloop was a prize. She was a Spanish war sloop of fourteen guns, with a crew of forty-seven. Of equal interest were her seven to eight thousand pieces of eight on board, with which
she had intended to buy provisions at Cap François for the garrison.[41] This
particular action displayed Warren as the clever, alert, and active officer
which characteristics his brother officers would in time themselves per-
ceive. The same day *Squirrel* destroyed another vessel that the Spanish
crew had beached. With his prize in company, Warren thereupon returned
to Charleston, after having been replaced on his station.

The expedition now began in earnest. Oglethorpe, leading the land
forces, struck south across the St. Johns River and overwhelmed the garrison of Fort San Iago, fifteen miles from St. Augustine, on 10 May, taking
almost sixty prisoners, some small cannon, and small arms. His troops also
captured two galleys sent to the relief of the fort. Two weeks later, with 300
of his own men and 350 under command of the South Carolinian Col.
Alexander Vandussen, Oglethorpe marched to Fort Negro, two miles from
St. Augustine. They found the fort abandoned and sent a force to the very
walls of the castle. In the meantime, all the naval vessels had converged off
St. Augustine bar, and on 5 June a council of war was held: "Oglethorpe
having desired to know the longest time his Majesty's ships can stay upon
this coast, and having examined the pilots of his maj. ships 'twas unanimously agreed by the Council, that . . . ships cannot stay longer with safety
upon this coast than the 5 July next."[42]

The sea officers feared that the possibility of hurricanes was too great a
risk on an unprotected coast. For the present, the council agreed to land
two hundred seamen on a nearby island. Oglethorpe was to land an equal
number of troops. Final briefings took place on 11 June. Under Warren's
command, the force took possession of the island the next day, without
opposition from the Spanish and despite a very heavy surf. There he or-

dered the erection of a battery of naval guns and manned by sailors, while simultaneously Colonel Vandussen erected his own battery on another island. For the first time the castle came under fire. On 15 June the Spanish sallied forth at dawn in great strength to attack Fort Negro, which Vandussen had garrisoned with 130 Highlanders and aboriginals, in order to blockade the town on the land side and raid the environs of the town at night. The Spanish attack was completely successful: most of the defenders were killed or taken prisoner. The prisoners, all Highlanders, were stripped of their clothing, had their hands bound, and were paraded into St. Augustine, where they were kept four months and then sent to Havana.[43] The loss of Fort Negro proved a major setback, for it left the town open to reinforcements and fresh supplies, while the colonials had too few men to attempt to retake and garrison it. Despite this reversal, on 21 June Oglethorpe sent the Spanish governor a summons to surrender that was curtly refused.[44] Plans for the assault were then discussed by the land officers, who felt that success greatly depended on the prior destruction of the Spanish galleys, which had several times demonstrated their usefulness as very accurate floating batteries.

The sea officers were asked to help. Pearse held a council of war to consider the matter; it unanimously rejected the proposal of a boat attack on the galleys—then moored above the town out of the range of the attacking batteries. The council pointed out that the ships were already severely undermanned with more than three hundred seamen ashore helping with the batteries and moving stores. Of greater importance, it was judged to be too hazardous "as the boats must pass the castle and town under discharge of their cannon, within shot of their musquetry for above one mile, before they can come at the galleys."[45] Pearse feared failure. He saw his seamen being devastated, his inability to man his warships, their seizure by the Spanish, the routing of the land forces, and his own disgrace. After receiving the results of the council's deliberations, Vandussen held a conference in his tent with Warren, Laws, and Townshend in attendance. They agreed that an attack on the galleys was practicable if there was enough water for the boats at half tide. Warren sent Tyrrell that night to sound the channel, and he came back with a positive report. Vandussen then offered not only men and boats but also soldiers to provide covering fire along the whole length of the shoreline, where the channel lay close to St. Eustatius Island. This forced Pearse to reconsider the matter; he had never bothered to go ashore and see the situation for himself nor make any alternative proposal to Vandussen, but instead "sent on shore to enquire more particularly how it might with any probability of success be carried into execution, and find upon examination that the difficulties that would attend upon this enter-prize, had not been so thoroughly inquired into by the proposers, as it should have been as the Weight of such an Undertaking requires."[46] As he failed to supply details, it is impossible to judge the soundness of his criti-cism. He took the opportunity to remind Oglethorpe of his determination to quit that coast on 5 July.

There was now no hope of a successful siege. With the squadron gone, there would be too few men to defend the island battery. The Spanish would be free to move in and out of the port. Vandussen suggested that a sloop be kept at Matanzas, a small harbor a few miles to the south, but it was found to be an unsuitable anchorage and quite unprotected from strong winds. He then suggested that two hundred seamen be left behind to help man the battery, but this a naval council of war rejected.[47] When Warren carried this last decision to the land officers, it was decided to break off the siege at once. The Spanish attempted to take advantage of the new situation and sallied forth in great strength on 5 July, but were quickly beaten back. As a parting gesture, Oglethorpe sent Pearse "a few oranges, which our men took out of the gardens under the walls," when pursuing the fleeing Spanish troops.[48] With all the naval guns safely embarked on the ships together with all the provisions, Oglethorpe, in broad daylight, marched away "with drums beating and colours flying," to the great re-joicing of the Spaniards and the din of pealing church bells.[49] Until a few days before, the besieged garrison had been very short of food, and its occupants had turned to eating cats and rats.[50] Supplies had reached them overland, at a moment when there was serious talk of surrender. Now their anxiety vanished.

There was no possibility of renewing the siege once the hurricane sea-son had passed. The South Carolina officers would have found it very dif-ficult to serve under General Oglethorpe, who they felt had proved incom-petent. Vandussen said of him: "he trifles away his time in doing of nothing, and yet seems always in a hurry."[51] Pearse dispersed the squadron to their several stations, sending one to the St. Johns River to be on hand to come to the aid of Georgia should the Spanish attempt to seize the initia-tive. His explanation of the failure was that the fortress "was found much stronger, better fortified, and mann'd, than expected; and the number of men General Oglethorpe had with him were so few, that they could make no attack."[52] Oglethorpe put the blame on the squadron, which, after doing such good service, deserted him. Warren was thoroughly disgusted. To the Admiralty he spoke of the siege only as "that unfortunate occasion" and the "ill-success that attended His Majesty's arms," emphasizing that it was Pearse, not he, who commanded the sea forces.[53] To his London agents, Messrs. Samuel and William Baker, he was more explicit, calling the attack "ill-concerted and worse conducted."[54] With great feeling he added, "I hope I shall never have any part in such an expedition again."

War, 1740–1744

The West Indies and New York

From the Florida coast Warren returned to New York where he found orders long awaiting him from Admiral Vernon at Jamaica. Vernon was so short of naval stores that he had been forced to send to New England for masts and had asked Warren to give Capt. Francis Perceval of *Astrea*—employed to purchase and freight the so-called "sticks," naval jargon for masts, bowsprits, topmasts, yards, and spars—all possible help.[1] He was then to "see him safe into the sea as far as you shall think there is any danger of his falling in with any force of the enemy's."[2]

For some decades since the 1690s, New England pine had been shipped to the English dockyards under contract, but the market in the West Indies was more recent. Only in 1711 was the first evidence found for the wartime supply of masts, bowsprits, yards, and spars from New England to Jamaica.[3] With peace in 1713, Jamaica and Antigua were cut off from the New England supply, which continued to flow to England. Thereafter the West Indies were supplied from England. Yet at moments of acute shortages, when excessive prices were demanded for all forms of naval stores in the local West Indies markets, the naval commanders had no choice but to pay highly inflated prices for the needed sticks. In 1738 the commander of the Jamaica squadron was authorized to deal directly with New England. Sir Chaloner Ogle had relied on shipments by merchant vessels, but with war against Spain, his successors employed prize vessels, of which *Astrea* was one and *Bien Aimé* another, a policy initiated by Vernon.[4]

Perceval had to undertake his business with the New Englanders alone, but Warren saw Vernon's orders as an open invitation to spend the winter in the West Indies rather than locked in the ice of Boston Bay. It was in the third week of October, with the mastship safely in Kingston, that Warren came under Vernon's command.

Vernon had been sent to the West Indies in the summer of 1739 to carry out a war plan that envisaged the capture of the two most important trade centers on the Spanish Main, Portobelo and Cartagena. This, it had been hoped, would cause Spain severe economic hardship and force a quick peace, thus gaining for the British government and its rapacious merchants the commercial advantages for which they had so long been agitating. Vernon's success in November at Portobelo had made him a national hero and raised great expectations of further victories. In March 1740, Chagres "the headquarters of the Spanish *guardacostas,* and one of the leading ports for treasure" was taken.[5] These initial successes came without significant support from the military. In this the campaign conformed to Vernon's conception of warfare in the Caribbean, where the army was largely unnecessary, and if present would be devastated by disease while consuming scarce victuals. The navy, by contrast, could provide the necessary mobility to curtail Spanish trade in the West Indies and thereby force open her ports to Britain's commerce. Yet his fleet required a constant supply of ordnance and naval stores, shortages of which had so hampered his squadron that it had spent the summer of 1740 on the defensive, confined to protecting trade. A week before Warren joined him, Vernon learned that Adm. Rodrigo de Torres had reached the West Indies with a squadron of twelve sail. The only news from England was of the expeditionary force, under Rear Admiral Ogle, lying idle at Spithead because of a serious shortage of seamen. Yet when Ogle's squadron reached Jamaica in January 1741, British naval supremacy in the region was unchallenged.[6]

For his part, Warren spent his time in the West Indies establishing his reputation as a highly successful and fortunate hunter of prizes, a reputation that by the end of the war was unmatched by any other commander. His successes this first winter had only a small impact on the war with Spain but served both to enrich himself and his crew and to mold the latter into a very alert and highly experienced ship's company. Not all the prizes were lightly defended merchant vessels; a number were heavily armed privateers almost as strong as *Squirrel* herself. Warren's first West Indian prize fell to him on 28 October, the next on 6 November; both tried to pass his inspection as French vessels, but through insistent questioning Warren was able to find adequate discrepancies in the stories each enemy crew told to warrant their arrests. A third prize fell to him in December, two more in January, and two others in February. In May his eighth encounter produced a dangerous engagement:

At 4 p.m. [I] saw a sloop lying under a bluffrock at an anchor night coming off shore; could not get near her with the Ship; I sent the boat in who finding her armed came off upon which I sent her in again to watch her motions & make proper signals if she should attempt to go out; at day light we stood in and came to anchor as Near as we could possibly venture & veered away in to 2½ fathoms where we soon drove them from their vessel, man'd our boats who boarded her under a brisk fire from the enemys small arms & swivel guns which they had planted ashore; we at the same time scaling the rocks & bushes to favour our people's boarding who when they got possession of her found her rudder was unhung & she fast aground & very much shattered by our shot therefore gave directions to set her on fire which they immediately did had one man killed & 12 wounded in this action.[7]

The battle had also cost *Squirrel* twenty half-barrels of powder and four hundred shot, with some damage to her rigging and sails. It earned for Warren a letter of thanks from the Jamaica assembly.

Though Warren spent much of his time patrolling, he was occasionally sent on important reconnaissance missions, the most significant of which occurred in February 1741. The previous November Vernon had learned of the departure to the West Indies of a French fleet that he expected would work in conjunction with the Spanish, even though France and Britain were not then at war. With the almost simultaneous arrival of the expeditionary force under Ogle, Vernon had only to determine which target to strike and when. As intelligence was of importance, Vernon sent Warren to reconnoiter Cartagena to discover if the Spanish fleet was there and to return with all speed to an agreed rendezvous.[8] Warren found but six men-of-war and a number of merchantmen. He returned at once to Vernon, who wrote in great relief to Admiral Wager and the Duke of Newcastle: "I thank God I can acquaint your Grace, Capt. Warren in the *Squirrel* joined me here the 23rd, happily in the very instant I wanted him, as we are just watered, and ready to sail."[9]

Vernon's delight is easily understood, for the day had witnessed a final council of war where the decision to attack Cartagena had been made, and now he knew the way was clear. Vernon had also learned the day before that the French fleet had departed the West Indies for home. *Squirrel* was ordered to Jamaica to clean, secure fresh provisions, and join the fleet at

Cartagena. It was at Port Royal, so recently clogged with men-of-war and dozens of troop transports, that Warren experienced for the second time since becoming a captain fatal disease among his crew. In less than three weeks thirteen men had died, including his best friend on board, surgeon Alexander Ramsey, and John Vandriesen, the surgeon's mate. Was it yellow fever, scurvy, or that prime killer through all the ages, typhus? Warren gives no hint.

Founded in 1533, Cartagena de las Indias was "the largest, richest, and most populous city on the mainland of Spanish America and its chief center of trade."[10] The city stood on the very coast, yet could not be approached from the sea. Its harbor was a vast lagoon with two entrances: Boca Grande, suitable only for small craft, and eight miles away Boca Chica, a narrow but deep channel. In between lay the island of Terra Bomba. Chica was powerfully defended by four forts and a fascine battery; Fort Santiago and Fort San Felipe on the seaward side of Terra Bomba were small with but eighteen guns between them. At the lagoon end of Chica, built on a shoal, was Fort San Jose, mounting sixteen guns, but the chief obstacle was Fort San Luis with sixty-eight guns. Once these forts were silenced, a fleet could sail into the harbor, only to face prevailing winds. Even then Cartagena was defended by its own city walls and more forts, especially San Lazaro. Despite these defenses the city had thrice fallen to the enemy: once to pirates, to Drake in 1585, and to the French in 1697.

Vernon had set himself a formidable task. On 9 March Santiago and San Felipe were bombarded and silenced. The army under Gen. Thomas Wentworth then began the investment of San Luis with a most inadequate artillery train, while a naval force stormed and captured the fascine battery. Warren arrived on the scene just in time to witness the fall of San Luis and San Jose. The warships now sailed into the lagoon and two of the defending forts were vacated by the Spanish—only San Lazaro remained. Here the British successes ended. The momentum was lost for the army was delayed; when the attack was made on 9 April, it struck not at dawn but in full daylight. The scaling ladders were too short (the Spanish had hastily deepened the surrounding trench unnoticed), and the attackers suffered more than six hundred casualties. Wentworth, badly shaken, nevertheless proposed a regular siege and asked Vernon for help in erecting a battery. An unfriendly correspondence ensued making cooperation impossible; the invaders withdrew after destroying all of the Spanish warships in the harbor and stripping and disabling the fallen forts.

Warren did not witness this unexpected debacle. Four days after he reached Cartagena, Vernon had ordered him to cruise the Cuban coast for five weeks. Only in mid-June, when once again *Squirrel* was cleaning at Port Royal, did he learn the dismal news from the returning fleet. His usefulness to Vernon at Jamaica was over, and at the end of the month he was ordered to return to his station at Boston. On his way there, Warren sailed first for New York, which he reached on 20 June. He had been away nine months, but news of his exploits had long preceded him. Even his nephew, William Johnson, in the wilds of the Mohawk valley, had constant reports from Mrs. Warren: "The welcome news you likewise send me of my dear uncle's safety, and the hopes of seeing him soon, together with the news here of his great & daily success (for the continuance of which I daily beseech the great God to prosper all his undertakings and shield him in all dangers) renders me incapable of expressing the vast pleasure and satisfaction it gives me."[11]

At New York, Warren found orders from the Admiralty to return home, escorting mastships from New England and any other trade that wished a convoy. Warren was in no great hurry to sail for England. Claiming the need to refit and clean his ship, he delayed at New York for nine weeks. William Johnson came down from Warrensbush, as the Mohawk property came to be called, and reported on his progress there. The summer before, Warren had lent his nephew £600, and now he advanced him a further £300.[12] He also conferred frequently with James DeLancey about his New York and New Jersey investments, which had expanded considerably since 1731. If his log is any guide, Warren appears to have spent most of his time ashore, leaving Richard Tyrrell, his lieutenant, to oversee the refitting of the frigate at Turtle Bay. If ever Warren visited the Mohawk Valley this is the only interval when it could conceivably have happened. In the midst of war with Spain, it is very unlikely that the captain would have allowed himself to be caught at that great a distance from his ship.

Warren left New York at the end of July, sailing for Piscataqua to await the arrival of the mastship he was to convoy to the English dockyards. He brought with him as a passenger Thomas Penn, the proprietor of Pennsylvania. Warren idled at Piscataqua for five weeks, all the while as the guest of William Pepperrell. It was there that they discussed the possibility of France entering the war and the dangers it would create for the northern colonies. They frequently discussed the possibilities of a successful attack on the great fortress that for twenty years had been building at Louisbourg.[13] At length, on 19 October, with a moderate easterly wind and a beautiful, clear autumn day, Warren sailed with the bombship *Terrible*, two mastships, and three merchantmen. Off Newfoundland they ran into strong gales and fog, and one of the mastships became separated and fell into the enemy's hands, as Warren later learned when the owners, Messrs. Henniker and Howitt, complained to the Admiralty. However mortifying to Warren, he was able to satisfy the Admiralty that he had done all in his power to locate the missing ship: "Had she been my own I cou'd not have taken more care of her; for the truth of which I appeal to the rest of the ships under my convoy; and for the care and regard to His Majesty's trading subjects in general, I also beg leave to appeal to those concerned in trade to all the places where I have been stationed or employed."[14] The convoy reached Plymouth on 22 November, then made for Spithead, where Warren received orders to press men in the Downs before sailing for Deptford. There in January, the entire ship's company transferred to *Launceston*, and Warren's days as a small frigate commander were at an end. It was there as well that he received permission to go to London for treatment of his dislocated left shoulder, an accident that had taken place at Piscataqua, and that "render'd it almost useless, and very painful."[15]

Though *Launceston* was a new ship, she was poorly made. Throughout her service she sailed badly and was always excessively leaky; Warren never acquired the affection for her that he had for *Squirrel*. As a fifth rate of forty-four guns, she had a crew's complement of 280 and three lieutenants. One of these was the Hon. William Montagu, an erratic and contentious younger brother of the Earl of Sandwich, but as brave in combat as his captain. Another was Richard Tyrrell, who was determined to employ every opportunity allowed him to display his fighting skills. The third was Clark Gayton, who had just passed his lieutenant's examination but had seen much action as a mate on *Squirrel*.

Launceston always proved very difficult to man fully; with the Spanish war now entering its fourth year, the proportion of volunteers among the seamen was very low and that of pressed crew unusually high. This created discipline problems that Warren never before had encountered. Indeed it was as captain of *Launceston* that Warren first employed the lash.

Warren had been ordered to command the station ship at New York. It had been his own idea and when he had put it to Admiral Wager at the Admiralty it had been accepted. It had also been agreed that Warren would transport the newly designated governor, Capt. the Hon. George Clinton, to his post at New York. While awaiting Clinton, he was ordered to Portsmouth to serve under Adm. Philip Cavendish. Before sailing, Warren prepared a memorandum, on his own initiative but with encouragement from

Wager, entitled: "Proposals for the Better Employing his Majesty's Ships Stationed on the Coast of North America."[16] This he sent to Thomas Corbett, the secretary of the Board of Admiralty for consideration. His paper suggested that because the winter season provided sufficient protection to the northern colonies, the station ships at Boston and New York and one of those from Virginia should spend each winter in the West Indies. He was very specific about the route of their winter cruise: off the Spanish Main to the windward of Cartagena until early February, then to the coasts of Hispaniola and Cuba, placing the ships in an excellent position to intercept the trade just then getting under way between Vera Cruz and Havana and the Spanish privateers, "who fit out at Havana about that time, in order to cruise on our trade to the northward." From late March this small squadron would then head northwards with one ship detached to cruise along the Florida coast, collecting intelligence later at both Georgia and South Carolina. The New York ship would proceed northward about sixty leagues off the coast and the Boston ship about a hundred, "the spreading the ships in this manner wou'd be the most likely way to meet any privateers cruising on our trade, & to retake any ships that shou'd fall into their hands." Warren also suggested that much closer cooperation should be encouraged between the respective governments through frequent communication among the sea officers and the installment of station ship captains as useful members of their colonial councils.

It was a sensible plan and had the great merit of deriving much from successful experience. It also had a very characteristic element of concern for Warren's personal advancement. If the plan were to be adopted, Warren expected to command the new squadron while an appointment to the council of New York had recently become the first object of his political ambition. The report lay unconsidered until August when—at Warren's prompting—the Admiralty Board read and amended it. Their views, as expressed in their orders to Warren, were even more flattering. Warren, at the approach of winter, was to leave New York with the New England station ship *Gosport* in company and assume command as senior captain of all ships at Barbados and the Leeward Islands. There he was to protect trade, cruise against enemy privateers, and report on "the routes which Spanish ships coming from Europe make in the American sea and at what places they usually touch for intelligence or refreshment, and accordingly endeavour to intercept them."[17] In addition, he was to prepare a full report on the suitability of English Harbour, Antigua, as a site to develop an overseas base for refitting and cleaning ships of war.

Before learning of these exciting orders and while awaiting Clinton, Warren was sent on three cruises, one to the Spanish coast and two in the Channel. The first, in company with his cousin, Capt. Edward Aylmer in *Port Mahon,* was highly successful. Warren took the Spanish privateer *Peregrina* of fourteen guns and a crew of 140 and retook four of the enemy's prizes including sixty Spanish prisoners.[18] He also intercepted an Irish sloop, laden with beer and butter, from trading with France.[19] *Peregrina* sailed so well and was so new that he wanted the Admiralty to commission her and give the command to Richard Tyrrell, who had brought her to England. She was commissioned in August, but Tyrrell remained with Warren.

On his second cruise, calm bedeviled him again and two privateers were able to row away from him, his only reward being a brigantine from Swansea, which he retook.[20] The novelty of cruising on the French and Spanish coasts and in the Channel soon wore off. When at the beginning of July Warren found himself sent out on yet a third cruise, Clinton still not being ready to leave for New York, he wrote a discouraged letter to his wife. This we learn of secondhand, for none of the many letters between Warren and his wife survives. Susannah's sister-in-law reported that "Sister Warren . . . received a letter last Sunday from Captain Warren dated 9 July he was then upon his third cruise was to be out three weeks & says he hope upon his return to set out for this place he wrote he had waited three months for the governor who now told him he met with so many disappointments he was afraid he should not get away this fall so that Captain Warren intended to ask leave to come without him & and says if he is refus'd will come passenger."[21]

Warren was not forced to this expedient; instead he received, on 20 August, the orders already mentioned, and this could only have been a delight to him.[22] Before leaving Spithead, he wrote in a friendly manner to the elusive Captain Clinton asking his support in being named to the first vacancy on the New York council, explaining: "I have no other view in this but as it may be to my fortune to settle in your country where I have a little fortune, Indeed equal to most of the degree I desire to be of there. It gives me some little rank above the common sort, and at the same time, an opportunity of doing service, to the country, and let me in a joke tell you one very material advantage. 'Twill give ones lady a very high place at a ring or ball."[23]

Clinton obliged him readily, but getting no immediate response, called on two members of the Board of Trade, Lord Monson and Martin Bladen, in April 1743.[24] In November Clinton wrote officially recommending Warren to one of the four vacant council places.[25] By January 1744, on receipt of the request, the appointment was approved, and Newcastle signed the mandamus on 23 March 1744.[26]

Warren did not confine his ambitions to the New York council. He soon realized that what kept Clinton in England were serious financial difficulties. Clinton, a mediocre sea officer, was extremely well connected but not well off. Seventeen years older than Warren, he was a younger son of the Earl of Lincoln. His elder brother, the heir to the title, married the sister of the Duke of Newcastle, who remained at the heart of government from 1724 until 1762. Clinton had entered the navy at the age of twenty-one, was promoted captain ten years later, and eventually, through seniority, became admiral of the fleet, even though he never served at sea beyond his captain's rank.[27] In 1737 when employment opportunities were scarce, he received the Mediterranean command, "the sweetest plum of all."[28] Upon learning in 1740 that he was to command a ship of the line in Ogle's squadron bound for the West Indies, he successfully petitioned Newcastle to be relieved of this unwanted posting.[29] Unable to live on his naval pay and the very small income given him by his father, he begged Newcastle for help.[30] The appointment to New York was the result, a perfect example of Newcastle's approach both to politics and his extended family.

On reaching New York in October 1742 and after consulting the De-Lanceys, Warren wrote to Clinton to suggest that he sell him the governorship, "as my affairs will oblige me to continue here, even without a ship I shou'd be glad to make a very advantageous proposal to you shou'd you not think it worth your while to come here."[31] Though Clinton declined this offer, Warren did not put the subject aside for long, returning persistently to the matter throughout his tenure on the various American stations.

Political business was not Warren's primary concern, for *Launceston* was in unseaworthy condition by the time she reached New York. Two severe gales had shattered her sails and rigging, the main topmast was sprung, and the spare one found to be rotten. Every seam needed caulking, for under a mainsail she took in a great abundance of water. It was impossible to keep her powder dry, and the pumps had to be manned constantly. It took almost two months to give her the appearance of seaworthiness. Warren left for the West Indies at the end of the first week in November, with the countryside blanketed by the first hard snowfall. He sailed unaccompanied by *Gosport*, for that summer she had been summoned southward to protect Georgia from a Spanish attack and had not yet returned north. Warren left word for her to join him at Antigua with all haste.[32]

Commodore Warren took command of his squadron at Carlisle Bay, Barbados, though most of his ships were then at Antigua, where he joined them on 10 December; he at once called the captains into conference.[33] He had a large force at his disposal, for besides *Launceston*, there was *Falmouth* (60), *Eltham* (44), *Scarborough* (24), *Lively* (20), the sloops *Otter* and *Pembroke's Prize*, and the bombship *Comet*. In addition, the 50–gun *Norwich* was expected to join them from the coast of Guinea and the 40–gun *Gosport* from Virginia. The Admiralty had never before concentrated so large a force in the Leeward Islands, and the prospect of achieving some local successes seemed very great.

In fact, Warren's squadron achieved almost nothing, for at the end of January 1743, Capt. Charles Knowles superseded him in command. Knowles arrived from England in the 70–gun *Suffolk* with another third rate, *Burford* (70), in company and orders to take most of the ships at Antigua under his command to carry out raids on the Spanish Main. Warren's new orders, which Knowles brought him from the Admiralty, required him to return to his station at New York and expressly forbade him "to interrupt or delay the service" on which Knowles was engaged, or to take any of the ships that had been assigned to Knowles.[34]

Like Warren, Knowles was an extremely active officer, very brave and eager for action; but, he had been made a captain only in 1737, a full ten years after Warren. Knowles had served as Admiral Vernon's trusted expert in the attacks on Portobelo, Chagres, and Cartagena and was even employed by the army as their surveyor. Yet it had taken twelve years for him to achieve the rank of lieutenant in 1730.

Though Warren was furious at being so slighted, he obeyed his orders. At once he wrote to Thomas Corbett and complained of his ill-usage:

> It wou'd have been very fortunate for me, that I had never come to these seas, on the footing I did, or that I had been thought capable of executing any commands here proper for an officer of my rank, for tho' I won't presume to say ('till better informed) that the superseding me in this command by a junior officer is owing to any dislike of their Lordships, from any misconduct, or demerit of mine, yet I humbly hope they will pardon me, when I assure them, it has that appearance with mankind, which puts me under the difficult task of clearing up my character, which I value equal with life and flatter'd myself I had supported in His Majesty's service, twenty-eight years, sixteen

of them captain, I therefore hope their Lordships from their great humanity will consider my situation, and disperse the cloud under which I now remain, that I may continue to serve my king and country, with that spirit, and zeal which I always professed.[35]

Here was Knowles, now carrying out orders that Warren himself had every reason to expect should have been his to undertake. Warren knew well how the rest of his profession would judge him, and was very anxious that the Admiralty should publicly demonstrate some act of goodwill to undo his present injury. Privately he wrote:

> I will with great truth venture to say, that if I had the capacity equal to my zeal for his Majesty's service, few in it wou'd have merited more of their Lordships favour. Nothing but the conviction of which, and the hope that their Lordships did not mean to treat me ill in this affair (in whatever light the world may look upon it) and support me in a climate where any chagrin is generally attended with the most fatal effects; should my conjecture in this point be just, I have still a character to clear up with mankind, which I apprehend can in no shape be done, but by their Lordships favour, and if I might presume to propose a method to convince the world that I was not superseded upon any dislike of theirs, or misconduct of mine. I think that of giving me the command of the North American ships to the number of four or five sail, with a distinction in rank to come to these seas in the winter season wou'd both clear up my character, and be a means of greatly distressing our present or future enemys here, by acting jointly or separately (with Mr Knowles if he continues) as the service may require.[36]

The Admiralty took this petition seriously to heart. They chose not to create a North American squadron but instead to appoint Warren the first commander in chief of all ships at Barbados and the Leeward Islands, with permission to fly a commodore's broad pendant. Knowles was given a similar appointment at the same time, but was to command only when Warren was away in the summer months on his New York station.[37] This compromise Warren accepted.

To conform to his orders, Warren took *Launceston* to cruise among the islands before coming into the Gulf Stream off the Florida coast and then northwards to New York. He netted three prizes: a sloop with a large cargo of hides bound for Havana from San Domingo, a brigantine privateer sailing for Vera Cruz from Cadiz, and a French merchantman from Martinique bound for Havana carrying goods the British considered contraband. All were sent to Jamaica to be condemned. Warren reached New York early in April with many of his crew "falling down of fluxes, fevers, & scurvy," and there poured out his grievances to his wife and the De Lanceys.[38] It is probable that he also wrote both to Admiral Norris and his agents, Messrs. Samuel and William Baker, to solicit the Admiralty on his behalf; the letters, however, have not survived.

Yet again *Launceston* needed a great deal of attention before Warren could take her cruising off the New York coast. He was twice at sea within six weeks. Both times he had on board a company of troops raised in New York to be employed as marines should any Spanish privateer be encountered. Yet after their adventures the summer before, the Spanish sent few privateers to North America, and Warren encountered none even though he ranged as far south as Charleston.

Warren had returned to New York when the new governor arrived on board *Loo* on 21 September, whereupon *Launceston* saluted him with seventeen guns.[39] Before he again sailed for the West Indies, Warren spent the next five weeks helping Clinton get settled in his new post. Clinton put his full confidence in the chief justice, James DeLancey, and from then until 1746 he retained absolute trust in him, bringing "his powers of patronage into play in behalf of DeLancey's friends."[40] Warren undoubtedly encouraged Clinton in this.

Again Warren had to leave his domestic and political life in New York to return to the dangers of sea life, with its almost inevitable mixture of rewards and disappointments. He took leave of his family, his wife who was again with child, and his friends and sailed from the Sandy Hook for the West Indies.[41] On reaching St. John's Road, Antigua, he received from Knowles the agreeable news of his appointment as commander in chief. He immediately hoisted his broad pendant in *Launceston* and was saluted with thirteen guns by the squadron. He then moved to the old 60–gun *Superbe*, taken from the French in 1710. She was a distinct improvement on the poorly built *Launceston*.

Warren was briefed on events since he last saw Knowles. He learned the full details of Knowles's two failures when he attacked the harbors of Puerto Cabello and La Guaira; the first the careening port of the Caracas Company, the latter the port of Caracas and an important center of trade. He had been bloodily repulsed both times at a cost of more than five hundred casualties and then retreated to Antigua, where he had confined the squadron to cruising and the protection of trade.

Warren commanded at sea, while Knowles hastened the building of naval yard facilities at English Harbour. Although the place had "long been recognized as a superb hurricane anchorage," only fifteen years earlier—in 1728—had initial efforts been made to equip it with a careening wharf and the necessary storehouses.[42] In 1742 both Capt. Edward Hawke and Capt. William Lisle had urged the improvement of its facilities. Lisle wanted a stone wharf on the western end with a more protected shore and prepared a detailed report for the Admiralty. Warren had read the report in December 1742 but had been given no time to make a thorough investigation before Knowles superseded him. Knowles had amended Lisle's report and received orders to undertake the work, which progressed rapidly with the help of slaves and the labor of Spanish prisoners of war.[43]

In the meantime Warren put to good use his now undisputed command. Besides *Superbe* and *Launceston*, his squadron included *Severne* (50), *Woolwich* (50), *Hastings* (40), *Lynn* (40), *Scarborough* (24), *Lyme* (20), *Deal Castle* (20), the sloop *Otter*, and the bombship *Comet*. These he kept at sea as much as possible. Several prizes were taken by the squadron, notably by Tyrrell, whom Warren had made captain of *Launceston*, and by Capt. Edward Herbert in *Woolwich*. In fact, there were few Spanish privateers left; those few remaining proceeded to sea only at grave risk to themselves, so dominant had the British navy become in those waters.

Warren's chief concern turned from the Spanish threat to the French. Warren was ignorant of the fact that, the October before, the treaty signed at Fontainebleau committed France to helping Spain recover Gibraltar and Minorca from England. Nor did he know that on 15 March France had formally declared war on England. He was equally unaware of the inconclusive battle off Toulon on 11 February between the English fleet and the combined French and Spanish fleets. Nevertheless, as winter gave way to spring, evidence rapidly accumulated that relations with France had altered profoundly. As early as 12 March Warren learned from the captain of the ordnance storeship *Salisbury* that *Aldborough* had been chased into the safety of port by French warships. But no word came from the Admiralty to confirm hostilities with France. On 9 April he wrote worriedly to Corbett: "The suspense in which I have constantly been, and still remain in, with regard to the uncertain situation of affairs, at home, had oblig'd me, to keep the ships under my command, within such limits, that I have had but little time to annoy the enemy, nor do more than protect the trade."[44] A week later he learned from an English merchant ship that Admiral Norris had gone to sea in search of the French fleet, and, from the newspapers, he first heard of Adm. Thomas Mathews's failure off Toulon. War, he felt, was bound to follow. He had reports that the French at Martinique were equipping privateers.[45]

On 21 April he was given a report that the Brest squadron had been dispersed in its projected invasion of England. Warren wrote to Corbett of his "uncertainty, as to the consequence of so extraordinary a step taken by the French, as attempting to invade our country and attacking Admiral Mathews, in conjunction with the Spaniards, whether after such an unparall'd breach of faith, and solemn treaties they are to be deem'd, As auxiliaries to the Spaniards, or principals in the war, as I am at a loss to know, I hope the latter, and that I shall soon hear of it."[46]

Warren at once concentrated his squadron and confined their cruising chiefly around the main French base of Martinique. He asked the governor of the Leeward Islands, William Mathew, to encourage the legislature to begin at once the erection of a guardhouse suitable for handling a large number of prisoners.[47] Warren informed him of his own plans for the defense of English Harbour, which included the building of a boom across the entrance. Warren felt the situation was grave enough to warrant searching all French vessels that came within sight of his squadron. On 1 May his policy changed dramatically. That day, upon searching a vessel from Le Havre, he found several letters with full accounts of the intended invasion of England in favor of the Pretender's son, Prince Charles Stuart, and the general expectation of a declaration of war. Convinced now that war had begun, Warren seized the vessel, together with two the next day from Bordeaux, and brought them into English Harbour to be condemned as prizes if a state of war truly existed, and if not, to be later released. He then ordered his captains to carry out a wholesale seizure of French shipping. At once he informed the governor of his decision, who in turn issued warnings to the other three islands under his jurisdiction.[48]

Warren then put to sea to join the scramble for prizes. The squadron was fortunate and took many ships. Warren, however, soon had to hasten back, for he had heard that the declaration of war had already reached Martinique. As he came within sight of Antigua, he stopped a sail from Dublin and was informed by the master, under oath, "that all the French at that place were stop'd, & their men taken into custody, & that a French war was hourly expected."[49] Then, on 23 May, *Comet* found a merchant ship from Cork carrying both the French and British declarations of war. The same day the sloop *Drake* arrived with the same news at last from the

Admiralty. "To the great joy of all the officers and seamen belonging to his Majesty's ships we declared war against the perfidious French, by hoisting a red flag at the topgallant mast head, reading the declaration of war and firing 21 guns."[50] The French prisoners from the fifteen prizes could hardly have misinterpreted that sound and the hurrahs that followed it.

There were no orders for Warren: he presumed they awaited him at New York and felt determined to sail at once. Very reluctantly he transferred his broad pendant from *Superbe* to the "exceeding leaky" *Launceston*.[51] By chance on his passage to New York, he met and took without the slightest difficulty *Saint François Xavier*, laden with five hundred hogsheads of sugar, some indigo, and cash to the value of about £3,000 in the form of gold and dollars.

Warren took the prize with him to New York, where she became the occasion of a serious dispute with the local collector of customs. As with all earlier prizes condemned at New York, foreign duties had been demanded on prize goods. Warren knew that other colonies exempted the produce carried on prizes. The matter was particularly important to Warren, for with a cargo of sugar, extra-heavy charges would be made under the Molasses Act. The prospect of his prize money vanishing stirred Warren to action. He appealed the collector's decision and, with the help of Governor Clinton and the DeLancey faction, got the assembly to pass a law exempting the goods from foreign duties. Let the historian of this incident take up the tale:

> The collector of the port was still adamant and turned for assistance to the Vice Admiralty Court. Judge Lewis Morris, Jr., could not have been unbiased in this case. And expansion of privateering was certain to bring him fat fees from prize cases. Whether through prejudice or precedent, he found in Warren's favour. But custom's officials are stubborn men and those at New York appealed to England. Governor Clinton rallied to the support of Warren and the privateersmen. In a letter to the Duke of Newcastle, he emphasized the "great expence" assumed by the city's merchants in fitting out privateers and stressed that the "nature of the duty claimed, would anticipate most of their gains" since the prize goods were mostly sugars.[52]

The governor's argument hardly applied to Warren, but the collector was a beaten man, and Warren became the richer by several hundred pounds sterling.[53]

His pleasure at taking so rich a prize vanished the moment he reached New York, for there his wife gave him the news of the deaths of two of his children and of his sister in Ireland, Anne Johnson. His children, the eldest, Elizabeth, and his only son Peter, had died in an influenza epidemic in March, a fortnight before his wife gave birth to another daughter, Susannah. A record of these doleful events was recounted in a letter his wife had sent to his nephew, William Johnson, almost two months earlier:

> I rec'd yr favour this day, of ye 2d of aprill & one before, which I should have answered, but my sore afflictions made me incapable. The loss of my two Dear Children hangs still very heavy on me, as does the loss of your mother, whose Death I much Lament. I have a letter from yr Father, who say she dyed ye 26th of January of a tedious decay occasioned by a Cholick and ague, he complains that you don't write to him, I am an unfit person at present to mention this melancholy affair at present to yu, for I have not spirits to give yu any Comfort and I hope allmighty God the great disposer of all things will comfort you.[54]

The agony of loss that Warren felt can easily be guessed. When seven years later he learned of the death of the only son of William Pepperrell, he wrote:

> I most sincerely condole with you on the great affliction with which you have been visited by the hand of providence in the death of your only son; But if I know you right, I think you have fortitude and resignation sufficient to bear it as becomes a good man, and to submit to the great power yet whose will it was to call him from this vain world, and to bereave you of so great an earthly comfort, as we look upon our children to be, but why should I, who have felt the same distress myself, say so much to renew your concern. My wife joins with me in wishing you to bear with patience this trial.[55]

To console himself, Warren threw his energy into getting *Launceston* again fit for sea. For seven weeks he had to employ twenty caulkers to fill her seams. Most of the powder was spoiled through dampness and had to be replaced—at three times the cost owing to its scarcity in the colony. It greatly perplexed Warren to be ashore with a French war just beginning. The defenseless state of the New York coastline also worried him, so he urged Clinton to ask the Admiralty to send additional ships to North

America. Clinton never received a favorable reply.[56] Warren also urged the governor to ask the legislature to outfit a guard ship as other colonies, especially in New England, had wisely done.[57]

This Clinton did in mid-July, but the assembly disagreed; when Clinton again broached the subject in March 1745, the assembly again declined to put the province to the expense.[58] This sharp difference between the governor and the elected body concerning just how the colony of New York should undertake the war with France led, in time, to a serious breakdown in government.

Unable to be at sea, Warren had time to turn his mind to strategic considerations. For the northern colonies the entry of France into the war had created serious difficulties. The news of the French declaration had reached Louisbourg three weeks before any American port heard word of it. Its governor, Jean-Baptiste-Louis Duquesnel, had at once fitted out two privateers and decided to attack Canso, which he regarded "as one of the most important British fishing posts in North America."[59] It had fallen even more quickly than Warren had predicted in 1739; when the first shots were fired, the commanding officer, Capt. Patrick Heron, had dashed out with a flag of truce. Before leaving with their prisoners, the French demolished the puny fortifications. Now Duquesnel's ambitions soared. He planned an attack on Annapolis Royal, whose garrison was no more numerous than Canso's had been, though with better fortifications and a more resolute commanding officer, Lt. Gov. Paul Mascarene. Despite the assistance of the Mi'kmaq and some Acadien inhabitants, the French attack failed.

Even before learning of the fall of Canso, Gov. William Shirley of Massachusetts had called on the general court of the colony to send reinforcements to the Bay of Fundy. The first of these had reached Annapolis Royal late in July, in time to frustrate the French designs there. The colony of New York did not feel equally committed, for its worries fixed on its extensive and ill-protected frontier with Canada. Warren's own settlement on the Mohawk was gravely threatened, while Albany itself would be exposed to attack if the *Canadiens* with their native allies decided to open hostilities in that quarter.

Warren dusted off an idea he had first expressed to the Admiralty in February 1743. At that time he said: "I think I cou'd make it appear that the dispossession of Canada and Cape Brettoon [sic], wou'd be of greater consequence to Great Britain than any other conquest that we may hope to make in a Spanish or French war, and our northern colony's are in a much

better situation now . . . the increase of the French subjects since that time
bearing no equality with that of our colonies."[60] Now in September 1744,
he repeated the suggestion to the Admiralty, adding details:

> I have made it my business to inform myself of their situation, as
> much as I cou'd to be sure nothing cou'd be a great acquisition to
> Great Britain, and its dominions, then the dispossessing the French of
> Cape Brettoon and Quebeck, by which the whole fur, and fish trade,
> wou'd be in our hands, a source of immense treasure, much greater to
> us alone if we had it, then now to both the French and us, for the
> constant feuds and animosity's, which they politically sow among the
> Indians, prevents their application to hunting for furs, and other
> valuable commodity's when on the contrary were we in possession of
> those places, we shou'd unite all the different nations of Indians to
> us, and to one another, some of which are so remote, that eye of
> Englishmen have not seen, nor any ear heard of, nor can it hardly be
> conceiv'd by us, what vast treasure it wou'd bring to our country,
> beside securing all his Majesty's subjects, upon the continent, in the
> quiet and peaceable possession of their lives, while so artful, and de-
> signing a people as the French are surrounding us, and using all their
> influence and application to get such [great] Nations of Indians [into]
> their interest and obedience, which if once accomplish'd will drive us
> into the sea.[61]

He reminded the secretary to the Admiralty that he had on an earlier
occasion written to him on the same subject "in a private and very long
letter gave you my sentiments upon this head." Then he had expressed
that his grave doubts of success "were owing to the navigation, the short-
ness of the summers, the want of good pilots and the mistakes people are
liable to (who have not very good intelligence) in making a disposition for
such an undertaking." He added, "I then recommended consulting the different governors and the legislatures of the colonies, with as much secrecy
as possible about it, and reducing their opinions, and the assistance they
wou'd give into proper form, to be laid before the ministry and their Lordships, who by that means wou'd be the best judges whether it is practicable,
and what force of ships &ca, wou'd be necessary from home." Warren believed that the British North American colonies, "upon proper application,
wou'd all assist in proportion to the good effect they shou'd conceive it
wou'd have on each of them."[62]

There were few men in either America or England whose ambitions went so far, perhaps only Governor Shirley of Massachusetts, although there is no evidence that even he had thought the matter out as thoroughly as had Warren.[63] In this letter, Warren stated all the essentials of the problem and expressed the widely felt impression that although the French were not numerous, their alliance with the native tribes made them so and enabled them to fence in the American colonies. Altogether it is a remarkable document from a sea officer, and unprecedented for those who had served in American waters. Warren's sources of information were, of course, excellent. The DeLanceys had sixty years of experience in the fur trade; they knew well both the Iroquois—especially the Mohawk—and the French merchants who were sometimes their rivals and sometimes their clients. William Johnson too, in his years on the frontier, had acquired unmatched experience of the confederacy of tribes. In addition, Warren's time in Boston had afforded numerous occasions for discussing the seriousness of the French threat. He acquired the usual prejudices, marked by a strong jealousy of French achievements and the conviction that they should be driven from North America. The difficulties he saw would be great, but the rewards of peace and prosperity would make the risks acceptable.

Shortly before he was due to leave New York for the West Indies, Warren received reports that a small squadron of warships was rumored to be on its way from France to Louisbourg to act as escort to several rich East India merchant ships that had orders to rendezvous there. He decided to attempt an attack and, as he said, thereby make his fortune. With *Launceston* and *Hastings,* the Virginia station ship commanded by Lord Alexander Banff, and whatever colonial privateers and guard ships were willing to join him, he would make all haste for Louisbourg. He was prepared to take the risk that the French warships might be of a superior armament. He informed Clinton and wrote to Shirley, asking for his cooperation.[64] The plan came to nothing, for *Hastings* was not ready for sea and Banff unwilling to leave his station; moreover, Shirley was angered by Warren's presumption in planning an attack on French shipping when two months earlier he had been unable to send help to reinforce Annapolis Royal.[65] Warren abandoned the project only when fierce gales tore at *Launceston,* again opening her seams. He instead bore south for Barbados. At once his good fortune returned, for within sight of the island he captured a Martinique privateer, *Maria Carlotta,* mounting eighteen guns and carrying a crew of eighty-seven. The prisoners were exchanged shortly afterwards for an equivalent number of English seamen brought from Martinique under a flag of truce.[66]

This proved to be Warren's last tour of duty in the West Indies, and the strain on the navy of waging war with both Spain and France was evident to him the moment he reached Antigua. The first indication was the increasing difficulty of maintaining the blockade of Martinique and Guadeloupe, which he had begun in April. At first, the French had suffered a shortage of provisions and an inability to dispatch privateers. By June, with Knowles in command, almost 150 vessels were locked up and unable to sail. This had changed in September, for on hearing the rumor of a French squadron on its way to the West Indies, Knowles had been obliged to realign his squadron in an attempt to intercept it. This forced the lifting of the English blockade, though the rumor proved false.

Now in December, the squadron plainly showed the cost of keeping active at sea for so many months, despite a careful rotation for refitting. Warren found the squadron very short of both naval and ordnance stores, though beginning in May and throughout the summer he had appealed for fresh supplies.[67] In this way, the domination of the seas around the Leeward and Windward Islands by the British squadron began to be successfully challenged. In December 1744 the squadron had been unable to prevent five heavily armed and richly laden vessels from leaving Puerto Cabello and sailing home by the Mona Passage between Hispaniola and Puerto Rico. Knowles had been forewarned of the convoy's intentions and had, from the Mona Passage, dispatched *Superbe, Severn, Lynn,* and two sloops there to the ships in the squadron, but in vain.

Nothing better illustrated the squadron's inability to dominate the Caribbean than Warren's futile attempt to prevent the neutral Dutch and Danes from supplying the French. His squadron captured a sufficient number of vessels from St. Eustatius and Curaçao, as well as off St. Thomas, Martinique, and Guadeloupe because of suspicions that they had been trading with the French. As neutrals, they were within their rights as long as warlike stores were not involved unless the islands were actually being blockaded. Then all trade became contraband. Because Warren and Knowles had hoped to starve the French islands, any supply of food acquired strategic importance. To the Admiralty, Warren expressed his belief that there was no other method of putting a stop to this trade "but by looking upon the French Islands, as blockaded by our ships, and therefore seize provision as other contraband."[68] The trouble was that the squadron had ceased effectively to blockade Martinique, and the rest of the islands received only passing notice. The squadron increasingly had to content itself with patrolling among the islands, protecting English and colonial trade, and taking prizes where it could. At the end of January, Warren wrote to the governor of St. Eustatius, Johannis Heyliger, and accused his merchants—since the outbreak of war between France and Great Britain—of supplying the French islands with all sorts of provisions and stores "proper for war, in manifest breach, and violation of treaty's and the neutrality that shou'd be religiously observed, by party's in that strict amity" in direct contradiction of such friendship which he hoped would always characterize relations between Britain and the Dutch Republic.[69] He ended with a warning that "I look upon Martinique, and the other islands here, belonging to the French, as blockaded, and invested, by the ships under my command and that I have given them directions, to seize, and bring into port, in order to be prosecuted, according to law, all ships and vessels, under what colours Soever, that they meet with carrying them contraband stores, or provisions, while they are so invested, and blockaded." This high-handed attitude was adequately rebutted by the governor, who merely reminded Warren that he had no evidence whatsoever of Martinique or any other French island being invested or blockaded. "I have this day heard from two of those places which are not invested, nor blockaded, and from whence their privateers frequently go out, and return, without interruption, there being none of his Majesty's ships, before their ports, to oppose them," was the gist of his argument.[70] He also denied that any ships from his island had supplied the French with warlike stores.

When Admiral Davers arrived at Antigua on his way to relieve Admiral Ogle at Jamaica, Warren consulted with him about the problem with neutrals. As Davers disagreed with Warren, the commodore was obliged to alter his orders to his captains. Henceforth, they were not to molest neutral shipping, but suspected ships were to be searched for contraband stores.[71]

The whole argument could easily have been settled if the Admiralty had been prepared to carry out a series of expeditions against the French bases, as they had against those of Spain between 1739 and 1743. If such expeditions had been planned and had succeeded, the Dutch and the Danes would have had no French colony to supply. Such was not the case, for the entry of France into the war had thrown British squadrons in the West Indies—at Jamaica, Antigua, and Barbados—on the defensive, as long as powerful French and Spanish fleets, even when in port, tied down the bulk of the British fleet in European waters.

Warren was one of the very few officers who attempted to influence the

Admiralty to adopt a more vigorous policy. Often he recommended that a "Flying squadron, of about five good ships" be sent each winter.[72] This was a far cry from the grand expeditionary force under Vernon or even that assembled for Knowles in 1743. Warren thought of it as a powerful raiding force rather than a strategic weapon of decisive proportions: "If there had been such this winter, whoever had commanded them, might have distress'd the enemys of his Majesty greatly and acquir'd honour and fortune to themselves, not inferior to that of Mr Anson" on his round-the-world voyage which ended in 1744.

Warren's primary task then was to protect British trade, and this he found a difficult responsibility to discharge. The abundance of flags of truce from Martinique told the clear tale that the French, now with many privateers afloat, were taking as many trading vessels as they lost. Where the French suffered more was in the loss of privateers, for, without benefit of a protecting squadron, these became their first line of defense and only offensive weapon. Yet from the end of November, when Warren reached the West Indies, until the end of February the squadron had taken only three French privateers. Warren had personally been responsible for two, and in February Capt. Richard Tiddeman in *Deal Castle* had taken one with a crew of 124, including ten carriage guns and twenty swivel—the most heavily armed privateer yet encountered. Still, the French had hardly been swept from the seas.

Several times Warren argued that losses among English and colonial shipping were too often the fault of the merchant captains. Warren, and every other captain, had always found merchantmen difficult to regulate in convoy: they did not obey signals, and they did not adhere to the appointed rendezvous. He advised the Admiralty to warn merchants always to send their ships bound for the West Indies first to Antigua. In fact, they took a wide variety of routes to avoid the enemy. Warren wanted them all to take the same route in order to provide adequate protection. Yet he was very doubtful of securing their agreement: "and while they continue to act as they do at present, were the whole British fleet employ'd here for their protection only, they could not secure them from falling often into the Hands of the Enemy."[73] Warren was particularly annoyed at having to answer a complaint from several Barbados merchants, conveyed to him in a letter from the Admiralty, dated 17 September 1744, and therefore arising from the previous spring. In replying, Warren took the criticism personally, for he had always exerted great effort toward maintaining close relations with merchants wherever he had been stationed: London, Boston,

New York, Charleston, Kingston, Carlisle Bay, or English Harbour. His defense, however sound, was in fact an admission of failure:

> If it had not much the appearance of vanity, I cou'd send their Lordships publick testimonies, of the satisfaction I have given in general here, and to that island in particular, from where the complaint has arisen. Whither it happened that those vessels were taken in my time, or not, I cant say, but believe the journals of the squadron will show. Then and in Mr Knowles's time, there were always cruisers to windward in the proper tracks of the trade, to all the islands . . . The trade never was deny'd convoy in my absence . . . The *Argyle* and *Otter* have been kept at Barbados, attending them, the one three weeks at a time, the other five. Most of these vessels . . . were Sloops, from the northern colonies . . . for tho' I very well know that there is not more honour in any community, or set of people, than in general may be found in the trading part of His Majesty's subjects, yet even they will allow, that rule is not without exceptions, and that they have, as well as other flocks their scabby sheep and those I fear, and have great reason to believe, tho' tis not to be legally prov'd, many of them being highly insur'd go into the enemys paths, in order to make a better market by their insurance, then they can do by their traffick.[74]

The very size of the British and colonial trade with the West Indies made it, in war, a target larger and hence more vulnerable than that of the French. With vessels coming from English and Irish ports, from the African coast, and from every continental colony and outpost from Newfoundland to Georgia, the French were presented with as enticing a target as had been the British, when in 1739 they set about ravishing the trade of Spanish America. However much Warren had the merchants' interests at heart and however energetic his squadron, unless the French Antilles bases were destroyed or their capacity to outfit privateers curtailed, Warren would have to admit to failure, as not all the British merchant fleet could be protected at all times.

It was not the merchant vessels alone that were vulnerable. On 9 February, Warren at last received the much-needed naval and ordnance stores for his squadron. They had come under convoy of *Weymouth* (60), with Warwick Calmady as captain. *Weymouth*, designed by the Admiralty as a suitable ship from which Warren could fly his red broad pendant, however, had a remarkably short life in the Leeward Islands.[75] On 12 February, when Warren was ashore with Knowles and Admiral Davers—who had just arrived from England with three warships, a sloop, and a convoy of trade—word was brought to them at lunch of a sea fight blazing just outside the harbor entrance. Warren raced for *Woolwich*, "the readiest ship," and took her out of the harbor within twenty minutes.[76] Tyrrell followed in *Launceston* "then on a heel" in less than an hour. Later, Calmady took out *Weymouth*, with Knowles aboard, in company with *Lynn*. Warren quickly came up with the sloop *Mercury*, which he found so knocked about that she was barely able to sail, and learned that she had been caught by the fire of the 36–gun *Santa Teresa*, a recently built privateer from Havana. Warren pressed on and came up to the bombship *Comet* shortly before dark. She had been made a Spanish prize, but when Warren began his pursuit she was abandoned by her captors, who took with them *Comet*'s captain, Richard Spry.[77] Warren kept to windward all night, as the fleeing privateer appeared to be making for Guadeloupe. At dawn the next day, with no sail in sight, Warren retreated to Antigua. *Launceston*, as instructed by Warren, chased to leeward all night but saw nothing at dawn; only by two long tacks was she able to return to Antigua on 22 February. Meanwhile, both *Weymouth* and *Lynn*, having roughly guessed the course the Spanish would take, saw them the next day, but could not overtake the prey. *Weymouth* never reached the safety of Freeman's Bay. At 1:00 a.m. on 17 February, by mistaking Antigua for Montserrat, she went aground three miles off St. John's Road, where Admiral Davers and his squadron lay at anchor. She could not be saved. By 11:00 in the morning, the ship had bilged and her masts had gone over the side. The entire crew was rescued with all contents, except those in her hold, and of course the hull. Davers at once summoned a court martial of which Warren was a member; Calmady was acquitted.[78] One of his lieutenants, on watch at the fatal moment, was mulcted six months' pay and severely reprimanded. The master was declared incapable of ever again serving as an officer. The pilot was found guilty of neglect of duty, sentenced to two years in the Marshalsea prison, and declared incapable of ever again piloting one of His Majesty's ships. It was a sorry moment in the history of seamanship and denied Warren the ship he had wanted ever since he had accepted *Launceston* three years earlier.

The court martial had hardly concluded when Warren received a most important communication from Governor Shirley of Massachusetts. The letter was dated 29 January and reached Warren on 23 February. It told of the colony's decision both to attack Louisbourg and to ask for the assistance of some of the warships stationed in the West Indies. A similar letter had been sent at the same time to Sir Chaloner Ogle, commander of the Jamaica squadron. Ogle, long out of touch with American affairs, in no way felt obliged to take action. He advised his successor that it was not in his power to comply with Shirley's request. It did not occur to Ogle that he might take his homeward-bound squadron, consisting of *Cumberland* (80), *Ripon* (60), *Montague* (60), *Assistance* (50), and the 20–gun frigate *Experience,* northward to give what help he could before continuing on to England.

At first Warren appeared to react in much the same manner, but he must have been tantalized by Shirley's offer "to come yourself and take upon you the command of the expedition." However much he may have wanted to accept, his responsibilities in the Leeward Islands clearly dictated his movements. He called a council of war with Knowles, Francis Holbourne, William Lisle, James Douglass, and Richard Tyrrell in attendance. After considering both Shirley's letter and the scheme to attack Louisbourg, Warren felt obliged to agree with the rest that the project appeared not to have the sanction of the home government. In view of the loss of *Weymouth,* any further diminution of strength would greatly weaken the squadron, then expecting daily the appearance of a French squadron, and would be of "no great service" to the expedition. It was agreed that Warren would send *Mermaid* at once to her station at New York, *Launceston* to her new station at New England, and he would remain himself in *Superbe* until a reply had been received from England via an express to be carried there with all haste by *Mercury,* now seaworthy again after her recent battle.[79] Warren assured the Admiralty that these decisions were "conformable to my own, and all the captains opinions."[80]

Matters did not lie long there. On 8 March, just as Warren was preparing to take *Superbe* on a cruise, the sloop *Hind* arrived from England with a commission for Warren from the Admiralty, together with new instructions. The commission was dated 1 January and the instructions were sent by Corbett three days later, all of this weeks before the ministry had learned of Shirley's intention to raise an expeditionary force against Cape Breton. They were very similar to the dispatches the Duke of Newcastle had sent to both Clinton and Shirley the same day. Both had been asked to give Warren whatever assistance he requested: "either of men, provisions, or shipping, to enable him to proceed either to the relief and succour of Annapolis Royal, or of any other of his Majesty's forts, or settlements, or for making any attempt upon the enemy."[81] Newcastle and the Admiralty thought that if Warren raided French fisheries and commerce, he would more than satisfy their purposes.

Though there was no mention of the Louisbourg expedition, Warren, as the first commander in chief in North America, could hardly avoid being involved. Warren was not particularly pleased with the turn of events. He summoned his captains again, and despite their opposition in view of the certain news which *Hind* had also brought of a French squadron on its way to Martinique, Warren determined not only to sail at once but to take *Superbe* with him.[82] The Admiralty had given him permission to take four ships, of which *Weymouth*—now a wreck—was one, and *Hastings,* which had never joined the squadron from Virginia as directed, was another.

This decision caused a great deal of ill feeling. The governor and assembly of Antigua "complained in the strongest terms of the danger to which the islands and the trade would be exposed by his departure."[83] Knowles complained to the governor and council of Antigua who, with those at St. Christopher's and Montserrat (both having already complained to Warren), directed humble addresses on the topic to the sovereign.[84] Knowles initially refused to take command of the squadron if *Superbe* was removed, or even to quit the ship "without you suspend or dismiss" him from her command.[85] Warren summoned two captains to carry to Knowles his direct order, which even that intemperate officer dared not refuse. Warren's very high opinion of this officer was shaken. "I am uneasy to differ with you in opinion," he wrote Knowles, "because I have ever until now, paid the greatest deference to yours."[86]

When Warren wrote to the Admiralty, he requested to be summoned home to England if Knowles's grievance against him was upheld.[87] It is worth noting that his resentment, in February 1743, at being superseded by Knowles had been wholly directed against the Admiralty, and he had at that time spoken of Knowles's "genteel behaviour on his arrival."[88] He had accepted his junior very kindly when he had returned to Antigua the following winter and at all times succeeded in working in close harmony with him. When Knowles had been criticized by the Admiralty for alleged extravagance in the building of the facilities at English Harbour, Warren defended him, saying that his economy would "save the government a considerable sum of money."[89] When Knowles suggested to Warren the need for a second storehouse and an apartment for a storekeeper, he fully agreed "being persuaded it will be a great saving, to the government, to have the storekeeper on the spot," and gave him permission, and only then asked the Navy Board to ratify it.[90] When hostilities with France began, he put complete faith in Knowles to fortify English Harbour.[91] When Knowles was threatened with imprisonment for debt, Warren immediately commissioned a prize Knowles had taken, without seeking Navy Board approval, thereby saving "a good officer from going to jail," and explained to the Admiralty that the service would have suffered more through his absence from overseeing the works at English Harbour than twice the value of the vessel, which had cost £2,666.[92] Even as he now wrote, warning the Admiralty that they could expect a complaint against him from Knowles, he spoke of him as "a very good officer," appreciating his difficulty and recommending the Admiralty to "make him amends, by sending him a better ship, as soon as possible."[93] He also asked that if the Admiralty found his decision insupportable: "I pray to be call'd home, to account for my actions, face to face, and I flatter myself, that they will find my motives, will appear, such as will not subject me, to their censure, to avoid which, has ever been my highest ambition, and it is with the greatest reluctance, I trouble their Lordships on a subject of this kind, which through the whole course of my servitude, in the Navy, never happened to me before, with any body."[94]

In fact, Warren was taking the greatest risk of his entire naval career. He was committed to supporting an expedition that it was not yet certain the government had sanctioned, which would be principally dependent on raw colonial levies, led by men devoid of military experience. He was weakening the Leeward Islands squadron by one ship of the line more than the Admiralty had calculated, at a moment when there were clear indications of the imminent arrival of a French squadron. *Hind* herself had seen the enemy off the Canaries. Even to disoblige the merchants and council of Antigua, with whom, as usual, he was on excellent terms, could have been no easy decision for him. There was every reason to doubt the wisdom of his present course of action, yet there was now clearly no doubt in his mind that he should go, and as quickly as possible, with the strongest force he dared take.

A View of the Town and Harbour of Louisbourg, ca. 1745. By permission of the British Library, c-2716.

Capture of Louisbourg, by Peter Monamy. By permission of the National Maritime Museum, Greenwich, England, A7943.

Above: *Battle of Finisterre, 1747*, by S. Scott. By permission of the National Maritime Museum, Greenwich, England, neg. 1314.

Left: *The Naval Nurse or Modern Commander*, engraving by R. Attwold. By permission of the British Library, c-2725.

Humours of the Westminster Election, or the scald-miserable Independent Electors in ye suds, July 1747. By permission of the British Library, c-2723.

The Honest Sailor (Sir Peter Warren, Vice Admiral of the White Squadron), engraving by N. Parr, publ. by Dickenson. By permission of the National Maritime Museum, Greenwich, England, neg. B3443.

Sir Peter Warren, Vice Admiral of the White. By permission of the Huntington Library and Art Gallery, San Marino, California.

Engraved by Ridley.

Sir Peter Warren, Vice Admiral of the Red Squadron, engraving by William Ridley. By permission of the National Maritime Museum, Greenwich, England, PU2784.

Sir Peter Warren, Vice Admiral of the Red, 1751, by Thomas Hudson, engraving by Johan Faber. By permission of the National Maritime Museum, Greenwich, England, B1977.

Detail of bust of Sir Peter Warren, by Louis François Roubiliac. By permission of the Huntington Library and Art Gallery, San Marino, California.

Sir John Norris, by C. Knapton. By permission of the National Maritime Museum, Greenwich, England, neg. 1319.

Sir William Pepperrell, by John Smibert. By permission of the Peabody Essex Museum, Salem, Massachusetts.

Admiral Sir Charles Knowles, Admiral of the Royal Navy, Governor of Louisbourg, 1746. By permission of the Athenaeum, Portsmouth, New Hampshire.

Richard Tyrrel, by Thomas Hudson. By permission of the National Maritime Museum, Greenwich, England, neg. 1894.

Westbury House, front view, ca. 1900.

Westbury House, rear view, ca. 1900.

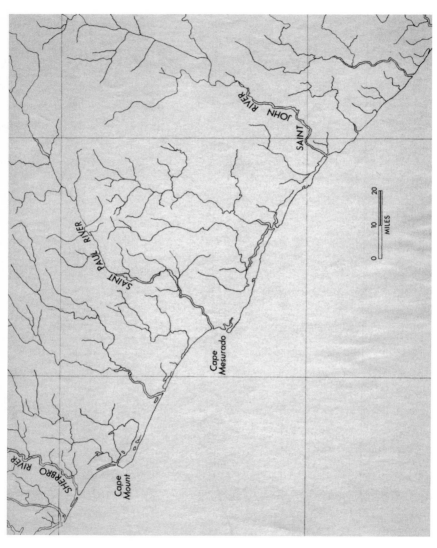

Grain Coast, West Africa.

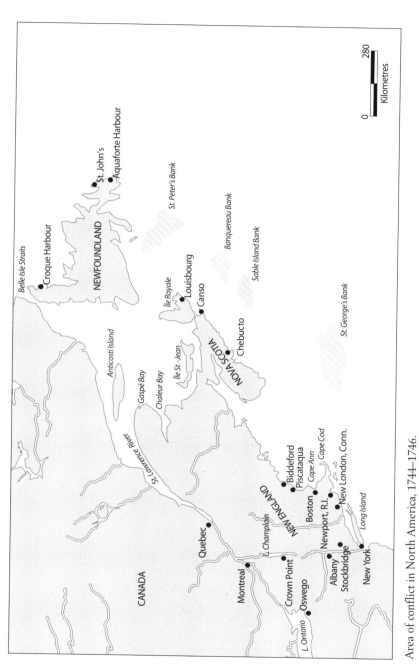

Area of conflict in North America, 1744–1746.

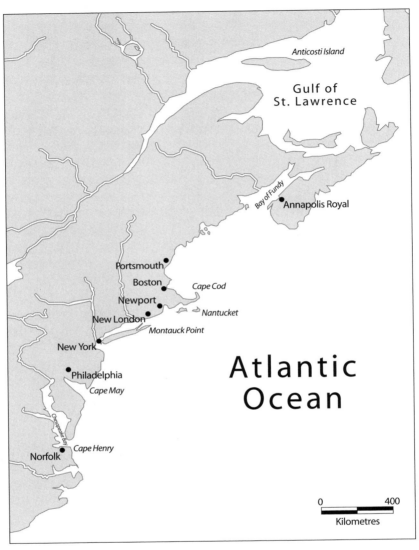

Anticosti Island

Gulf of
St. Lawrence

Bay of Fundy

● Annapolis Royal

Portsmouth ●

Boston ●   Cape Cod

Newport ●

New London ●   Nantucket

Montauck Point

New York ●

● Philadelphia

Cape May

Chesapeake Bay

Cape Henry

Norfolk ●

Atlantic
Ocean

0   400
Kilometres

Eastern coastline of North America between Cape Breton and Virginia.

4

The Siege of Louisbourg, 1745

As Warren made the two-thousand-mile passage from Antigua to Canso, the rendezvous for the expeditionary force, he had much time to consider the wisdom of the New England initiative. He felt compelled to write two lengthy letters to Adm. George Anson, recently named to the Board of Admiralty. He referred to an earlier suggestion by Anson of an "[e]xpedition in embrio against Cape Breton," and to his own private correspondence with Thomas Corbett on the need to capture Louisbourg.[1] One letter is filled with foreboding:

> I think it wou'd be in vain to attempt Lewisbourg, without a moral certainty of success. As it is a regular fortification, and has always a strong garrison, of regular troops, in it, I submit whether it is not likely, that it will hold out a siege longer, than the season will allow the besiegers (if not numerous enough, to take it by storm) to keep the field, and what can they do in that case in the winter? It is certain if ships go into the harbour to attack it the people must determine to succeed or dye. . . . The navigation is bad, and the weather foggy and no proper place to anchor any where near Lewisbourg.

Despite the difficulties, he assured Anson that he would exert himself to the fullest to allow every chance of success. Yet his idea of a suitable expeditionary force was quite different from what Shirley had indicated in his letter. Warren wanted regular troops from England and a proper artillery train—all protected with an adequately equipped squadron. Colonial troops and vessels would also play their part.

Shirley himself had held similar views when he first began seriously to consider attacking Cape Breton. By December 1744 he was shown a plan for a surprise attack on Louisbourg by William Vaughan, "a successful fishing and lumbering entrepreneur" of Maine, and John Bradstreet, a captain in the 40th Foot, who had been captured when Canso fell.[2] The scheme called for an independent colonial expedition, in which surprise would more than compensate for the absence of a naval squadron and siege artillery. On 9 January the Massachusetts general court considered the plan at "an unprecedented secret session."[3] The scheme amounted to a daring raid of two thousand volunteers, who with luck and the blessings of divine providence "might make themselves masters of the town and Harbor."[4] The first reaction of the members was that it had no hope of success. A committee was formed, and after two days' debate declared itself almost unanimously opposed to the scheme, chiefly because the committee doubted New England's ability to procure the men, arms, provisions, and transport needed to mount the attack. Shirley was then forced to admit failure and wrote to Newcastle, urging the ministry to take the initiative and mount an expedition to destroy the French menace, telling him of the general court's decision to support such an effort.[5] Vaughan refused to accept the verdict of the committee. He found one hundred Marblehead fishermen who promised to furnish vessels to carry thirty-five hundred men. Vaughan then set about contacting some two hundred of the most influential men of Boston to urge the general court to reconsider the idea. He rekindled Shirley's interest and was allowed to have Bradstreet and others who had personal knowledge of Louisbourg to be present when the committee met. The committee was won over, and its new resolution, favorable to the expedition, passed in the house of representatives on 25 January. Massachusetts then solicited the help of the neighboring governments of New York, the Jerseys, Pennsylvania, New Hampshire, Connecticut, and Rhode Island. A commanding officer, William Pepperrell, was appointed. Pepperrell, a highly successful merchant with many years of experience in the general court and as president of the council, was without military experience. As colonel of the Maine militia, he had done little more than inspect the frontier defenses. Yet he was a popular choice, and the desire for plunder soon swelled the enlistment rolls.[6] As the merchants strained their resources to fill the orders for provisions, a motley fleet of transports and escorts collected in Boston harbor. On 24 March the fleet proceeded to the rendezvous at Canso.

The expeditionary force had gone to sea only when Shirley had received Warren's reply to his letter. The news was confined to his closest advisors; the crew sailed in ignorance. Without warning, on 9 April, the situation changed: news reached Boston that Warren was on his way with three ships. The same day the news reached New York, and Susannah Warren left at once for Boston, hoping to find her husband there.[7] Shirley received the news with mixed feelings; additional strength while welcomed was not essential to the success of an expedition that for weeks he had been arguing could be achieved by New Englanders alone. Warren had been critical of the scheme. The tone of his letter was clear; he thought it rash. Shirley at once realized that the unified command under William Pepperrell would now be threatened.[8] Warren would expect to command at sea and this division of authority might jeopardize the entire expedition. To Pepperrell, he wrote at once: "It is a general observation that the land and sea forces when joined upon the same expedition seldom or never agree. I am perswaded it will not be so between you and Commodore Warren, as any misunderstanding might prove fatal."[9] He believed that Pepperrell was not one to pick a quarrel, but having to work side by side with a proud and experienced professional, he stood every chance of becoming the object of criticism. Shirley implored Pepperrell in every letter he wrote to him that month to keep Warren fully informed so there would be no cause for complaint. Pepperrell took this advice very much to heart, and his remarkably regular correspondence with Warren constitutes one of the principal sources for the history of the siege. Shirley's concern was somewhat eased when he received Warren's next letter, delivered on 22 April by the purser of *Superbe*. He now told Pepperrell that "Warren's heart seems by his letter to be intirely set upon the reduction of the place."[10] Again he implored Pepperrell "let the utmost harmony be preserved between you, as what must (under God) secure your success more than anything." He informed the general that Warren's commission gave him the command of all ships and vessels to the north of Virginia, so that he must transfer to Warren, without delay, the command of those privateers and colony cruisers already involved in the expedition.

Warren reached Canso on the morning of 23 April, having spent five days in St. Margaret's Bay on the Nova Scotia coast. He had sent ahead from Antigua orders to Captain Durell of *Bien Aimé* not to sail home with mastships, as his previous orders had instructed him, but to join the expedition at Canso. Durell had received Warren's letter just as he was on the point of sailing from Piscataqua for Portsmouth. He at once adhered to his new instructions and joined the squadron at Canso.

The eleven vessels that now came under Warren's command were quite diverse but small and in many ways the ideal complement to the much larger warships.[11] Once the troops were safely landed, Warren had as many small sailing craft as he desired to carry messages to Boston, Canso, and Annapolis Royal, to correspond with Pepperrell on land, and to ensure the complete effectiveness of the blockade of Louisbourg by sea. He also used the vessels, under command of *Eltham*, to devastate the French fishing villages on the Cape Breton coast. He provisioned his squadron with their help; he had prisoners carried to Boston in them; and he employed the largest of them, *Molineux, Caesar, Shirley, Prince of Orange, Boston Packet, Massachusetts,* and *Fame,* in his line of battle. Once they had grown accustomed to using proper signals and to carrying out his orders with enthusiasm and dispatch, they greatly pleased Warren with their performance. He had occasion later to speak highly of their captains and crews alike.

Even so, the problems facing both Warren and Pepperrell were immense. The fortifications, begun in 1718 five years after the town was founded, had grown prodigiously by 1745, presenting an imposing barrier to the untrained eye. The town looked out to a large harbor and was protected on the landward side by two bastions and two demi-bastions, with a ditch covertway and glacis. A curtain wall ran the full three-quarters of a mile connecting these bastions, with one end anchored on the rocky ocean coast and the other on the shore of the harbor. The harbor mouth was almost a mile across and the channel between ten and twelve fathoms deep. It was well protected by a 36–gun battery on an island near the middle and by numerous scarcely submerged reefs that effectively reduced the passage by half. If a hostile force managed to break into the harbor, it would have immediately come under fire from the 42–pounders located in an isolated battery—the Grand battery—on the mainland about one mile northeast of the town and commanding not only the entrance into the harbor, but every part of it.[12] The town was garrisoned by more than five hundred regulars, some of whom were Swiss, and as many as nine hundred militia.[13] Pepperrell's chief concerns, once his troops had landed, were discipline, siege artillery, and a successful plan of attack. The first he never solved; the second solved itself when the French abandoned the Grand battery and failed to spike efficiently the great guns they left behind. The third evolved slowly. Warren's overriding apprehension was that the siege would have to be abandoned if a French squadron more powerful than his own arrived off Louisbourg. His other major worry was the short season, which made speed essential if the besiegers were to succeed. Equally troubling was the prospect, too real on a coast known for its fogs, of French ships slipping through his blockade and bringing reinforcements and fresh provisions to the garrison.

There were no French warships in harbor when Warren's squadron arrived, but this caused no particular concern for the garrison. Strategy upon the outbreak of war had been determined ten years earlier, when the Comte de Maurepas, the French *ministre de la marine,* had determined that to take the fortress Britain would have to dispatch troops from England in concert with an impressive naval force. In the interval needed to outfit such an expeditionary force, France, having evaluated the menace, could then reinforce Louisbourg in plenty of time to raise the siege, if it had already begun.[14]

Despite the impressive appearance of the fortress there were serious shortcomings. These were well known to successive engineers and commandants at Louisbourg. In violation of the principles of fortification, the fortress walls were commanded by low hills, from which one could see without difficulty over the walls into the town. The climate, notably poor in the immediate Louisbourg vicinity, played havoc with the work of the masons and carpenters. The season when work could be undertaken on the fortifications was brief, while damp conditions often prevented the mortar from setting adequately. Moreover, the winter's cycle of frost and thaw undermined even the most successful summer's work. As the walls were in danger of falling into the surrounding ditch within a few years of their completion, a system of revetting had been devised by which planks were spiked into beams held in the masonry by iron clamps. Even by the summer of 1745 some of the walls had yet to be repaired in this manner. Furthermore, surrounding hills overshadowed the Grand battery, isolated as it was from the main fortifications. Finally there was a shortage of guns and gun carriages, so that by the spring of 1745 only about 60 percent of the embrasures had guns mounted.

When news of the 1744 outbreak of war reached Louisbourg, Governor Duquesnel had at once taken the offensive, as we have seen.[15] Privateers were commissioned to prey on British and New England fishing and trading vessels off Newfoundland and elsewhere. Canso was attacked and seized, the buildings and wharfs burned, and booty captured.[16] Not all went well for the French, as losses among fishing vessels and even privateers began to be reported.[17] More serious than these setbacks was the state of the garrison's morale. The garrison was neither well disciplined nor altogether trustworthy. Late in December 1744 most of the soldiers mutinied. Except for the small artillery company, with the sergeants and corporals of the French companies, the officers found themselves isolated. Complaints focused on exploitation that the men had suffered at the officers' hands. In particular, they were angered by the shortage of firewood and at their inadequate clothing.[18] The mutiny ended only when concessions were made to the men by their officers. That winter discipline remained lax, even to the point where soldiers helped themselves to goods in the town's shops, after naming their own prices. Thus a divided and rather intimidated population anxiously awaited the end of winter. From the new commandant (Duquesnel had died in October) to the average town citizen, all expected in 1745 some form of retaliation for the loss of Canso and the abortive attack on Annapolis Royal the year before. It was thus no great surprise when vessels, thought to be enemy, were first sighted off the coast in March.[19] Nor was there even much alarm when continued sightings were reported throughout April and early May. It was believed that the anticipated arrival at Louisbourg of French naval reinforcements, already requested, would nullify any plans brewing in Boston or elsewhere. The governor, Louis Dupont Duchambon, had requested the year before that a ship of the line and two frigates augment Louisbourg's naval defenses in the summer of 1745, instead of the usual solitary frigate.[20]

Whatever may have been Warren's thoughts about the wisdom of the expedition, when faced with the situation he was determined to do all in his power to "promote the success" of the affair.[21] From his earliest letters to Pepperrell, which were of a friendly and obliging nature, he insisted time was of the essence and employed such phrases as "[d]ispatch is the life of business"[22] and "delays may frustrate all our hopes."[23] His memory of St. Augustine was clearly before him. Warren asked for and welcomed Pepperrell's suggestions in the disposition of the ships, and the latter did not refrain from giving his opinion. At the same time, Warren felt at liberty, in view of the very friendly reception Pepperrell had given him, to make suggestions about the conduct of the siege. They cooperated in small matters too. Pepperrell was successful in finding clothes for Warren's seamen, many of whom were "almost naked."[24] Warren was concerned that some of the schooners should be sent fishing to keep the troops supplied with fresh food,[25] and he sent lemons, claret, and rum to Pepperrell and his officers.[26] Warren also readily ordered *Mermaid* to help escort the force from Canso to Cape Breton; he expressed his great delight at the successful New England landing and the defeat of the small French force sent too late to repulse them. To assist in the landing, he made a feint with the rest of the squadron—then consisting of about thirteen hundred officers, seamen, and marines with 220 guns—as if he were preparing to sail into the harbor.[27] Pepperrell, on his part, congratulated Warren on the taking of three small prizes "which tho' in themselves of little consequence may prove a great disadvantage to the enemy by depriving them thereby of transporting men or stores for their relief."[28]

Until the expeditionary force actually appeared off Louisbourg, Duchambon was not certain of its existence, although he had increasing evidence that New England privateers were on his coasts.[29] At least one French contemporary account describes the town as blockaded in the last week of April.[30] Before the expedition anchored in Gabarus Bay, Duchambon had sent a small force to patrol the anticipated landing, while summoning militiamen from outlying settlements partly by having the bells of the principal buildings continuously peal.[31] Fearful of the British warships sailing virtually unopposed into the harbor, he reinforced the troops already sent to Gabarus Bay so that the New Englanders, when they landed, faced perhaps eighty militia and thirty soldiers.[32] This masking force, having suffered light casualties, was quickly scattered by the New Englanders. A hastily summoned council of war approved the abandonment of the Grand battery once the guns were spiked.[33]

Warren was encouraged both by the news of the early capture of the Grand battery and by the fact that its guns were found to be improperly spiked—so that soon they began to play upon the town they had been built to protect. Warren's hopes rose greatly, as they had throughout the American camp: "I am glad to find so glorious a spirit in our *Americans*, it will greatly recommend them, to their mother country, and if they can make this acquisition, it will be the greatest to them in particular, and to our country in general, than has for many years been made."[34]

Warren also correctly concluded that the French planned to make their defense within the town itself. The next objective he suggested should be the Island battery. Its fall would make it impossible for the sea blockade to fail; the town would then starve. Should Pepperrell attack the island, Warren was ready to offer him men and boats to ensure its success. After consulting his council of war, Pepperrell immediately replied that it was of the "utmost consequence to get possession of the Island battery," and the attempt would be made once a battery had been erected to fire on the town.[35] Pepperrell of course welcomed the offer of seamen and boats. In doing this, he was adhering strictly to his original instructions from Shirley that called for attacks first on the Grand and Island batteries before the main siege of the town began.

In fact, Pepperrell labored to bring his men to their duties: including fortifying a base camp, erecting storehouses and rude huts, and collecting

firewood. The site chosen was along the side of a brook about two kilome-
ters from the town's walls but obscured by low hills and scrub forest. Later
a picket line was erected for its protection and cannon placed at intervals. It
took almost a fortnight to disembark all the supplies. Roads had to be fash-
ioned in the marshy land before wooden sledges could move the cannon,
with their shot, shells, and powder. Successive batteries were raised until
the most advanced was little more than two hundred meters from the west
gate.

While Pepperrell's men were thus heavily engaged, Warren summoned
several of his captains to prepare a plan of attack. When this was sent to
Pepperrell, Warren made it abundantly clear that it was a mere proposal:
"As I wou'd be far from being obstinate in my opinion, I shall always be
ready, to join in any other plan, that may be thought more conducive to the
attaining the end, for which we are all come here, which will be the greatest
acquisition, to our country, in general, to the northern colonies in particular, and an everlasting honour, to every person contributing thereto."[36]
Their plan called for an attacking force of seven hundred to eight hundred
men, of whom five hundred would be soldiers and the rest seamen. It
named no commanding officer, though it provided details about how the
men should be armed, what signals should be used, and what arrangements ought to be made for casualties. It suggested the use of passwords. It
proposed that a feint be made on the town itself, an hour or two before the
attack. The plan made provision for either a day or a night attack. Once the
attack was made, the squadron, with several of the colony vessels, would
sail into the harbor, immediately fire on that undefended harbor side of the
town, and exploit the success as quickly as possible.

The sea officers' plan, clearly going beyond a simple attack on an isolated battery, which raised the prospect of "the sudden reduction of
Louisbourg," was considered the next day, 5 May, by Pepperrell's council.[37]
No sea officer was present. The council did not amend the plan; it postponed it indefinitely.

This news brought Warren ashore, and on the next day he attended
Pepperrell's council of war and joined with the general in drafting a sum-
mons for the governor to surrender Louisbourg and with it all of Cape
Breton. After a symbolic cannonade, the summons was carried under a flag
of truce by Lieutenant Agnue, the senior marine officer in the squadron.
This was politely but absolutely rejected by Governor Duchambon, who
refused to consider the question "except after the most vigorous attack."
Until then his response would be from "the mouths of our cannon."[38]

When Duchambon's reply was read to the assembled troops, it was greeted with such a display of bravado that the council decided at once to make an attempt on the Island battery. Warren summoned ninety men under an officer from *Superbe* and fifty-five men from *Launceston*. Volunteers from the New England troops were called for. Command was given to John Gorham, who had led the assault troops the day they landed. Warren offered £500 to be divided equally among the force to spur on the effort. It was all in vain, for Gorham returned without having made an attempt owing to the tremendous surf lashing the rocky island shore. On the succeeding two nights the troops, still assisted by the seamen and marines, again prepared for the attack that was to be made in conjunction with a feint against the town. The surf again proved too dangerous, although the real cause of failure on the second night was the unwillingness of the New England troops to storm the town. It was apparently Warren who, among the senior officers, first perceived the uneasiness among the men and at once brought it to the attention of Pepperrell. The general called a council of war that cancelled the proposed attack.

Much of the next day, 10 May, was spent in preparing a revised plan of operations.[39] It called for further efforts against the Island battery and for the erection of a number of fascine batteries, to intensify the bombardment of the town before an assault could again be contemplated. In the next two weeks, several more attempts to organize a raid on the Island battery were made, all based from the Grand battery, the last on 26 May. In the meantime, the provincial officers carried out the erection of batteries with spirit. They concentrated them to the north and northwest of the town, the closest within musket shot of the French. Thousands of cannon balls and hundreds of mortar shells rained on the town, inflicting great damage to many buildings. The west flank of the main bastion was reduced to a massive pile of rubble. The west gate and the nearest bastion to it suffered serious damage as well. Still, the general ordered no assault on the walls.

As time wore on, the fortress, despite its battering, continued to fly the French flag. Indeed on two occasions the French garrison mounted sorties. The more important occurred on 16 May, when a force of one hundred militia under a retired infantry officer and a sergeant from the Swiss company set off with ten days' worth of rations, each man armed with a musket and fifty balls. Spotted as they embarked in three boats to cross the harbor to the lighthouse, a nasty but brief exchange of fire ensued. The French party escaped into the surrounding forest and linked up with about forty Mi'kmaq, who had earlier captured about twenty New England pillagers. This formidable force was later attacked by New England soldiers, in a costly two-hour battle in which each side claimed victory.[40]

Warren early on began to display clear signs of impatience at what he perceived to be dilatoriness on the part of the troops. On returning to sea on 11 May, he began writing to the governors of all the northern colonies, as Pepperrell had requested, to ask their support. He had doubts about their value: "I hope my letters, to the respective governors, from New York to Virginia inclusive, will have some weight, but it will be a great while before wee can expect any succours from them, shou'd they be ever so inclinable to assist us. I fear it will take up so much time, to reduce Lewisbourg by blockading that I cou'd wish more vigorous measure were advisable."[41] To assist Pepperrell, Warren sent two more gunners in addition to those he had already assigned for duty ashore. He had intimated to Pepperrell that he would like daily accounts of the siege's progress, and, with a gentle reminder on 15 May, Pepperrell obliged him. Warren's sense of urgency increased rather than diminished when news reached him that reinforcements were on the way from England. From Newfoundland came news that five or six warships were soon expected, but it was a rumor rather than certain orders. From Boston came word of the arrival of *Princess Mary* (60), which after repairs to her bowsprit was proceeding to Louisbourg. *Hector* (44) was also on her way. Warren's comment to the general was "You may judge, by the sea force that are coming to our assistance, how much the government, at home, has the success of this expedition, at heart, and for God sake, let us use all our efforts not to disappoint them in it. I must own It gives me great concern that no one advantage has yet been acquired, by our troops from the enemy, except the Grand battery, which they abandoned."[42] He repeated his wish that there could be a quicker solution to the capture of Louisbourg than by blockade.

Less pressed than Pepperrell in his day-to-day cares, Warren was able to give time to the preparation of a plan of assault once Louisbourg was sufficiently battered. It was in no sense an attempt by Warren to assume command of the expedition. Instead, it was a restatement of the use to which the squadron could be put when the decisive moment came. Warren and his captains assumed that the French would defend with all their resources the area surrounding the breach, and it would therefore be necessary to split their own forces by attempting the walls with scaling ladders. This would necessitate a larger force than Pepperrell had under his command.

Warren suggested that for a brief time the squadron might abandon its cruising, leaving but two small colonial vessels to guard the mouth of Louisbourg harbor. The rest would gather in Gabarus Bay as near to the fortress as possible and land about fifteen hundred sailors and marines, leaving some as guards and others as scouts in case an enemy fleet should be sighted. They would then rejoin the main army at its assembly point before the attack was effected and there rest and refresh themselves. When the attack was made, they would form up in regular companies, with a warning that "to shrink, or put back, or utter any words to induce others so to do, shou'd be punished with death."[43] Seamen and whale boatmen based at the Grand battery would join in the attack on the town from that quarter. Warren concluded: "as this scheme must fail or succeed, in one night, 'tis propos'd, that the men from the ships shou'd stay no longer on shore, but go immediately on board their respective ships in order to cruise, or execute, any other scheme, that may be agreed on, upon the failure of this."

This was a substantial alteration from his proposals of 4 May. The Island battery had made the difference. For, as Warren admitted in the letter accompanying the plan that his three captains and the two colonial captains, John Rous and Daniel Fones, had signed, he now thought it impossible with his limited naval force to attempt a passage into Louisbourg harbor. The Island battery, still untouched, effectively constrained him.

Warren of course did not expect the plan to be implemented until the breach was ready; he was not surprised when he learned that Pepperrell's council deferred consideration until a later moment. The general received it "with grateful pleasure, particularly I note your prudent and great thoughtfulness to bring to a happy issue the affair before us of so much consequence."[44] His criticisms were candid and friendly; he entered into some of the difficulties he was facing with the undisciplined troops and difficult terrain and expressed the hope that Warren's "patience will not tire." He expressed his understanding of Warren's fears about a superior enemy naval force arriving suddenly on the scene. Before Warren received this communication, he sent the general a draft of his proposed orders to the squadron and colony vessels, adding: "If we fail in all these attempts give me leave to assure you if at a general council it shall be thought practicable and advisable to go in against the town and batterys with all our naval force of every kind I shall be very ready and willing to do it."[45] He also begged forgiveness for being so anxious to bring the expedition to a head; but both the unpredictability of the wind and weather, "especially in this uncouth climate," and the knowledge that the coast of America as far as the Carolinas was unguarded by any station ship bore heavily on him.

Warren's fears of French warships were well founded. At the end of January, Maurepas, *ministre de la marine,* had dispatched the 32–gun frigate *Renommée* to Louisbourg. *Renommée* was a marvelous ship, more heavily gunned than the usual English frigate she could outsail them all. When at length she was captured in 1747, her design, in modified form, became the basis of a new class of English frigates.[46] Another frigate, *Mars,* was to be sent in March, while *Castor,* launched at Quebec and then being readied for sea duty, was to join them. By mid-April *Renommée* had reached Louisbourg but had been unable to enter the harbor because of severe ice conditions. She then cruised toward Canso, where she exchanged fire with the Rhode Island cruiser *Tartar,* then escorting the Connecticut contingent to the rendezvous at Canso. *Tartar* and the convoy escaped, while *Renommée* cruised southwards. Unable later to sail northeast because of contrary winds, she had returned to France without testing the effectiveness of Warren's blockade of Louisbourg.[47] Of this piece of good fortune Warren remained ignorant for some time.

Meanwhile, *Mars* had taken so long to fit for sea that *Vigilant,*[48] a new 64–gun ship, was sent in her place, departing Brest on 15 April.[49] She came laden with powder and other provisions and a full complement of more than five hundred seamen and marines. On her passage she took two English merchant vessels and sent them ahead to Louisbourg with prize crews. At about noon on 19 May, she approached the entrance to Louisbourg harbor from the southwest. This surprised Warren, for he had been led to believe that French ships normally made their landfall to the northeast of the harbor. Nevertheless Warren was ready, having received intelligence from a prize taken the day before by *Tartar* that a French squadron of four ships of the line and three frigates "may be daily expected here."[50] He had strung out the squadron, with *Launceston* about thirty-five leagues north of Louisbourg lighthouse, *Eltham* and *Superbe* off the harbor's mouth, and *Massachusetts, Shirley,* and *Mermaid* to the south. *Mermaid* first spotted the strange sail; she at once signaled the rest of the squadron and sailed away from *Vigilant,* drawing her on for more than an hour and exchanging fire from the stern guns. At length *Vigilant's* captain, the Marquis de la Maisonfort, perceived his peril and came about, reversing his course and giving *Mermaid* a broadside as he did so.[51]

Now *Mermaid* and the rest of the squadron gave chase. Capt. James

Douglass remained on *Vigilant's* starboard quarter and twice put her helm about to send a broadside into her rigging. Not until 6:00 in the evening did the rest of the squadron come within range, when Captain Rous in *Shirley* began firing with effect from his bow chaser. A half-hour later, *Superbe* began exchanging broadsides. An hour after that *Eltham* came up and at once was struck by one of *Vigilant's* broadsides. The battle raged on into the night amid thick bands of swirling fog. With her sails and rigging shattered and torn and more than sixty of her crew now casualties, *Vigilant* struck her colors and sued for quarter about 9:00 p.m., wearing under *Superbe's* stern. *Superbe* herself was so knocked about that she could not board the prize, so Warren ordered *Mermaid* to steer south-southeast after her, together with *Eltham*. All night Capt. Richard Tiddeman, though wounded, kept his crew knotting and splicing, so that by four o'clock the next morning she was able to join the others, who signaled their presence in the thick fog. A prize crew was sent on board, and slowly *Vigilant* was escorted to an anchorage in Gabarus Bay, to the great relief and joy of the troops and the crew of *Launceston*, which had been too far north to engage in the fray.

The taking of *Vigilant* was a mixed blessing. To ensure that the besieged population knew of their loss Warren convinced Pepperrell to allow their noble prisoner, the Marquis de la Maisonfort, to correspond with Governor Duchambon.[52] The besieged garrison had seen the tragedy develop and it sorely affected their spirits. As French morale sank, that of the fleet and the troops besieging the fortress rose. Pepperrell sent Warren his heartiest congratulations and considered it "a happy omen of our success against Louisbourg."[53] Hundreds of barrels of powder answered a pressing need keenly felt by the New England gunners. *Vigilant* also carried several unmounted guns; these too were valuable, together with her food supplies.[54]

Her capture created two real problems: first, it produced overnight five hundred prisoners, all of whom had to be fed and guarded; second, the vessel needed a new crew, as Warren decided at once to commission *Vigilant* for the king's service. Some of this crew and all of the officers were taken from the warships, and Captain Douglass was given the command with William Montagu appointed to take post in *Mermaid* in his place. Warren appealed to Pepperrell for crew members "to man her, as soon as possible, in order to make us strong enough, for any squadron of the enemys, that may come here, I assure all such Men as you shall let us have, for her, that they shall be discharg'd, upon our arrival at Boston."[55] Pepperrell had already stripped the troop transports to man *Shirley* and could offer no help because so many of his own troops were ill or otherwise occupied. Some of the prisoners were soon transported to Boston, under the escort of *Molineux* and *Caesar*, while the remaining prisoners were kept in shackles aboard transport vessels moored in Gabarus Bay.

If Warren was to lose the services of the two colonial cruisers, he was more than compensated by the arrival of *Princess Mary* on 23 May and *Hector* on 24 May. Aboard the first was Capt. James Macdonald, who already had war experience in Flanders and was "well-respected by the Duke of Newcastle." Macdonald now commanded those marines whom Warren decided to land to assist in the attack on Louisbourg.[56]

These two warships had been dispatched from England following a hastily called meeting of the Admiralty Board to consider Shirley's four dispatches between 5 January and 1 February, which had been carried to London by Joshua Loring.[57] Loring had stayed but twelve hours before he was sent on board *Princess Mary*, which sailed at once with *Hector* to help the expeditionary force. They arrived off Louisbourg at a fortuitous moment, for the appearance of *Vigilant* had heightened Warren's apprehension of the arrival of the rest of the French squadron "hourly expected here both from France and the West Indies."[58] Warren at once informed the two new commanders, Richard Edwards and Frederick Cornwall, as well as the marine captain of his 16 May plan to land more than fifteen hundred seamen on shore for the time necessary to assist in an attack on the fortress.

This plan was soon scrapped and replaced by a bolder enterprise. Once *Vigilant* was repaired, the whole squadron—warships and colony cruisers, schooners and transports carrying some sixteen hundred of Pepperrell's men—would force a passage into the harbor. The squadron, together with the marines under the command of Macdonald, would then attack the lightly defended harbor side. The new plan with Warren's accompanying letter began with an apology, "I am sorry to give you, the trouble, of so many plans of operation, against the garrison of Lewisbourg, and beg leave to assure you, most candidly, that they have been such, as appear'd best, to my weak judgment, under the several circumstances, that you were in, at the different times of my proposing them."[59] The next day Warren held a further consultation with all his captains present. He secured their agreement and issued his detailed orders. *Hector* was to lead with *Fame* on the offside abreast, then *Eltham* with *Shirley* abreast, *Superbe* with *Massachusetts* abreast, then, in line, *Princess Mary, Mermaid, Launceston, Bien Aimé, Molineux,* and *Boston Packet,* each a cable and a half apart. No ship was to begin firing until it was properly anchored, and only when it was sure "the smoke of their guns will not be a prejudice to the rest."[60] *Tartar* and *Defence* were to anchor with the transports and schooners in the part of the harbor farthest from the town and, on a signal from the commodore, set off in their boats, led by *Superbe* in the middle of the line, to land in the town across the wharf.

The plan presumed that the Island battery first had to be neutralized. On the night of 26 May, Pepperrell sent against it a force of four hundred from the Grand battery. It was bloodily repulsed, with almost two hundred killed, wounded, and captured, completely souring Pepperrell's council on any further attempts.[61] The council also rejected Warren's latest plan by pointing out that sixteen hundred could not be spared with more than one thousand either sick or patrolling the interior in search of two parties of Mi'kmaq and French that had been reported in the area.[62] The council helpfully offered five hundred men to be drafted from the cruisers and transports to man *Vigilant,* under the terms Warren had offered. The squadron was free to "proceed into the harbor at the time agreed upon in such manner" as Warren thought best.[63] Whenever the attack was made, five hundred men were to be carried by boats from the Grand battery, together with whatever number of marines and seamen Warren could spare, all then to hurl themselves over the wharf and into the town. Another five hundred were to scale the walls on the southeast face as a diversionary move; the main attack, however, was to be directed against the west gate, where upwards of one thousand troops would gather leaving the rest to man the batteries.

Though it was the most substantial commitment to an assault the council had taken since its aborted decision of 9 May, it did not greatly please Warren, who after consulting his captains again replied to Pepperrell: "I am very sorry no plan of mine, tho' approv'd of, by all my captains, has been so fortunate, as to meet with your approbation, or have any weight with you, I flatter'd myself, from the little knowledge, I have endeavour'd to acquire, in military affairs, my advice singly, wou'd have had some influence, in the conducting of the present expedition."[64] He felt that his plan must not have been adequately understood by the council and so sent Capt. Philip Durell, then commanding *Eltham,* to elaborate the plan.[65] Durell, having spent the winter before in Boston, would have met most of Pepperrell's council. Macdonald, who had already been ashore and had complained to Warren that the New Englanders not only failed to guard their trenches but did not concentrate their fire at the west gate to effect an early breach, went along as Warren's military spokesman. Warren felt that under his plan he could concentrate at least two thousand men in the vicinity of the west gate, while Pepperrell's plan would place no more than one thousand men there. Warren saw no way of covering the movements of the assault force from the Royal battery. Moreover, he wanted to know why there was no mention of an attack on the Island battery: "Everybody will allow, that the going in, with the ships, before the taking [of] the Island battery, or reducing the Circular or any other of the town's battery's, will be a bold attempt, where there is no retreat, it is therefore worthy of Englishmen." Almost as an afterthought he remarked: "if the Island battery was taken, it wou'd be a much more reasonable one, but what can be, shou'd be done, for the honour of his Majesty's arms."[66]

Not until after the letter was sent did Warren receive Pepperrell's of 28 May, which gave a few details of the heavy losses the New Englanders had suffered in their futile attempt of the night of 26–27 May. When Warren learned the news, he expressed his deep sorrow, ending his very long letter by stressing the need for harmony between land and sea officers. He hoped that his always candid suggestions had not been misconstrued and assured Pepperrell that he had no desire to give him "the least offense, for I sincerely wish you well."

Warren, in fact, had upset some of Pepperrell's council with his tactless references to indolence, when it was rather their inexperience that taxed his patience. Some may have resented his detailed plans and orders to his squadron, which were far more meticulous than their own. Though Pepperrell gave him almost daily sketches of the situation on land, Warren failed to realize how inadequate a picture he possessed, particularly of the morale of the New England troops and their officers. What irritated Warren in particular was the land officers' failure to grasp what he himself clearly saw: the mobility Pepperrell's force could acquire if the squadron was used as far more than a blockading force. Perhaps if he had been given more opportunities of meeting the council, their shortsightedness in this matter would have vanished.

Their caution was understandable, not as resentment against Warren's supposed pretensions to command, which he denied having and clearly did not possess, but as the realization of their own increasing attrition through sickness. There simply were not enough troops to assault Louisbourg. Warren's strength, which they had never really considered their own however much Warren tried to impress it on them, grew, and this he felt entitled him to a larger voice in the affairs of the siege.

One immediate advantage of Warren having sent Durell and Macdonald ashore was the interest generated in the idea of erecting a battery near the lighthouse to fire on the Island battery from a height and at a distance of about two-thirds of a mile. The site was already occupied by New England troops, who in May had repulsed an attack of about a hundred French militiamen transported from the town in three shallops. The idea of erecting a battery at the lighthouse had apparently first been suggested by Brigadier Waldo, who commanded the troops at the Grand battery.[67] When Durell and Macdonald first heard of the idea, they realized its possibilities at once. Warren recommended it to Pepperrell as "of the greatest consequence."[68] The next day he added: "We are of the opinion that the battery at the light house shou'd be carry'd on, as soon as possible to annoy the Island battery, Captain Durell informing me, it will be of infinite service, as it will greatly facilitate the entrance of the ships into the harbour."[69]

Warren was at once concerned with the problem of getting the guns and carriages to the lighthouse and asked the general to call on him if assistance was needed, reminding him that "the carriages and every thing belonging to them shou'd be landed at the same time." Pepperrell assured him that the battery was being erected in great haste, the six 12–pounders and a mortar being carried by schooner from Gabarus Bay to a point more than a mile east of the lighthouse and dragged up the steep cliffs.

Pepperrell encouraged Warren to give the New Englanders every assistance to hurry the battery; the work, however, was done by 320 provincials under Gorham. On 7 June, with the battery still not ready, Warren again summoned his captains and suggested that the squadron force a passage into the harbor. They insisted on first silencing the Island battery and suggested that the squadron could assist in the bombardment.[70] Warren accepted this advice and asked Pepperrell for pilots who were more familiar with the harbor's mouth than those then on board the warships. Pepperrell promptly complied. To his great relief, Warren saw the Lighthouse battery open fire three days later and to such good effect that the French gunners had to flee their now-exposed positions. The barracks were destroyed and the magazine blown up; in a matter of days the principal obstacle to his entry into the harbor was removed.

Ever since Durell and Macdonald had returned from conferring with Pepperrell and his senior officers, Warren had recognized the need for more frequent face-to-face meetings between his captains and Pepperrell's council. Fog and easterly winds prevented several attempts: "I long for a general consultation with you, and your council, in conjunction with the captains, of the squadron, but it will not be prudent by any means, with the wind easterly, to have our ships to leeward of Lewisbourg, for fear of any ships of force getting in, from the eastward, but the wind westerly wee may lye close in with your Camp for a few hours which wou'd be suffi-cient, to determine upon the best plan of operation, that wee can pro-pose."[71] With his constant apprehension of a French squadron appearing at any moment, he dared not come ashore with his captains. Later that same day his wish was realized. Pepperrell and five of his senior officers joined Warren, Calmady, Douglass, Montagu, and Tiddeman on board *Superbe*. No final decision was taken about the nature of the attack to be made on Louisbourg, but it was agreed that the moment was not ripe. The batteries had not yet achieved their anticipated results, while Warren was particu-larly anxious to see the effect on the Island battery.

In the meantime, the vexatious matter of manning *Vigilant* was solved. The French prisoners would be taken to Boston in a number of transports and colonial cruisers with very reduced crews. That in turn would free up provincial soldiers with sea-going experience to be assigned to *Vigilant*, along with able seamen removed from other the ships in the squadron.[72] Of far greater importance, the consultation firmly re-established the har-mony between the council and the captains such that the testiness that had surfaced in both Pepperrell's and Warren's letters now vanished.

Warren also readily agreed to write to the captured captain of *Vigilant*, as one professional to another, to complain of the barbarous way in which a number of New England soldiers had been put to death while prisoners of the French and Mi'kmaq in the interior.[73] On 6 June Warren wrote to the captain contrasting the excellent manner in which the marquis, his offic-ers, and seamen had been treated in comparison to the inhumanity the New Englanders had suffered.[74] De la Maisonfort obliged and wrote the next day, assuring Duchambon that he and his officers were treated *"non pas en prisonnier, mais comme leur bons amis"* [not as prisoners, but as their good friends].[75]

Here matters stood until 10:00 a.m. on Sunday, 9 June, when *Launces-ton* sighted a strange sail, signaled the rest of the squadron, and, cleared for action, gave chase. The long-awaited French squadron was thought to be at hand; to Warren's great surprise and pleasure, the sail was the 50–gun *Chester*. Her commander, Capt. Francis Geary, brought him the news that the Admiralty had sent three warships to reinforce Warren's squadron at Louisbourg. Early in March word had been received in London of a force of warships and transports fitting out at Brest, and Canada was thought to be its destination. When, a week later, firm news of Shirley's intended attack on Cape Breton came to hand, the Admiralty expressed great concern lest the French armament escape across the Atlantic, learn of the New England force, and make for Louisbourg. Adm. William Martin was ordered to sea, putting out from Plymouth on 21 March, and within a week he had certain news of the French squadron being already at sea, its destination still uncertain. Martin chased westward for four days and then detached *Chester*, with *Sunderland* and *Canterbury*—both of sixty guns, to continue the chase and to warn Warren. In fact, the French squadron made for the West Indies, returning unhindered with the trade in August.

This happy act of precaution by Admiral Martin quite altered Warren's attitude toward the siege. He now felt sure of victory and wanted to bring matters to a head as quickly as possible; at once he suggested to Pepperrell that a final discussion be arranged to work out the details.[76] He spoke of "our present prospect of success, which I think very great, therefore hope soon to keep a good house together, and give the ladys of Lewisbourg a gallant ball."[77] Pepperrell's pleasure and relief were almost equal to Warren's, whom he assured, "I shall be doing everything in my power for the success of your Enterprize."[78]

The next day, the general officers went aboard *Superbe* and while celebrating the anniversary of the coronation of George II they received Warren's assurances that the squadron would sail into Louisbourg harbor. The consultation of officers took place, and Warren's plan was adopted.[79] It was a compromise between his suggestion of 24 May and the council's plan of the same day. Whereas he had, in the first instance, asked for a thousand troops on board his ships, after six hundred others had manned *Vigilant*, now with *Vigilant* at sea he settled for an additional five hundred to come aboard his ships by other means, something that the council had not before conceded. Although before the council had wanted the force from the Grand battery to attack in whale boats, they now agreed that they should, at a given signal, go aboard the five men-of-war in the center of the line, together with one-third of the crew in each ship of the squadron. On the landside of Louisbourg, one thousand men would attack the west gate breach; Warren's force would amount to twice that number. The next day, Warren had to alter these instructions slightly, for in addition to *Sunderland* and *Canterbury*—with a prize in company, came *Lark* (44) bringing an ordnance storeship with cannon and powder. *Lark*'s captain, John Wickham, had been dispatched from Plymouth to convoy ships to Virginia via Newfoundland and at St. John's had found Warren's orders awaiting him to hasten to Louisbourg. On his passage he had met the other ships.

Lark was now added to Warren's line of battle. With his squadron in line, Warren would be able to bombard the least-defended side of the town with his port guns, more than three hundred in number. With all his ships busily being barricaded with moss and bulkheads and cabins knocked down to take in the large number of additional men, Warren called his captains to a final briefing. In view of the sorry state of the troops on shore, the only possibility they saw of taking Louisbourg was for the squadron to enter the harbor: "We have duly considered the dishonour it may bring upon his Majesty's arms, not to attempt the attack with the squadron now here, are therefore unanimously of the opinion that we should go into the harbour, and use our utmost endeavour to reduce it to his Majesty's obedience."[80] Following Warren, each of the commanders of the ten warships declared his approval. This done, Warren wrote to Pepperrell "that we wait only for the men you are so good to supply our ships with, and a fair wind, to go in and attack the town with the vigour that becomes Englishmen and we don't in the least doubt but you will do the same by land."[81] The New Englanders went on board later that day, but the wind came from the southwest. Warren postponed the attack until the next day and went ashore to inform Pepperrell. His main purpose was, however, to address the troops. Pepperrell obliged him by forming up the army and Warren then made "an Excellent speech Well worth writing down,"[82] saying, "He'd rather leave his body at Louisbourg than not take the city," and reminding them that their general "could not take the city with the land forces neither could he with the sea forces without the assistance of each other."[83] He was given "three cheerful huzzas."[84] The contrast in the troops' behavior compared with 9 May could not have been greater.

The New Englanders and Englishmen alike were denied their heroic moment. They did not have to test the wisdom of their plans and the mettle of their men, as Duchambon sued for peace. The governor began to look for ways to effect both a profitable and honorable surrender once he saw the desperate situation to which the Island battery had been reduced. He received a petition, which he himself might have inspired, from some of Louisbourg's most influential inhabitants, who advocated surrendering the town rather than permitting it to be pillaged. There was no dishonor in attempting to protect personal possessions and business inventories under adverse circumstances. Duchambon had ordered his chief engineer and captain of artillery to submit reports on the state of the defenses. The dauphin demi-bastion was in ruins, the right flank of the king's bastion had been demolished, and the breach at the west gate allowed the enemy to rush the walls without even having to use ladders. Most serious was the utter destruction of the Island battery.[85] The captain of artillery noted that of the 670 barrels of powder available at the outset of the siege only forty-seven remained, while all the fuses had been used.[86] As far as provisions were concerned, the royal storehouses still held some 2,500 cwt. of flour, 200 cwt. of bread, 300 cwt. of lard, 500 cwt. of vegetables, 100 barrels of wine, and 300 barrels of molasses alone, besides additional provisions in the hands of the townspeople.[87] A council of war heard these disheartening reports read and determined unanimously to ask for terms. The principal reasons given were the increased strength of the enemy, the weakness of west gate defenses, the short supply of powder owing to the blockade, and the damaged state of the town.

Negotiations began forthwith. An officer was sent to Warren and Pepperrell, who at once replied, giving the governor until early the next morning to accept the terms first proposed to him on 7 May.[88] Instead, the French submitted sixteen articles of surrender, asking that all the inhabitants be permitted to remain in the colony or be evacuated to France, the West Indies, or Canada, taking with them all their effects at the expense of His Majesty. Those who chose to depart were to be allowed to sell their personal effects and real estate. Missionaries were to be permitted to continue their work among the Mi'kmaq, while the practice of Catholicism by those among the French who remained behind was to be tolerated. The wounded were to be cared for and repatriated when they had recovered. A reciprocal exchange of prisoners was to take place. They also asked to march out with the honors of war: bearing their arms, with bayonets fixed, drums beating, and colors flying. The commandant was to be permitted to remove his personal effects in two covered wagons, while anyone who wished could leave the fortress-town *masqués ou déguisés.*[89]

As Warren and Pepperrell believed that a force of about seven hundred *Canadiens* and Mi'kmaq were on the march toward Louisbourg, they agreed to much of this.[90] In fact, this relief force got no further than Tatamagouche harbor before being turned back by three New England vessels: *Tartar, Resolution,* and *Bonetta.* In addition, French inhabitants were to be treated with the "utmost humanity."[91] Transportation would be at the expense of the British government, while the inhabitants and garrison were allowed to remove whatever personal effects they could carry. All non-commissioned officers and soldiers were to surrender immediately, with their arms placed on board a warship, while the commissioned officers and townsmen were to be confined to their homes. The practice of their religion was permitted until their return to France. Warren and Pepperrell insisted upon all military personnel returning to France, to avoid risking any increase in Quebec's military strength, and by this juncture Warren was already contemplating the conquest of Canada in its entirety. New England prisoners were to be released immediately, while all the French officers and men were to refrain from any warlike action against Britain or her allies for a full year. To ensure the rapid conclusion of the negotiations, the Island battery was to be handed over by six o'clock that very evening, when the squadron would be free to enter the harbor unmolested. The honors of war were granted, as Warren wrote to Duchambon, "in consideration of your gallant defence."[92]

Warren returned to his ship before the details of both the transfer of the fortress keys and the dispatch of troops to occupy the town had been settled. This occasioned some irritation as a result. The evening of 16 June, Warren sent Durell, a French-speaking Jerseyman, as a hostage. The next morning when the fog cleared, the squadron was cheered by the sight of the Union Jack flying over the Island battery, which at dawn had been occupied by Macdonald at the head of four hundred marines. At one o'clock in the afternoon, *Eltham* entered the harbor with the commodore on board.

When Warren landed at the town's quay to be greeted by the governor, this brought two men nurtured in the strict code governing the honors of war face to face. He found the governor somewhat dismayed by a letter he had just received from Pepperrell, who had demanded that the town be delivered to him later that afternoon.[93] The letter required Duchambon to act in a manner significantly different from the agreed articles of capitulation, as Pepperrell wanted Duchambon to order his troops to place all their arms in the magazine "where they shall be safe, and delivered to you the day they are to march out of the town."[94] It was a marked act of mistrust on the part of the New Englanders who formed Pepperrell's council and who undoubtedly advised him in drafting the letter. An explanation can be found in Warren's letter to Pepperrell written the night before. Warren's decision to send Durell to Duchambon must have appeared to Pepperrell and his council as an attempt to steal the glory from the army. To combat this, the council decided to dispatch a detachment under John Bradstreet the next afternoon, 17 June, to take possession of the town and fort. Haste was vital unless Warren, his ships, and his marines, appeared in the harbor and town first. This resulted in the council's decision not to await the ratification of the articles of capitulation and took place not from inexperience, as some authors have hinted, but as a deliberate act. Pepperrell was too experienced in business not to know that a contract had to be signed before a deal was completed.

Warren, doubly annoyed as the letter took no notice of him, felt that Pepperrell had displayed publicly a serious lack of faith in him. He felt the hurt more particularly since he had ended his own letter, the night before, with his expressed desire to work openly and in harmony with Pepperrell and his council, now that fortune had smiled on them, bringing them into daily communication with each other as victors of Louisbourg. Warren immediately complained to Pepperrell "of a kind of jealousy which I thought you wou'd never conceive of me after my letter to you of last night."[95] In that letter Warren had said:

I rejoice at our success, be assured sir that I shall always be glad of your approbation of my conduct, I beg we may all behave to the prisoners that fall under our protection by the chance of war with that humanity & honour becoming English officers, and bee persuaded it will add greatly to the reputation which we acquire by the reduction of this formidable garrison, I believe you will think it right to send an express both to England and Boston as soon as possible, I will write no letter but what I will show you, that you maybe convinced, that I do you and all the gentlemen employ'd on this expedition all the honour in my power.[96]

Before coming ashore, Warren had also written to Duchambon to ask that the keys of the city be delivered up to him.[97] This rather high-handed behavior on his part emphasized both the importance he placed on the squadron's contribution to the success as well as his concern over the ability of New England officers to keep their troops properly disciplined.

In any event, the incident in no way damaged the regard the two men had for each other, although it created something of a sensation in Boston, growing far out of proportion to its actual significance. Warren had his way, for Duchambon handed him the keys of the fortifications, and when the New Englanders marched up to the city, Warren handed them to Pepperrell.

During the next three hours the rest of the squadron, including the New England vessels, their prizes, and transports crowded into the harbor. At the same time the New England troops marched through the Maurepas Gate along the rue d'Orléans, and past the hospital to the parade ground in front of the King's Bastion barracks. There the troops received the customary salute from the surviving French garrison, which was drawn up in order. The French flag was struck, and the British colors were hoisted in its place, whereupon the whole squadron saluted with a discharge of their great guns. The siege had ended; the capitulation, effected without serious incident, brought honor to both sides.

Warren did all in his power to assist Pepperrell and his council in their first weeks as the new government of Louisbourg. They were at first fully occupied in hastily bringing all their guns, stores, and provisions into the fort, while Warren landed many of his seamen who policed the city. The French soldiers were then embarked on the warships in preparation for their return to France and were, of course, guarded by the marines. Warren suggested the appointment of necessary officials, including fort and town majors, storekeeper of the ordnance, master gunner, and judge of the admiralty court.[98] He also prepared an elaborate system of warning signals for use either by day or by night in case Louisbourg was alarmed.[99] He put Captain Durell, "a good draftsman," to the task of preparing detailed drawings of the town and its fortifications.[100] He wrote to the governors of all the colonies in North America asking them again for immediate assistance, particularly for men "arm'd and victual'd for at least seven or eight months" to garrison Louisbourg until the ministry's plans for the place were known.[101] He first sent Captain Montagu with a dispatch to London giving news of the success but then advised that the New England captain, John Rous, "a very deserving man, and has done his country great service," be sent as well to ensure that the news was received at the earliest possible moment.[102] He suggested to Pepperrell that all the necessary provisions for winter and the materials for the repair of the fortress and town be paid for by drawing bills on the British government, as the colonies "had already been at very great expence."[103] At his suggestion, a joint letter was sent to Newcastle, the first of many such cooperative efforts, to congratulate him on the successful siege of forty-nine days. They emphasized the "timely assistance of the squadron of his Majesty's ships" and expressed the hope not only that the capture of Louisbourg fortress would be "thought of great advantage to his Majesty's dominions, especially in North America and that immediate care will be taken for the defence and maintenance thereof by the nation [but] also that his Majesty's subjects who voluntarily engag'd in the expedition will be entitled to such favour from his Majesty as will animate them to make further progress against the settlements of the French King in America."[104]

Warren had expressed his wish to Pepperrell that both land and sea officers and men receive preferment, that those who had been maimed would receive some pension, as well as the widows of those men who had lost their lives. He was fully conscious that the soldiers in particular had been greatly disappointed by their lack of plunder.[105] In his first letter to the Admiralty, he strongly recommended the general to His Majesty's care: "As the general who is a gentleman of a very considerable fortune in New England, had no inducement to bring him to this expedition, but that of honour and the service of his country, if his Majesty would be graciously pleas'd to confer on him the honour of knight baronet, that it might descend to his posterity."[106] Warren and Pepperrell had no doubt that their success was as great as it was unexpected and that there was no question but that Louisbourg should be retained, repaired, and adequately defended. They saw it also as a stepping-stone to other ventures against the French in America, perhaps in the end leading to dispossessing the French of all their territorial possessions on the continent. They also wanted to establish a civil government throughout Cape Breton—with Louisbourg as a free port—with power to grant land "upon the easiest terms."[107] Warren, in particular, seemed convinced that the mistakes at Canso, which had remained under military rule and had declined in importance, should not be repeated in any new territories seized from the French in North America.

Cape Breton and the Conquest of Canada, 1745–1746

"God has raised you up to be a father to these His Majesty's
North colonies in America, by giving us an interest in your heart
for the knowledge you have of our worth."[1]

Until His Majesty's intent was known about the future of Cape Breton, Warren had to busy himself with a hundred tasks, the most pressing being the dispatch of the French prisoners and inhabitants to France. He decided to strip *Launceston* of all but two of her guns and gun carriages and all other warlike stores to make as much room as possible. Carpenters swarmed over her to erect cabins for the French officers and their families. The first draft of 600 prisoners went on board on 19 June, 300 followed on 22 June, and a further 250 on 25 June. On the afternoon of 1 July, Duchambon and all the principal French officers boarded with their families and effects and sailed two days later in company with *Lark*. *Launceston's* entire company had been transferred earlier to *Superbe*, except the chief officers, and consequently was manned on her homeward passage by Frenchmen. They reached La Rochelle exactly a month later, the first of six cartel ships with Louisbourg prisoners.[2]

This done, Warren with Pepperrell organized the collection of a sufficient fuel supply for the winter. Gangs of men from among the troops and seamen set out in a dozen brigantines and schooners to different points on the island, St. Peter's, St. Anne's, and Île Madame, to cut hardwood and collect as much dry wood as possible. It was carried to the town and to the outlying garrisons in the Island battery and Grand battery, where it was corded, carted to the houses and barracks, stacked, and made ready for winter. A great many men were employed in this way—the prospect of earning a shilling a day was incentive enough. Notwithstanding this foresight, Warren underestimated the fuel needs and had to order both seamen and soldiers to cut and fetch more firewood as it was needed.[3] (Even though Cape Breton was well known for its rich coal deposits, very little coal was used.)

A more immediate problem was the repair of the town and fortifications. This chiefly concerned Pepperrell and his council, acting as the temporary government, but Warren lent his advice and assistance as well. On one occasion, he sharply criticized his colleagues for wasting their time "on trivial affairs, when the safety of this garrison which is of the greatest consequence is so much neglected."[4] This unsubstantiated accusation Pepperrell ignored, with the remark "as you have not pointed out any particular instance of my backwardness, I am at a loss to know what you refer to."[5] It was the last demonstration of impatience and was directed more at Pepperrell's colleagues than at the general himself, for whom Warren expressed the highest personal regard. Although the capture of Louisbourg had not made life any easier for Warren, he had little to complain about in the behavior of the council.

With Warren's approbation, John Henry Bastide, an engineering officer from Annapolis Royal who had come to Louisbourg about two weeks before the fort capitulated, was ordered to prepare a report on the most necessary repairs. These he estimated at a cost of £9,000, and was immediately appointed to oversee the work. Dozens of carpenters and masons and a small army of laborers converged on the ruins of the west gate and began repairing the roofs and chimneys of houses and barracks in the town as well as at the Grand and Island batteries. The guns used by the New Englanders and those taken off *Launceston* had to be dragged and hoisted into place on the ramparts. Other men were at work on the main barracks as well as the hospital, both of which had sustained considerable damage. Orders went out to New England for great quantities of windowpanes, pine and oak boards and planks, spikes and nails, bricks and mortar, wheelbarrows, shovels, and every kind of tool. Smiths were set to work fashioning gates for the storehouse, mending and re-hanging the bell in the citadel, and making and repairing tools and other hardware. The soldiers and seamen supplied the skills and labor, while some of the New England officers, who were almost all in trade, undertook to supply goods for the use of the garrison, by contracting with New England suppliers. As Pepperrell and Warren foresaw the need for a British garrison at Louisbourg much larger than the French had thought necessary, they ordered new barracks to be erected to accommodate seven hundred men.[6] This added considerably to Bastide's estimates.

All the while, Warren had to concern himself with the best disposal of his squadron. *Launceston*, as we have seen, had been sent home earlier, via France, with French prisoners. She sailed with *Lark*, which Warren ordered to return to her station at Newfoundland, after ensuring that the crew of *Launceston* made no attempt to take command of the ship and sail for Canada instead. In reply to urgent appeals both from Shirley and Clinton, he sent *Superbe* and *Wager*, which had arrived from Newfoundland on 3 July, for a six-week cruise as far south as Virginia.[7] *Shirley* was sent to England with dispatches. *Bien Aimé* and *Molineux* went to Boston with French prisoners, so too did *Hector* and *Eltham*; the former underwent repairs to her rigging before rejoining the squadron, and the latter proceeded with her much-delayed convoy of mastships to England. *Boston Packet* kept guard over the dozen small vessels engaged in collecting coal and wood. *Tartar* and *Resolution* were sent on an abortive attempt to make prisoners of the French inhabitants of Baie Verte, at the head of the Bay of Fundy. *Caesar, Fame, Massachusetts,* and the other colony cruisers were discharged.

This left the seaward defenses of Louisbourg entrusted to *Vigilant, Sunderland, Canterbury,* and *Princess Mary.* Warren ordered French colors to fly from the warships as well as the fortress and Island battery. His hope was to lure French shipping into the harbor before they realized the town had changed hands. On 18 June the squadron added *St. François Xavier,* with a cargo of wine, brandy, soap, vinegar, oil, and cloth from Bordeaux, to the nine prizes captured during the siege. She had sailed right to the harbor's mouth before *Chester* was towed out to make a prize of her.[8] Exactly a month later, one of the colony cruisers brought in a schooner from Quebec, laden with flour and other provisions. Then on 22 July, a very large ship appeared off Louisbourg that Warren thought to be a 60–gun warship. He at once sent out *Princess Mary* and *Canterbury* and made a prize of the 380–ton *Charmante,* a very rich East India vessel of twenty-eight guns and a crew of 109.[9] The unfortunate captain assured Warren that she was "except for Mr Anson's, as good a prize as has been taken in this war."[10] Then on 1 August, another East India ship, *Héron,* was made a prize by *Chester* and *Mermaid* with as little effort.[11] "Pretty Rich," Warren said of her, and added "by her we learn that the *Triton* is on her passage, and that this is the appointed rendezvous for their India trade, therefore 'tis to be hoped more of them will fall into our hands."[12] It was not an East India ship but one from Peru—*Notre Dame de la Déliverance,* with thirty-six guns and about sixty men—that fell the next victim to Warren's ruse the following day. She had sailed from Cadiz in 1741 and was fabulously rich, with her holds full of bullion, cocoa, Peruvian wool, and "Jesuits Bark."[13] She was on her homeward passage looking for safe convoy off Newfoundland in company with two other South Sea ships when she had encountered enemy privateers and fled to the supposed safety of Louisbourg, only to be made a prize.

The enormous good luck of the squadron not only made Warren's fortune but also, not surprisingly, aroused the jealousy of some of the New Englanders. Eventually, a lengthy and complicated court case was fought over *Notre Dame de la Déliverance* in an attempt to establish the rights of the colony cruisers to a share with the squadron in the prize money. The ship had been made a prize by *Sunderland* and *Chester* with *Boston Packet* giving the first warning of her approach, but this did not deter captains John Brett and Philip Durell and their crews from trying to lay sole claim to her. One of the New England army officers wrote bitterly: "'tis galling to little minds (who consider that the world is govern'd by an all wise God) that the army should both fight for & afterwards guard the city & yet they have none of the prizes which cost the men of war nothing more than go & meet them which we could do was the city afloat."[14] How widely this discontent was felt cannot really be known, but for some it clearly constituted a real grievance.

With his eighth part of the prize money and every prospect of being honored by the king, Peter Warren seemed at the height of his career. He now expected an admiral's flag: he stood very near the top of the list of post captains and had labored to keep his name before the Lords Commissioners of the Admiralty. Then with his squadron, he hoped either to be ordered to the West Indies or to England for leave, thereafter to return to North America in the spring of 1746 with an expeditionary force to conquer Canada. He was, as were many in his squadron, ill with scurvy, which he had developed the winter before; he begged the Admiralty for leave to recover his health "for since the commencement of the Spanish war, I have been so continuously at sea, and since that of the present expedition, have undergone the greatest fatigue and anxiety both of body and mind."[15]

He wanted to see the war through to its completion and then retire from the service to assume an appointment on land. He had told Anson in April 1745 that he was determined, so long as his health allowed, to remain active in the navy "'till ill treated, which I have no reason to apprehend, when you are at the Admiralty." He counted on Anson to advocate his promotion to admiral's rank.

At that period in his life his principal ambition was to be named governor of either New Jersey or New York. He informed Anson that "a retreat to America as a governor wou'd be more agreeable to me . . . then being lord high admiral."[16] He reminded his friend, who had only recently returned from his celebrated round-the-world voyage, that he was no

stranger to my marrying at New York, nor to Mrs Warren, as you plainly demonstrated, in your obliging favour, by kindly remembering her whose disposition if ever you took notice of it, is not greatly turn'd to pass her days in the *beau m[o]nd* but wou'd if possible, and it cou'd be made convenient to me, choose to take up her rest at New York among such of her relations as are left alive, her father and mother, having both paid the great debt to which all nature is sooner or later liable. Before, and at their death, I receiv'd what in that country is esteem'd a tolerable fortune, and indeed I think she has had a dear bargain of me, since so little of my time has been at her disposal, She had done better as a girl said to Solomon, [and] marry'd her own equal in her native land, as I think her deserving, I wou'd use all my endeavours to oblige her.

His friends had met with a friendly reception when the matter was first raised with the Duke of Newcastle and his brother, Henry Pelham, now running the government.

'Tis possible Mr Clinton may be better provided for in time, my having the Jersey government may be as an introduction to that of New York, where I shou'd be at the pinnacle of my ambition, and happiness, for I take it not to be so slippery as that to which we aspire, in a military way, where tho wee soar very high, we seldom can support ourselves long. I have the greatest regard, & esteem for Mr Clinton, and wou'd by no means interfere with any thing which shou'd concern his interest, as I have reason to believe, he will mention me as his friend to the Duke of Newcastle his nephew Lord Lincoln, and to Mr Pelham, and I am well assur'd my good friend Sir John Norris, who I have wrote often to on this subject, will heartily joyn you in any thing for my Service, and as I wou'd put you to as little trouble as possible, I pray you will give Mssrs Samuel and William Baker merchants, the latter an alderman of London, both my friends & correspondents, leave to wait on you, and to transmit your commands to me, on this or any other occasion.[17]

To Governor Clinton he wrote at the end of August, thanking him for his offer of support in succeeding the aged Lewis Morris as governor of New Jersey, adding:

> As the success which has attended me in this conquest has been a great addition to my fortune & I hope would be less to my reputation if please God I get home safe with the squadron. You know my attachments to New York. If at any time you shall think of leaving that government if you will use your good offices for me to succeed you I woud gladly be as grateful as you can wish. What I woud propose is to give you one third of all the profits of the government while I shoud continue there, and in case Mrs Clinton shoud survive you during that time I would allow her five hundred pound a year then.[18]

When Louisbourg fell, Warren wrote again to Anson, as well as to Norris, the Baker cousins, the Duke of Newcastle, and the Earl of Sandwich, all touching on the same theme. To ensure a good reception from him, he had sent the first news of the success by the hand of Sandwich's brother, Capt. William Montagu, whose career Warren had taken some pains to forward.

Montagu's news added the necessary detail to Warren's and Pepperrell's dispatches, and caused a great sensation. For a fortnight the name of Louisbourg was on everyone's lips, only to be supplanted by the startling news of the Young Pretender's landing in Scotland. There were bonfires in celebration, the Tower of London guns were fired, poems and broadsides published, loyal greetings drafted, public houses renamed. Warren became a hero, his behavior and success were contrasted everywhere with those unfortunate individuals implicated in the courts martial that followed the inglorious affair off Toulon in February 1744. It shifted attention from the continent, where the Pragmatic Army, with Dutch, Austrian, and English contingents, had been defeated in May by the French at Fontenoy.

For the first time ever, North American affairs took center stage in London. The ministry was greatly surprised both by the success and by the popular acclaim it received. When the king, then in Hanover, learned of it, he expressed "his highest satisfaction."[19] To Carteret, now the Earl of Granville, it was "the first opening we had of the dawn of glory."[20] Pitt called it a "national success,"[21] informing Pelham: "I would never restore Cape Breton."[22] The Duke of Bedford, then first lord of Admiralty, made his determination to retain Cape Breton widely known, and Sandwich was of like mind. Pelham, ever concerned at the cost of war and in principle unsympathetic to it, came soon to see Louisbourg as a serious obstacle to peace and the cause of future difficulties with France. The Earl of Chesterfield agreed with him, observing that Cape Breton had quickly become "the darling object of the whole nation; it is ten times more popular than ever Gibraltar was, and people are laying in their claims, and protesting already against the restitution of it on any account."[23] Newcastle and his principal advisor, Lord Chancellor Hardwicke, were ambiguous in their reaction: the news was not unwelcome and the conquest could serve as the basis for new enterprises in North America, or it could act as a powerful inducement to pursue peace negotiations.

Warren's friends of course, were greatly pleased at his success, and in their congratulations exaggerated the role he had played. The Baker cousins wrote: "We heartily join in the joy & satisfaction which every body is zealous to express for the acquisition of the Island of Cape Breton; we have a particular pleasure in it, because you were the principal instrument of so great & glorious a conquest, we find the behaviour of all the concerned in the expedition has given great satisfaction, particularly that part of the execution of which we presume to be entirely by your direction, we mean the sending the French all off the Island, and obliging them to go to Old France, the scheme was exceedingly right, & the immediate putting it into execution right also." They added: "Mr. Pelham tells W.[illiam] B.[aker] that you had wrote to his brother the Duke of Newcastle about the Jersey government, & also that you hint towards that of New York hereafter . . . The first we think you are sure of, fall when it will, the other we believe with the friendship of the present governor and your own merit may be obtained; but it is supposed that you still intend to continue in your services at sea while the war lasts." They further noted that

this also agrees with Mr Anson's opinion, who professes great friendship for you as an old acquaintance. Our W.B. waited upon him on the receipt of your letter, he says he will be always regardful of doing you any service, & believes nothing you ask but will be granted, yet at same time said there was some demur about a request you had made of having a grant of the late governor's house at Louisbourg . . . Also he said you had an inclination to have an appointment of the government of Cape Breton. That, also was new to our W.B. Might we advise, it should be that you seek first to be made an admiral, & all these things will be added unto you. Mr Anson told our W.B. that the Duke of Bedford had wrote to Hanover the night before . . . to desire an order from his Majesty to appoint you to a flagg, and which he doubted not would be sent to him.[24]

The reaction of the ministry, which Warren had so longed for, reached him by the hand of Captain Rous on 24 September. It was all he could have reasonably expected. Warren had been given a commission as rear admiral of the blue squadron.[25] Warren hoisted his flag at the mizzen top masthead of *Superbe* and received salutes from both the squadron and the fortress. With the commission came letters from Newcastle, the Admiralty, and personal letters from Anson, Sandwich, Norris, and the Bakers, all overflowing with praise and congratulations. Much to Warren's consternation, Newcastle had recommended him as the first British governor of Cape Breton.

He immediately wrote to all his friends, as well as to Newcastle and Bedford, begging not to be named, or if this had already been done, to send a replacement with the squadron earmarked for Louisbourg in the spring of 1746. To his friends Anson and Sandwich, he pleaded ill health; to Newcastle and Bedford, his desire "to serve in the sphere in which I from my infancy have been bred, and in which I flatter myself I am capable of doing his Majesty and my country most service."[26]

Warren was of course delighted with the government's intention to retain and defend Louisbourg and the plans to send two regiments, then stationed at Gibraltar, to garrison the town. He was also very pleased that the New Englanders had not been overlooked: Pepperrell was to be made a baronet with command of one of the two new American regiments that were to be raised; Governor Shirley was to have command of the other. The government had under consideration the matter of pensions for widows and those so maimed that they could no longer provide for themselves or their families. Equally satisfying was the Admiralty's acquiescence in Warren's decision to commission *Vigilant* and its agreement to purchase the frigate *Shirley*.

William Shirley took no delight in Warren's honors. He had come to Louisbourg in August accompanied by his wife, and, incidentally, Oliver DeLancey, Susannah Warren, and the two Warren children, to deal with the New England troops whose loud demands to be sent home bordered on mutiny. Shirley took three days to consider how he should express his disappointment. On 27 September he penned a missive to Pelham, with whom he had maintained a frequent private correspondence, in which he contrasted the rather empty thanks he received with Warren's shower of honors. He insinuated that Warren had refused his appeal in the summer of 1744 to sail *Launceston* to Annapolis Royal when Shirley thought it in grave danger of falling into French hands, but instead preferred to pursue a French East India ship then in Louisbourg harbor. He pointed out Warren's absolute refusal to assist the New England expedition to Cape Breton when he was first asked. "I say, sir, when I compare my services in respect of Nova Scotia and this acquisition to his Majesty's dominions with Mr Warren's," he wrote, "who besides gaining near seventy thousand pounds sterling (the direct consequence of this expedition, wholly formed, set on foot and carried into execution, in New England, by myself, and into which he was forced by his orders) is immediately distinguished with a flag, a government, and as I further hear the dignity of a baronet, & compare the fate of his services, with that of my own, which seem degraded below those of Mr Warren or Sir William Pepperrell . . . by the superior marks of his Majesty's favour shown to them, I must acknowledge that it gives me no small concern & makes me less able to bear the loss of my health which I have almost wholly destroyed in the publick service."[27] These were bitter words indeed.

Having thus vented his spleen, Shirley was able to end the lengthy letter by expressing a very high opinion of Warren's zeal for the service of the king, "which he follows with indefatigable diligence and honest, warm heart; and I had the utmost dependence on him when I first determined to set the expedition on foot; and no gentleman could have served his Majesty more faithfully and successfully in his situation, than he did after he entered upon the service of the expedition, or better deserves the marks of his Majesty's favour; and in particular I am persuaded, his being appointed governor of this place will be much for the security of it, and for his Majesty's service."

During the two months that Shirley remained in Cape Breton, Warren had every opportunity to sense the governor's disappointments and dissatisfaction, with which he would have largely sympathized, even as he would have hotly denied the interpretation Shirley had placed on some of his actions. Warren had a very high opinion of the governor and had described him in July 1745 to the Admiralty as "a gentleman of honour, temper and good sense, and greatly beloved by all his Majesty's subjects under his government, upon whom he has such an influence, and they such a reliance upon his integrity, that he can do what he pleases with them, and I beg leave to assure their Lordships that his Majesty has not more loyal subjects in any part of his dominions then in his colonies."[28] They had known each other from the days when Warren had served on the New England station, and there appears always to have been a certain element of rivalry between the two, noticeable particularly on Shirley's side. They were destined to spend many weeks together with their paths crossing many times before the end of 1746. It was fortunate indeed that their general aims concerning the future of the French king's dominions in North America ran a parallel course and were very similar.

For the time being they were concerned, as was General Pepperrell, with the defense of Louisbourg. The New England troops had not been much placated by being told that their terms of service did not end with the capture of Louisbourg, as they argued, but extended to garrison duty until relieved by fresh troops either from the colonies or Great Britain. Nevertheless, many were allowed to return home, chiefly those who were sick and rendered incapable of doing their duty. Those who were the sole support of their families were also given special consideration. By mid-September more than twelve hundred had left Cape Breton. Of the less than two thousand who remained, many were destined not to survive the winter. Dysentery reached epidemic proportions and, when added to the serious shortage of food and the much-altered diet, led to a significantly higher mortality rate. By June, Warren and Pepperrell had buried more than twelve hundred men. At first they had hoped that the onset of the bitter cold of winter would cause the sickness to abate, but the infection lingered until spring.

The seamen and marines from *Vigilant* and *Chester*, whom Warren retained "as well to prevent desertion in the troops, as to strengthen the garrison," suffered far less.[29] They were segregated in the Grand battery, and this must have accounted in part for their good state of health, although Warren attributed it to diet: "their being more accustomed to a salt diet than these latter, who when at home have great plenty of roots, milk, and other wholesome food that can't possibly be come at here."[30] He also felt that the method of cooking employed by the New Englanders might have been partly to blame.

With a much reduced and sickly garrison, and with no prospect of getting fresh supplies or reinforcements before spring, Warren had to face the possibility of a surprise attack by a force of *Canadiens* and Mi'kmaq. He had first heard the rumor in November from inhabitants of Île St.-Jean (now Prince Edward Island), who by the terms of capitulation were to be returned to France. It was immediately resolved to remove all the heavy guns from the Grand battery to avoid "[s]plitting upon the same rock the

French did."[31] Without heavy artillery, Warren foresaw little hope of such a lightly armed detachment retaking the town.

Earlier, Warren had been alarmed by reports from Capt. John Wickham in *Lark* at Newfoundland of several French warships at anchor in Carouse Bay on the northeast coast of that island. He feared that the French intended to attack either Newfoundland or the fishing fleet, then making ready to return to Portugal. On 30 September he held a council of war with his captains, Brett, Calmady, Douglass, Edwards, and Hore. It was decided to send *Princess Mary, Sunderland, Canterbury,* and *Superbe* with the two East India ships and the treasure to assist *Lark* and ensure the safe return of the fishing vessels and any merchant ships bound for England.[32] Warren also gave orders to build a boom across the harbor mouth and to cover it with one of the French prizes that he commissioned as fireship *Louisbourg.* Scouting vessels were at once dispatched about the coasts of Cape Breton Island, to Annapolis Royal, to Newfoundland, and along the New England coast to gain further intelligence. This alarm, like that of the possible attack by the *Canadiens,* came to nothing but contributed to the anxiety under which Warren and Pepperrell labored that winter.

Warren still had time enough, beyond the immediate flurry of day-to-day business, to encourage both Newcastle and the Admiralty to view Cape Breton as a permanent British settlement. Its capture, Warren believed, threw open the whole of Canada to British conquest and hence the entire North American continent. Aligning himself with a few colonial officials, Warren urged the ministry to broaden its conception of the war with France and consider, for the first time since 1711, an invasion of Canada by land and sea.[33]

For the moment Warren hoped that Louisbourg would develop as a major port, with a small squadron based there to be employed against French fishing vessels in the summer, to escort the North American and West Indies trade to British ports in the autumn, and to patrol the West Indies in the winter months.[34] The idea of using Louisbourg as a rendezvous for trade, a role Havana played for the Spanish, was never seriously investigated but did encounter sharp professional criticism from Commodore Knowles.[35]

To maintain such a squadron, Warren advised that Louisbourg become a naval base with proper careening facilities where the squadron could refit. One of its considerable advantages was that desertion was exceedingly difficult in such a remote place.[36] This last proposal the Admiralty adopted, despite opposition by Knowles.[37]

To deal with the captures made during and after the siege, Warren established a Vice Admiralty Court. When informed that he lacked the authority, the court's sentences were nullified.[38] Orders to establish such a court were received only a year later in June 1746. The officials—judge, registrar, and marshal—were all New Englanders and Warren's nominees.[39] It is uncertain whether the court ever transacted any business because its records have vanished.

Warren was concerned about the settlement of both Cape Breton and Nova Scotia. Of fundamental importance was the establishment of a civil government of the sort found in Nova Scotia, otherwise few would be attracted to the settlement while governed by a military regime. To encourage settlers, Warren also recommended that Louisbourg be named a free port to afford it a trading advantage over other North American ports. This radical idea, first embraced in the West Indies only twenty years later, was ignored by the ministry perhaps because it was opposed by Shirley.[40] Warren suggested that newcomers be granted land free of quit-rents for an unspecified period of years.[41] To encourage both settlers from New England and Protestants from Germany of the sort he had encountered in New York, Warren suggested that religious toleration be extended to dissenters.[42] With Cape Breton free of military government and Louisbourg a free port, the island had every prospect of flourishing, he believed, and so might repay the heavy cost to Britain that would be incurred in the first years of the colony's life.

Warren also wanted a small fort erected at St. Anne's harbor, the principal settlement on the island after Louisbourg. It would make an excellent base for the fishery, and with several "improved farms about it" some of the provisions needed by the Louisbourg garrison could be raised there.[43] The rest of the provisions would be more cheaply supplied from the colonies rather than being sent from England, as the Admiralty had first intended.[44]

On 29 October Warren and Shirley sent Bedford, as first lord of Admiralty, their assessment of the need to lay plans for the conquest of Canada, which would, among other benefits, guarantee the survival and development of Cape Breton. With Canada conquered, not only would the wealth of the fisheries pass to the British but also the great fur trade and the unknown riches of the interior.

The Admiralty granted Warren's request to be relieved of the governorship of Cape Breton for health reasons.[45] He formally resigned only on 2 June 1746, when Commodore Charles Knowles was named his successor, principally due to his knowledge of fortifications.[46] Before coming ashore, Knowles sent Warren a conciliatory message acknowledging his culpability in the dispute over *Superbe* at Antigua the year before. Knowles arrived in the 60–gun *Norwich* with *Canterbury*, on which Warren's brother-in-law, Oliver DeLancey, was a passenger. They arrived on 23 May, a fortnight after Vice Adm. Isaac Townsend in *Kingston* (60), with *Pembroke* (60) and the newly commissioned *Kinsale* (44) escorting two ordnance storeships. On 2 April the Gibraltar troops, having wintered at New York and Virginia, began arriving under convoy of *Fowey*, *Dover*, and *Torrington*, which—with the addition of new recruits from the colonies—ensured the security of the conquest. By April there was a surplus of provisions, and the morale of the New England troops who had survived the terrible winter rose dramatically at the prospect of soon returning to their families.

Before leaving, Warren summoned the entire garrison in the parade square outside the main barracks and addressed it for the last time. His words were directed principally to the New Englanders. The moment proved a rare example of a British military or naval commander addressing colonial troops with understanding, compassion, and respect, and as such Warren's reported remarks are worth quoting.

> It is with very great pleasure I have call'd you together at this time, because I have it now in my power to gratify you in what you have so long, and earnestly wish'd for, and desir'd; I mean to return to your families, and settlements, after the great fatigues you have gone thro,' both in the reduction, & protection of this valuable acquisition.
>
> Your signal services upon this occasion shall never be forgot by me, and you may be assured I will . . . in person, whenever I return to Great Britain represent your services, and the importance of this conquest, to his Majesty, and the ministry, in the truest light. . . .
>
> I have seen with great concern, how much the officers and men have been crowded in their houses, since the arrival of the troops to relieve them, to prevent which, as much as possible, we have kept one of the regiments on board the transports, 'till we can prepare quarters for them in the hospital, which we are under the necessity of converting into a barrack; when that is done, and new barracks built, the materials for which are hourly expected, I hope there will be room to give houses to all such people as shall choose to settle in this place, and to allow such of the troops as are married proper conveniences out of the barracks.

Any persons who have an inclination to remain here as inhabitants, or to enlist into his Majesty's service, may depend upon my
protection; and the former shall always be at free liberty to leave this
place, whenever they please; and as nothing can contribute more to
the welfare of any government, and people than a religious discharge
of their duty, and a benevolent and brotherly behaviour to each other,
I, in the most earnest manner recommend this, gentlemen, to you all,
that as we are all one people under the best of kings, and happiest of
governments, we continue in one mind, doing all the good offices in
our power for each other. . . .

I sincerely wish you all a happy meeting with your familys, &
friends, and shall ever think it the greatest happiness that can attend
me, to have power equal to my inclination to serve every officer and
soldier that has been, in the least degree, instrumental in the reduction of this garrison to his Majesty's obedience, the securing which,
during the course of a long and severe winter, in which you suffered
the greatest hardships, and many brave men perished, 'till the arrival
of his Majesty's troops, highly merits the favour of your king and
country, which I hope will always be shown you.

You are very happy, Gentlemen, in the governors, and legislators of
your different provinces, who in all their letters to Sir William
Pepperrell & myself, express the greatest concern at the mortality
that raged among you last winter, and that they had it not in their
power to keep faith with you, by relieving you as soon as you expected after the reduction of this place; and such indeed was their care
for you that had not the two regiments from Gibraltar happily arriv'd
nor the levies gone on so well as they have done for the American
regiments, both here, and in the colonies, yet they were determined
at any expense, to raise men this spring to relieve you.[47]

He ended by assuring them that they could put the greatest faith in Admiral Townsend and his squadron. Should France make any attempt on the
city, "I am persuaded the same spirit that induced you to make this conquest, will prompt you to protect it."

Warren's final task before formally handing over the government was
the reconciliation of his accounts. For repairs alone, he and Pepperrell had
disbursed £16,318 5s. This together with the fuel, clothing, gunpowder,
and sundry other bills brought the total to £24,967 4s.[48] It had come from
their own private resources, and it took several years before the various
government offices audited these accounts and Warren was reimbursed.

Although Warren had been granted leave to recover his health at Boston, his orders of 14 March instructed him to concert measures with Shirley and other governors for "attempting new conquests upon the enemy."[49] Before leaving Louisbourg, Warren outlined to Townsend and Knowles what he thought could be achieved that summer. The Louisbourg defenses, still not repaired after their battering of the summer before, must be completed. He saw no possibility of living in harmony with the remaining French population, even those who had been allowed to remain on the island after the Louisbourg garrison had departed could not be trusted and would have to be repatriated. The approximately one thousand souls thought to be inhabiting Île St.-Jean were to be sent to France along with those at Baie Verte, at the head of the Bay of Fundy. The St. Lawrence was to be blockaded both to prevent provisions and troops from being sent to Canada and to familiarize sea officers with that great river of which Warren now believed he possessed a fairly good chart and suitable pilots. The squadron would cruise off the coast to detect any squadron bent upon the recapture of Louisbourg. Elsewhere in New England, vigorous patrolling of the northeast frontier would put an end to *Canadien* and Mi'kmaq raids. In New York, negotiations already begun with the Iroquois would continue in an attempt ultimately to align the tribe to the British interest and thus transform the Mohawk valley frontier from a threatened zone into a secure base for raids into Canada (and incidentally enhance the value of Warren's estate there). All the colonies were to organize their resources for the conquest of Canada, which he believed would be possible to undertake in 1747.

Warren never enjoyed the tranquility of the relatively unhurried summer for which he hoped. He was but three hours' sailing from Louisbourg in *Chester*, which Townsend had assigned him, when the sloop *Hinchinbroke* hove in sight with new orders from Newcastle and the Admiralty. The attack on Canada was not to be delayed until 1747, but was to be undertaken that very summer. As this altered the entire situation, Warren returned forthwith to Louisbourg to give the startling news to Townsend, who hastily called a council of war.[50] There it was decided to send *Kinsale* at once into the St. Lawrence. The plan to remove the population of Île St.-Jean was postponed because all available transports were then needed to carry the expeditionary force to Quebec.

Warren thereupon sailed for Boston to hasten the preparations to be undertaken by the colonies. He left with serious misgivings and in a deep state of depression. He was to command the squadron up the St. Lawrence, yet his doctors assured him that with the scurvy already so far advanced he could not possibly hope to survive. He was irritated that his and Shirley's advice had not been heeded. He saw no hope that the colonies—willing to contribute to the expedition—would have sufficient time to raise the necessary men and gather together their provisions. Even among the New Englanders who had been most zealous in the service of the king, there would be grave difficulties, as they had all been "discharg'd and gone from Lewisburg previous to the receipt of those instructions, and agreeable to the promise made them by Governor Shirley, I doubt very much whether it will be possible to make the necessary preparations and raise upon so very short notice a number of forces in the colonies, as will be sufficient in conjunction with those expected from England . . . to attempt the conquest of Canada this season, which is now far advanc'd."[51]

Warren feared failure, the great expense, the exasperation, and the disgrace that would be visited on the principal officers responsible for carrying the impossible instructions into execution. He saw his career ending in ruins simply because the scheme, however well conceived, was projected a year too soon. In addition to his letter to the Admiralty, Warren wrote to his old patron, Admiral Norris, of his disgust and surprise at his orders, especially as he and Shirley had frequently advised Newcastle "that nothing cou'd with any prospect of success be attempted against Canada this year; because in the raising of levies for such an attempt, the consent & concurrence of so many different governments is absolutely necessary and will take a great deal of time to procure."[52] He pleaded for the senior admiral's wisdom. "Pray, sir, do me the favour to resolve me whether it is the duty of an officer in my situation, if my health wou'd admit of my undertaking such a command, to do it against all probability of success, in my own opinion, and by that means put my country to an immense expense, lose a number of his Majesty's subjects to no purpose, and of course be censured himself which is always the consequence of a miscarriage, whether owing to misconduct or not." Rather, he believed, as he explained to Norris, "it may be done next spring with the greatest prospect of success. By the plan the troops are ordered to rendezvous at Louisbourg from the colonies the latter end or middle of May & to sail for the St. Lawrence the beginning of June. It was the 6th June before we receiv'd the plan, so you may judge how soon the men may be expected from the colonies, and I dare say those for England will not be at Louisbourg in all July, if they have such a passage as is common to large convoys, shou'd they sail from thence as soon as expected." In conclusion he wrote, "it is too late and too short a warning to prepare for an expedition of so much importance to our country, and for my own part, if it can be done with honour, I had rather give up all my pretensions to his Majesty's service than be a means of leading my country into so great an error and misfortune, but upon a well-concerted plan I shall be proud of the honour of being an instrument worthy of having my share in the execution of it. I persuade myself you were not of the council that resolv'd upon this scheme."

The ministry had reached its extraordinary decision on 3 April, in great haste, at a cabinet meeting attended by Hardwicke, Bedford, Harrington, Pelham, and Newcastle. Though the capture of Louisbourg had raised hopes for extending the conquests in North America, a decision about the precise measures to be taken was delayed at first by the seriousness of the Jacobite uprising, which required all available forces to be concentrated at home. Even in December 1745, when the Young Pretender began his long retreat from Derby, political reasons prevented effective planning for the 1746 campaign either in Europe or in North America. The political crisis came to a head only in mid-February, when the Pelhams and their friends resigned en bloc in a successful attempt to force the king from continuing to take the advice of his long-deposed minister—John Carteret, Lord Granville—and to give office to William Pitt.[53] Only then could plans be laid. Warren's melancholy account of the state of Louisbourg, written on 18 January, arrived at the beginning of March, occasioning some serious new thinking about America.[54] The king gave his consent to dispatch another one thousand men, some of whom were to be carried on the two men-of-war then preparing to sail for Cape Breton. This would ensure that the serious losses suffered by the New Englanders would be replaced. On 14 March orders were sent to Warren, Townsend, and Knowles but called for nothing more than the concentration of a large naval squadron at Cape Breton, the adequate garrisoning of Louisbourg to rebut any attempt at recapture by the French, and the vague concerting of measures among the colonies for further harassment of French settlements.

Ten days later the atmosphere changed. Bedford sent Newcastle a lengthy report strongly advising the conquest of Canada that season.[55] Newcastle promptly named Bedford to a committee with the master general of ordnance, the Duke of Montague, and Lt. Gen. James St. Clair as the other members. Their report, submitted on 30 March, endorsed Bedford's proposal and elaborated a plan of operations,[56] which called for a two-pronged attack on Canada. The first contingent would head up the St. Lawrence under the command of General St. Clair, with five thousand British regulars, thirty-five hundred of whom were to be convoyed from England and the rest taken from Louisbourg. No special arrangements were to be made for a siege train, the ships' guns being thought sufficient when used as shore batteries. If the convoy from England was ready in a month, the expedition could be mounted before Quebec by mid-July, time enough for its capture. The second prong of the attack was to be wholly a colonial venture. It called for an attack on Montréal, mounted at Albany, under the command of William Gooch, the lieutenant governor of Virginia. From Albany, the expedition was to make its way up the Hudson River to Lake Champlain, then to the Richelieu River, and eventually to Montréal, reinforced by whatever Iroquois allies could be collected. When the cabinet considered the plan four days later, those who had doubts arising from the warnings Warren had often sent—that the scheme, if it in any way depended on the support of the colonies, should be planned no earlier than 1747—remained silent. Henry Pelham and his brother, the Duke of Newcastle, put their weight behind it because of their political indebtedness to Bedford and his friends, the architects of the scheme; because both the admirals and the generals thought it practicable; because its success would bring considerable diplomatic rewards as well as parliamentary support; and, of course, because it was known to be popular in the country.[57] It now only remained to draft suitable instructions to the sea officers in America and to the colonial governors concerned, and to set in motion the hasty preparations at home that the plan demanded.[58] With matters in the hands of the experts, Bedford, with undoubted satisfaction, retreated to Bath on 22 April.

When Warren reached Boston on 24 June, he found Shirley equally aghast at the plans of the ministry, but they agreed to keep their pessimism to themselves and do all in their power to raise the necessary troops. Shirley had been pleasantly surprised at the speed with which New England recruits had joined his and Pepperrell's regiments once recruiting began in earnest in March, and he hoped that the new levies would be forthcoming just as quickly.[59] Although Warren was somewhat heartened by this news, he feared that "the season advances faster than the levies."[60] The same lament continued in all his letters throughout the summer. By the end of August, almost five thousand men had been raised in the New England colonies and another twenty-one hundred elsewhere; both Shirley and Warren thought it an insufficient force for the expedition to Canada, even when the British regulars were added.[61] As the weeks went by, they both grew exceedingly doubtful that the troops had sailed from

England. By August, Townsend was convinced that even if St. Clair were soon to appear, nothing could be attempted, while Warren began to think of returning home "with the plan from the colonies for the execution of it next spring if approved by his Majesty."[62] In the meantime, Warren dispatched one hundred cattle, through Messrs. Apthorp and Sparhawk, to Louisbourg for St. Clair, should he arrive. So great was the rush of business that Warren never left Boston to make a tour of several colonies to encourage the recruiting drive and embolden the colonial officials and legislators. Townsend, for his part, sent ships into the St. Lawrence, where a number of insignificant prizes were taken, disrupting the French riverine fishery. The plan to remove the population of Île St.-Jean was revived, but the French escaped into the interior, after killing members of the British landing party.

As the possibility grew that the thousands of men recruited for the Canada expedition would not be used in 1746, an alternative plan developed. It was suggested that an attack on the French fortress of Crown Point be attempted. There, some ninety miles northeast of Albany on the western shore of Lake Champlain, the French in 1731 had erected a fortress, Fort Frédéric. This, Warren and Shirley believed, was the "key of Canada on the land side & the place of rendezvous, from whence the enemy not only may make incursions upon most of his Majesty's colonies, & have begun already to commit great devastations, but very much annoy that part of his Majesty's land forces, which . . . is design'd to penetrate into Canada from Albany."[63] It was thought necessary before any such scheme was undertaken to ensure at least the neutrality of the Iroquois in the Mohawk valley before committing a large force to the risk. All summer Governor Clinton of New York negotiated with the Mohawk, and with the particular assistance of William Johnson, Warren's nephew, their support was obtained.[64] This unexpected good news reached Warren early in September, and he reveled in what proved to be the only positive development in America the entire summer.

Just as Shirley and Warren were trying to salvage something from the efforts of the colonies, the ministry at home was abandoning the St. Clair expedition. Adverse winds had prevented the transports from reaching Plymouth from the Downs until 12 June. The fleet sailed on 15 June but was becalmed almost at once; then contrary winds developed, forcing it back to Spithead. In the meantime, the wisdom of sending the fleet was called in question by the report that a great French fleet was collecting at Brest. Admiral Martin, who put to sea on 2 May from Plymouth, discovered on 19 June that the French were at Rochefort with part of a Spanish squadron. He was greatly outnumbered, and deciding wrongly that the enemy force was destined for Ireland rather than Cape Breton, as he had earlier suspected, he withdrew to guard the Channel rather than move south off Cape Finisterre, the best station to intercept a fleet bound for Louisbourg and Canada. This move enabled Jean-Baptiste-Louis-Frédéric de Roye de la Rochefoucauld, Duc d'Enville, the French admiral, to quit the French coast unhindered and to make for Nova Scotia, where his orders carried him. The news threw the ministry into a flurry; St. Clair was ordered to rejoin the task force and sail to America for the protection of Cape Breton, Nova Scotia, and Newfoundland. As it was too late to attempt the conquest of Canada, St. Clair was now ordered to winter in America and then proceed on the great task in the spring of 1747. He was ready to sail only on 6 August, but the fleet, now under the command of Adm. Richard Lestock, again faced contrary winds and could not get past St. Helen's. On 23 August the plan to invade Canada was abandoned for that year, a decision endorsed by Anson, who remarked to Bedford: "I was extremely pleased with the account of the American expedition being laid aside for the present . . . There is no man in this Kingdom who thinks that putting the American scheme in execution, will be a righter measure or have more good consequences to this country than I do, but the season being so far advanced made it dangerous to attempt it."[65]

For their part, the French, as soon as they learned of the fall of Louisbourg, determined on its recapture the following year. There would be no question of peace with England without the restoration of the fortress and island. To avoid the embarrassment of having to bargain for it at some future peace conference they would seize it by war. Late in December 1745, the main outlines of the plan to re-establish France's position in North America had been decided by the *ministre de la marine,* le comte de Maurepas. Command was given to Jean-Baptiste-Louis-Frédéric, Duc d'Enville.[66] His fleet, with an expeditionary force, was to rendezvous in the great uninhabited harbor of Chebucto, Nova Scotia, toward the end of May. Its first duty was to prevent any enemy attempt on Canada via the St. Lawrence. Its next duty was to besiege Annapolis Royal, Louisbourg, and Placentia in Newfoundland. If all went well, the force was then even to consider attacking the coastal settlements of New England, including Boston. Delays in bringing the fleet together and provisioning the troops prevented d'Enville from sailing until 11 June.

The fleet consisted of the flagship *Northumberland* (70), *Trident* (64),

Ardent (64), *Mars* (64), *Alcide* (64), *Borée* (64), *Léopard* (64), *Caribou* (56), *Diamant* (56), and *Tigre* (50); the frigates *Renommée* (30), *Mégère* (30), and *Mutine* (24); the sloops *Palme* (10) and *Perle* (8); the bombships *Argonaute* and *Parfaite;* the hospital ship *Mercure;* and fifteen troop transports with nineteen vessels carrying provisions. Adverse winds and calms contributed to a very long passage, during which many of the seamen and soldiers fell ill. Not until the end of August was the coast of Nova Scotia sighted, and then the fleet was buffeted by a violent storm. Facing thick offshore fog banks characteristic of that coast in summer, only by 9 September did the fleet begin to limp into the comparative shelter of Chebucto. The ships were in a shattered condition; many seamen and soldiers had died on the passage and many more were desperately ill. The Duc d'Enville himself had contracted scurvy and died on 16 September; hundreds more followed him in the next few days.

Now there was no question of launching an attack on any of the English or New England forts or settlements, as all efforts were directed toward survival. Command passed to Contre-amiral Constantin-Louis d'Estourmel, whose mind became so unhinged at the sight of the force dying about him that in a fit of depression three days later he fell on his sword in a failed attempt at suicide.[67] Jacques-Pierre de Taffanel, Marquis de la Jonquière, the next senior officer, took command.[68] He was determined at least to besiege Annapolis Royal and to send to Quebec four provision ships, which he knew were greatly needed. As contrary winds prevented him from reaching the Bay of Fundy, he reluctantly gave the order three days later to make for France after sailing from Chebucto on 13 October.

Though the Duc d'Enville's expedition was considered a serious disaster by the French, it gave those in America many anxious moments. Admiral Martin had sent early warning to Louisbourg of the French fleet's preparations and possible destination and this news had reached Townsend on 5 July. The vice admiral at once sent the sloop *Albany* to notify Shirley and Warren at Boston.[69] At almost the same moment, Warren received a still earlier warning from the Admiralty of the same preparations.[70] Warren at first thought the French arrangements were more likely designed to strengthen Canada than to attack Louisbourg and encouraged Townsend to station ships constantly in the St. Lawrence. With the British warships already in North America and those expected daily with the St. Clair expedition, there was little chance of Louisbourg being taken. It greatly complicated matters, however, for if the French fleet appeared it would have to be dealt with before the descent on Canada was undertaken. Warren sent

Chester, commanded by Richard Spry, to cruise to the northwest and provide early warning of the approach of any hostile squadron. Spry returned
on 8 August, having met only a small merchant vessel that had reported a
sighting on 27 May of a fleet of twelve large ships to the west of the English coast. As there were no transports sighted, Warren accurately concluded that it could be neither the French fleet nor the St. Clair expedition,
and therefore was most likely Admiral Martin's squadron.

By the beginning of September, Warren experienced some anxiety
about the safety of Annapolis Royal. From information received by Gov.
Paul Mascarene on the inadequacies of the fortifications there,[71] Warren
concluded that the French would be well advised to attack that fortress first
and, if successful, "add upwards of five thousand fighting Nova Scotians to
any other force that they may be able to collect from Canada, besides the
addition of a large body of Indians."[72] Then they would be able to concentrate a truly formidable body of men for the assault on Louisbourg. Warren ordered *Chester* to sail at once for Annapolis Royal to join *Shirley,*
already there, and suggested to Townsend that St. Clair be asked for five
hundred troops to garrison the place during the winter, as it would then be
too late to send the expedition to Quebec.

Actual evidence of the presence of d'Enville's fleet reached Louisbourg
and Boston on 6 and 12 September. At Louisbourg, *Kinsale* brought in one
of the provision ships bound for Quebec that had left La Rochelle with the
fleet. The master, Antoine Rodriguez, gave a very accurate though somewhat exaggerated account of the size of the armament and the number of
troops aboard. The next day a schooner from Marblehead reached Louisbourg with news of having sighted several strange warships off the Nova
Scotia coast, a report that prompted Townsend to send cruisers to range
southwards from Louisbourg.[73]

Before this news reached Warren, he had his own information of the
French arrival. His and Shirley's immediate concern was for the safety of
Annapolis Royal, where they at once dispatched three hundred troops,
with seven hundred to follow, all being drawn from the intended expedition to Crown Point.[74] Warren sent a half dozen vessels to make contact
with Admiral Lestock to warn him of the French fleet.[75] He also cautioned
Capt. James Douglass, in command of the station ship at Newfoundland, as
well as the captains stationed in American colonies to the south. He was in
some anxiety about the fate of the sloop *Hinchinbroke,* which he had sent
to Louisbourg with a considerable quantity of coin for the garrison,
shortly before the news of the French reached Boston. It was some time

before he learned of her safe arrival there on 17 September, her precious cargo intact, with a full report on the French and that she had been sent into the Bay of Fundy by Townsend to help defend Annapolis Royal.[76]

Although Warren was greatly concerned about where the French "fury will fall," he was equally excited by the prospect of doing battle with them.[77] He applied to Townsend for a ship, fully expecting to be placed under Admiral Lestock's command and to have some share in "the destruction of those gasconading French chaps."[78] He admitted to Captain Douglass that it would give him "high pleasure," and privately to Corbett he spoke of his impatience to know "where the thunder of the French fleet is to fall.[79] But God send Mr Lestock here to let his roar first upon them in which I sincerely wish to bear a part."[80]

Warren and his colleagues learned of the withdrawal of the French fleet much earlier than the cancellation of the Canada expedition. On 24 October Warren had the full story of the disasters the French had suffered and of their extreme vulnerability during their time in Chebucto harbor. He learned too of their abortive plans to attack Annapolis Royal. He did not gloat over the French losses, guessing accurately at the horror they had suffered. In truth, he was much relieved by their withdrawal. His only worry was that the Marquis de la Jonquière had supplied the Acadiens and the Mi'kmaq with muskets and ammunition and several small vessels that the French squadron had taken as prizes. He gave both Mascarene and Knowles notice of this. It remained only for him to summon *Chester* from Annapolis Royal and give Shirley what assistance he could to hasten the preparations for the Crown Point expedition.

Shortly after, Warren decided to return to England, so he sent his family to winter in New York and hastily wound up his affairs both there and in Massachusetts. Reasoning that he would be returning to America the following spring to command the squadron for the conquest of Canada, his separation, he thought, would not be excessively prolonged. In June he had heard of the death of the governor of New Jersey and had at once applied to his friends for their assistance in securing the appointment. He sent letters to Adm. Sir John Norris, to whom he confided that he was negotiating with Governor Clinton; to Corbett, he petitioned, "pray why may I not serve at sea and be nam'd to a government during the war."[81] He made a direct application to the Duke of Newcastle, but if he wrote to Sandwich and Anson the letters have not survived. To Samuel and William Baker he wrote: "I have an account of the death of Mr Morris governor of New Jersey, and have wrote to his grace the Duke of Newcastle to favour me with the government, with a prospect of succeeding Mr Clinton when it shall be agreeable to him to leave New York. I must desire the favour that you will solicit this affair for me, in the best manner you can, with all my friends."[82]

Their efforts were unavailing, for the appointment went to Jonathan Belcher, William Shirley's predecessor at Boston. Whatever the factors favoring Belcher's appointment, there were two powerful ones against Warren's. He had successfully impressed the ministry with news of his precarious health and his need for a leave of absence; this made him a doubtful prospect and offered them a useful excuse that they chose to employ. Of more importance was his appointment to command the naval squadron for the attack on Canada. This would occupy him fully throughout the summer and autumn of 1746, and, if it succeeded, he would probably have to spend the winter as governor of Quebec. This effectively ruled out whatever inclination Newcastle and his brother had of making him Lewis Morris's successor. Early October brought Warren news that he had failed in this bid.[83] In the turmoil of the moment, with the prospect of d'Enville's fleet about to seize the initiative in America, he had little time for chagrin.

Two months after the fall of Louisbourg and with several rich prizes to his name, Warren offered to purchase the governorship of New York from George Clinton.[84] This had been the beginning of a negotiation that Warren was prevented from completing in the summer of 1746 by business pressures, which kept him constantly at Boston. Clinton had replied, asking for £5,500.[85] Warren thought it "a great deal too much especially if I have to give up my half pay of an admiral, which will be daily growing."[86] He added that he would be "very happy as a private gentleman while you remain our governor." He made no counteroffer, sticking to his original proposals. It was left to Clinton to resume the matter six months later:

On looking over your first proposal, I find it would be impossible to accept of it by reason of its interfering with my half pay which is more than what you offer. That nothing but a sum can do it . . . I imagine you will be going for England in the fall that if anything is to be done before you go for when in England it will be to late as letters miscarry daily therefore the sooner we can agree the better but as I mentioned before to must be possible without my half pay being a hindrance for any thing else. Now my dear sir, I deal ingenuously with you by telling you I am determined to leave this government in case I can get any body to take it off my hands without being a suf-

ferer which I doubt not I will meet, however had much rather it was
you as your desirous of being here and upon the strength of that
imagine we don't differ in the thing but shoud it not succeed as much
as I dislike the place & ways of the people, yet rather than hurt my
family am determined to stay 'till I have meet with an offer worth
waiting for.[87]

He expressed his confidence that they could come to an agreement, or that
someone else in England would be glad of the appointment on the terms
Clinton proffered. Above all, they were to ensure that their friends in England should understand the terms of their agreement, should it be made,
and carry out their part "that they may know what they go upon that there
may be no mistake in a matter of that consequence."

Warren found the letter friendly and obliging and made a counteroffer:
"tho I give up a much better thing for it, I would either give you three
thousand pounds or over one third of the income of that government during your and Mrs. Clinton's life and my holding it."[88] The letter was carried to New York and thence to Albany, where Clinton was spending the
summer in negotiations with the Iroquois, by Oliver DeLancey, who told
Clinton of Warren's intentions to come to New York. This pleased Clinton,
who observed that Warren had omitted the word "sterling." He estimated
that one-third of the income amounted to about NY£800. As the sum was
uncertain, he would settle for the lump sum together with a guaranteed
£400 sterling a year "during Mrs Clinton's and my life and your holding
the government."[89] Clinton considered the matter as good as settled; he
would apply for leave to return home and then secure Warren's appointment, but he advised Warren that "this must be kept a great secret for
should it be known there are people in England ready enough to attempt
getting it."

In September Warren sent a reply to Clinton but its contents are unknown, and though it must have been favorable, it clearly did not clinch
the deal.[90] There is no evidence that Warren changed his attitude toward
the government of New York by the time he sailed from Boston for England late in November. His last surviving letter to Clinton in 1746, written on 20 October, in reply to a very agreeable letter of Clinton's, full of
praise for William Johnson's successes with the Iroquois, was a very
friendly expression of pleasure at the excellent service Warren's nephew
had undertaken by helping the governor to bring the difficult negotiations
with the native tribes to a successful conclusion: "I propose to kiss your
hand at New York about the middle of next month," Warren had written.[91]

He had to alter his plans and took his wife and children only as far as Rhode Island before sending them ahead to New York and returning hastily to Boston. It is then fair to conclude that their arrangement, still unsettled by the end of 1746, needed very little to become a bargain.

Rear Adm. Peter Warren never became governor of any colony other than Cape Breton. His ambitions for the New York appointment were swept away in the factional bickering and jealousies of New York colonial politics. Warren's brother-in-law, New York's chief justice James DeLancey, had supported Governor Clinton for three years but now dramatically altered his policy. By trying to make life unbearable for the governor, DeLancey hoped to force his early resignation. As Warren's own objectives, such as confronting the power of France in North America and securing an alliance with the Iroquois Confederacy, closely mirrored the policies Clinton had been pursuing, he had no desire to upset the governor. Nor had Warren the least reason to upset his new patron, the Duke of Newcastle, whose sister had married Clinton's brother. At least until the end of 1747 Warren believed that the divisiveness now evident in New York's politics would evaporate. Instead, his letters to Clinton, designed to bring about an accommodation through compromise, merely drew from his colleague the accusation, as Clinton complained that Warren "stiks at nothing for the sake of his own interest and friends, however prejudicial to mine."[92]

The political price Warren paid for being identified with the DeLancey faction was high. Clinton's determination to battle his detractors cost Warren the realization of his foremost ambition of becoming a governor in a strategically important and commercially expanding North American colony. His importance to the DeLancey faction was limited to helping secure, in 1747, James DeLancey's commission as New York's lieutenant governor and the appointment in 1748 of Robert Charles, Warren's secretary, as agent for the New York assembly in London.[93]

The Western Squadron, 1747–1748

"The navy of France was so much reduced, as to be no longer formidable; and this may be truly said to have been the only advantage that Britain gained by the war."[1]

If Warren was still dreaming of a colonial governorship when he reached Spithead on Christmas Eve in 1746, a different fate awaited him. While the war lasted, it was no longer in American waters or the West Indies that he was to make his mark, although this at first was not apparent. He was summoned to appear early in the New Year before a meeting of the cabinet council to reiterate his views about a future expedition to Canada, expressed most recently in the letter he signed jointly with Governor Shirley two months earlier.[2] That proposal called for a naval force of eighteen ships of the line with attending frigates and sloops to rendezvous on the Cape Breton coast either at Spanish River (now Sydney) or Louisbourg. About one-third of the force, he proposed, would remain stationed off Cape Breton to ensure that no French armament entered the St. Lawrence River. The remaining naval force would then escort to Quebec twelve thousand of the twenty-two thousand men to be enlisted in the colonies in support of the British regulars shipped from England. The other ten thousand colonials were to march against Montréal at the same time. The colonial forces were to be mustered, as far as possible, as a separate force alongside the British regulars.

If Warren was correct in his estimate of the naval force needed to conquer Canada, his advice killed whatever enthusiasm was left in the cabinet for further American adventures. When the cabinet decided not to send the force Warren and Shirley had recommended, but a smaller one instead, they asked for Warren's assessment as to what forces would be needed for a less ambitious deployment. Warren responded in two documents, both dated 17 January, one a personal letter to Newcastle, the second a proposal signed jointly with George Clarke, the former lieutenant governor of New York, and William Bollan, agent in London for the colony of Massachusetts. Warren recommended that a civil government be established in Nova Scotia to hasten its settlement with loyal Protestants, that a fort fit for five hundred men be erected on Chebucto harbor with a smaller one for one hundred men at Canso. Requisite forces included a squadron of eight ships of the line, two sloops, and a fireship, with two thousand troops. As the "security of Nova Scotia and the frontiers of the neighboring colonies very much depended on the friendship of the Indians," he recommended that a system of gifts, in the manner of the French, be adopted.[3] The annual sum recommended was £500. He also advised both the building of a fort and the construction of armed vessels to patrol Lake Ontario and thereby interrupt French trade to the Mississippi.

Appropriate orders were delayed for seven weeks. On 5 March Warren was given command of *Devonshire* (66) as a flagship, with three 60–gun ships, four 50–gun ships including *Panther* and *Chester*, and five frigates including *Adventure* (44) and *Shirley* (24), and two sloops.[4] He ordered *Panther* to escort the trade bound for Newfoundland,[5] while *Adventure* was sent to her Carolina station.[6] The rest would act together as his squadron.

Three weeks later, from information received by the Admiralty, Warren's orders were cancelled. The Admiralty learned that the French planned to dispatch two heavily escorted convoys, one to India, the other to Canada. So large was the rumored force that a small squadron off Belle Isle withdrew to Plymouth, leaving but one frigate, *Ambuscade* (40), to cruise down the French coast. Early on 28 March she encountered *Auguste* (34), and in rough weather initiated battle that she broke off when two large French warships bore down on her. The storm sank the badly damaged *Auguste*, capsized *Légère*, and drove *Chasseur* ashore a wreck. Of this French squadron, only three reached the coast of India. With this new intelligence of French naval preparations, the cabinet council, with Anson and Warren present, decided to concentrate the navy in home waters. By abandoning the plan to send Warren's squadron to the Gulf of St. Lawrence, it could strengthen the force of what was becoming known as the Western squadron instead. Commodore Knowles at Louisbourg was to be sent only three warships.

Warren was named second-in-command to Vice Adm. George Anson, with instructions that if any part of the Brest squadron managed to break loose into the Atlantic bound for North America, Warren was to sail "with a sufficient force" in pursuit.[7] These instructions were of some interest, as they evolved from ideas that Warren himself had first suggested to Anson early in 1746. He had asked to command a flying squadron of ten "good, clean sailing ships of the line, not too much limited by orders, but left to follow the enemy wherever I could trace them by intelligence or otherwise."[8] Not to be hedged in by overly detailed orders was an essential part of this idea. Now a year later in the spring of 1747, the Admiralty had given Anson and Warren that very latitude.

Anson was instructed to collect as large a fleet as could quickly be sent to sea to intercept and destroy "the ships of the enemy, their convoys outward and homeward bound," while protecting "the trade of his Majesty's subjects."[9] Anson was assigned eighteen ships of the line, five frigates, three sloops, and two bomb vessels. Warren, at Portsmouth, as his second-in-command acknowledged his appointment on 2 April.[10] With Anson in *Prince George* (80), they sailed on 6 April accompanied by *Lyon* (60), *Defiance* (60), *Princess Louisa* (60), *Chester* (60), *Pembroke* (60), *Bristol* (50), and the bombship *Terror*. The next day off Plymouth, they were joined by eleven ships: *Namur* (74), *Hampton Court* (70), *Monmouth* (64), *Prince Frederick* (64), *Nottingham* (60), *Eagle* (60), *Windsor* (60), *Falkland* (50), *Centurion* (54), the sloop *Otter*, and the cutter *Tavistock*. The rendezvous was twenty leagues off Belle Isle between 46°N and 47°30'N.

Initially the fleet lacked sufficient frigates to undertake the necessary scouting and had to employ the 50–gun *Falkland* and its single cutter. Only on 20 April did they receive information that led Anson to conclude that Brest was empty of ships ready for sea. With the unanimous advice of Warren and the captains, Anson shifted his position south across the Bay of Biscay to a point forty leagues north of Cape Ortegal, leaving the frigate *Inverness* (22) and the sloop *Viper* (10), which had joined him, to hasten further reinforcements to the new rendezvous as they arrived from Portsmouth and Plymouth. In his passage southwest, Anson exercised the fleet in a variety of formations, sending comments to Warren. In return Warren offered his old friend both suggestions and encouragement, firm in his own belief that they had taken the best course given the intelligence they had received.[11] As frigates in considerable numbers began to join the fleet, Anson was able to send them cruising along the Atlantic coast of France for further intelligence.

Their vigilance was rewarded on the morning of 3 May 1747 when the sloop *Falcon*, commanded by Richard Gwynn, reported a sighting the afternoon before of a fleet of thirty-eight sail steering westward at a distance of four or five leagues.[12] It was quickly calculated that the enemy must then be lying southwest of Anson's fleet. Shortly afterwards, when *Namur* sighted the French armament, Anson signaled a general chase—the first time in British naval annals such an order was recorded in advance of a battle—and within three hours the French were plainly in sight.

These were the squadrons of the Marquis de la Jonquière bound for Quebec, and of Grout de Saint-Georges heading for India. They consisted of *Invincible* (74), *Sérieux* (66), *Diamant* (56), *Rubis* (52), *Jason* (52), *Gloire* (46), *Black Prince* (36), *Apollon* (30), *Philibert* (30), *Emeraude* (24), *Vigilante* (22), *Modeste* (22), *Thétis* (20), *Dartmouth* (18), and twenty-four merchant vessels. The two 30–gun ships and *Thétis* were Compagnie des Indes vessels. The fleet had departed La Rochelle on 30 April and made for the Spanish coast across the Bay of Biscay before heading westward to Cape Ortegal and escaping into the open ocean.

By 1:00 p.m. the enemy was but a mile off, already shortening sail and forming in line of battle. In response, Anson began to form his powerful force in line abreast. Soon altering his plan, he signaled the fleet to form line of battle ahead. The principal reason behind such a move ensured that when action began, ships could support each other so that no single ship would be exposed for any length of time to overwhelming enemy fire. One drawback was that the maneuver was time consuming, and the enemy convoy began to make its escape. While executing line of battle, *Devonshire* soon closed on Anson's flagship, which was hove-to, allowing the two admirals to discuss briefly the situation through speaking trumpets. Warren apparently advised an immediate pursuit, but Anson preferred first to assemble his ships and then make a concentrated attack. It took the fleet almost two hours to come into line. With Warren's division leading, the van at first bore away in chase in succession instead, as Anson intended. He signaled Warren to reform the line and to steer larger—that is, to sail with the wind near or abaft the beam.[13] These signals allowed Anson to strike in the French center.

When the British at length formed line, la Jonquière, whose own line even included the largest East India ships—both certainly armed too lightly for the line—now for the first time understood the great strength of the English squadron. He immediately ordered a fighting retreat. When Anson saw la Jonquière's ships breaking line, suddenly putting up their helms and making more sail, he finally ordered a general chase. It was then about 3:15 p.m.

Warren's van division—*Centurion, Namur, Defiance* (60), *Windsor, Nottingham* (60), *Yarmouth* (64), and the flagship *Devonshire*—were the first to engage the French rear. As the French ships were disabled, they were taken by fresh warships when they joined battle. In the meantime those British ships first engaged, pressed on toward new targets before repeating the exercise. Warren's flagship closely fought la Jonquière's flagship and forced its capitulation.[14] Within three hours the entire French force, now badly disabled, had surrendered. One French officer noticed that despite the rough seas, the English were able to employ their great guns on the lowest gun deck, while the French were unable to do so.[15]

When the French began to flee, la Jonquière had detached the frigate *Emeraude* to escort the vanishing merchantmen ahead. On seeing this, Anson ordered *Falkland, Ambuscade,* and *Falcon* in pursuit. Now with the action over, Anson also sent *Monmouth, Nottingham,* and *Yarmouth* to join the pursuit of the vanishing merchantmen. Some twenty merchant vessels made their escape along with their escort, the frigate *Black Prince* (36). The frigate *Emeraude*, commanded by la Jonquière's son, reached Quebec safely on 24 June, with her troop reinforcements in company with five merchant vessels, two others arriving two days later.[16]

The French had suffered terribly, as the butcher's bill showed. Saint-Georges's ship had 125 dead and forty-eight wounded. La Jonquière's *Sérieux* lost 125 men with ninety-five wounded. McCarthy's *Rubis* reported forty-seven dead and twenty-eight wounded.[17] On Hocqart's *Diamant*, thirty were killed and fifteen wounded, and on *Gloire*, 101 were killed and thirty-one wounded. On *Jason* there were thirty-five who were killed or died from their wounds and another ten wounded. On *Invincible* eighty were killed and 171 wounded. *Philibert* suffered twenty-one dead and thirteen wounded.[18]

With much damage aloft, the ships of Warren's division that had been the most hotly engaged now needed considerable repairs at sea. Only then could the British fleet make for Portsmouth with their eighteen prizes. Anson's official description of the battle, sent to Portsmouth with Capt. Peter Denis of *Centurion*, curiously made no mention of Warren. This battle proved to be the last occasion when Warren's behavior had put his life at serious risk. His flagship had engaged successively both *Sérieux* and *Invincible*, the two largest French ships. None of this was described in Anson's dispatch, which later appeared in the newspapers, but one contemporary account attempted to balance the record as it related to *Invincible's* role:

A day, as famous for the scene it exhibited to the world, as infamous for the little notice taken of the principal actors in it! . . . For who could have thought that the hero, who commanded at the taking of Cape Breton, and who play'd so great a part in this action, together with that truly British young nobleman [Hon. William Montagu], who shew'd whose pupil he had been, by so exact and close an imitation of his patron's manner of fighting, should stand unnoticed in the panegyrical records of this day? But that there are men, who, by their partiality to themselves, would have all the fame of a glorious action their own, and the heroism of every brave man under them buried in oblivion.[19]

If Anson was silent about Warren, by contrast, Warren was effusive in his praise of his commander. He wrote to Bedford, begging the duke to mention nothing of the letter to Anson. "In my life I never served with more pleasure, nor saw half such pains taken to discipline the fleet. While I have the honour to continue in it, I will endeavour to follow his example, however short I may fall of it, and could wish to be commanded by him rather than command myself."[20] He wrote the same day to Anson, wishing him "a pleasant journey to town and that reception from your king and country which is so highly due to your merit."[21]

If Anson's rewards as fleet commander were greater—a peerage and £62,982 in prize money—Warren did not go unrewarded. He was made knight companion of the Order of the Bath and earned £31,496 in prize money.[22] Very shortly thereafter he was promoted vice admiral.

There were some words of praise. Warren acknowledged complimentary letters from his two principal patrons, the Duke of Bedford and the Earl of Sandwich. As well, Warren received fulsome congratulations from some in the American colonies. Pepperrell wrote of the pleasure he experienced on learning of his hand in defeating the French.[23] Josiah Willard, the secretary of Massachusetts, added his own congratulations to those of the council and house of representatives.[24] Lt. Gov. Cadwallader Colden of New York wrote of his "true heroic merit."[25] Gov. Jonathan Law of Connecticut saw Warren's role in the destruction of the French fleet "as being an instrument in the hand of God," by which he averted "the misery and destruction, with which the French threatened us." He added that "we can never forget the good services you did at Louisbourg for New England . . . without which we must have returned ashamed from so bold an enterprize."[26] There may have been others, but Governor Clinton of New York appears to have sent no such message. Nor was a word heard from War-ren's chief critic and rival, Commodore Knowles, still cooling his heels at Louisbourg, a place he detested.

When Anson returned to his seat on the Admiralty Board, Warren took the squadron to sea once again a fortnight after reaching Spithead. Before doing so, he hastened the repair of those ships involved in the Cape Or-tegal battle, both British and French. He had already selected *Invincible* for her strength and beauty as his future flagship.[27] Warren also had to deal with the captive French officers who were sent to quarters at Fareham. "I have ordered everything they desire," Warren informed his senior, "and two hogsheads of wine for their table."[28]

Warren used the short interval ashore to acquire an estate in Hamp-shire. For £8,500 he purchased the 554–acre Westbury Manor from the widow of Adm. Philip Cavendish.[29] Another £1,000 purchased all the fur-niture. A "very dear bargain," he told Anson, "which nothing but being your neighbour" could have convinced him to conclude the sale.[30] Anson earlier had bought nearby Soberton Manor. Warren's estate, of which about one-fifth was forested, was the principal seat in the parish of East Meon. The house, built probably in the 1690s, had a large pleasure garden and orangery laid out by Charles Bridgeman, the outstanding garden ar-chitect of his day. Standing on rising ground above the Meon River, it had a lovely view of the valley and surrounding downland. The tree-lined av-enue leading to the house crossed a bridge over the rivulet, which had been broadened into a pond. Near the house stood the twelfth-century chapel of St. Nicholas.[31]

For the next cruise, Warren anticipated an equally successful, if short, cam-paign. "May not I hope to go out a vice admiral with a prospect of getting soon to the Board," he told Anson. "I pin my whole faith upon you, and determine, if you will give me leave, to stand or fall with you."[32] He noted: "I am quite of your sentiment that we should continue to keep the nation pleased with our conduct. Could I be so happy to go again under your command, I should entertain great hopes of doing it. If I can't be so, you may command me to go at a moment's warning, though to the hazard of the little reputation I have acquired."

The speed with which Warren returned to sea with the fleet arose not from any anticipated movements of French naval units based at Brest or elsewhere but from intelligence of a large, well-escorted convoy home-ward bound from the Antilles.[33] Declining permission to go up to London to aid the passage of his outstanding Louisbourg accounts, Warren took *St. George* (90), *Devonshire*, *Monmouth*, *Nottingham* (60), *Hampshire* (50), the frigate *Ambuscade*, the sloop *Falcon*, and the fireship *Pluto* and set sail from Spithead on 3 June.[34] On board were six hundred soldiers. At Plymouth, after complaining of a shortage of frigates, Warren was assigned both *Grand Turk* and *Dagger*.

Before sailing Warren wrote of his anticipated pleasure at the end of this cruise of meeting Anson in Portsmouth with the captured St. Domingue fleet along with "two or more *Invincibles*."[35] As Anson, still in nominal command of the Western squadron, was to share half of all the prize money arising from Warren's activities, the rear admiral's hope was to make some financial return to Anson for the small fortune he had just acquired as a result of Anson's spectacular naval success. His last communication with Anson before he sailed from Spithead assured the admiral that he intended, as was his practice, to "be very communicative with the captains of our squadron . . . and . . . to let then know ones scheme or plan of operation."[36] He added jocularly, "Who knows, this cruise may bring forth Lord Westbury."

In the meantime, when the main body of the Western squadron came home to be refitted, several men-of-war and frigates remained on the French coast and off the Bay of Biscay, so great was British domination of home waters. Some of these were stragglers that, having departed British ports after Anson's fleet had sailed in April, had missed the battle off Cape Ortegal. Among these numbered *Kent* (70), *Hampton Court* (70), *Lyon* (60), *Eagle* (60), *Chester* (50), *Hector* (44), and *Dolphin* (44). With Warren's squadron now at sea but not yet at its proposed station, this force under its senior captain, Thomas Fox, came upon the very convoy Warren had been ordered to find and seize. There were some 120 sail, escorted by three French ships of the line, *Magnanime* (74), *Alcide* (64), and *Arc-en-ciel* (56). By noon on 21 June the British warships had drawn to within a distance of less than three miles of their prey. The French convoy thereupon divided, with some sailing to the northwest and the rest with their escorts eastward. Fox's squadron closed the gap only shortly before nightfall. At daybreak on 22 June, as the French warships had vanished, Fox detached *Eagle* to search to the northwest for the merchantmen. Gradually the British warships overtook the fleeing merchantmen and made their first prize before evening. The next day another forty-seven merchantmen were captured, but no less than sixty-four sailed safely into French ports with their naval escorts.

Meanwhile Warren's squadron had been at sea for almost three weeks. *Ambuscade* had been detached to look into Brest and Rochefort for intelligence. Indeed the Admiralty learned a good deal about French naval dispositions within ten days of Warren's departure.[37] Reports reaching the Admiralty suggested that Brest harbored twelve ships of the line ranging from fifty to eighty guns and ten frigates from twenty-four to forty-four guns, all of which were ready for sea. By contrast, none of the warships at Le Havre, Port Louis, Rochefort, or Toulon was ready for sea. At Isle d'Aix *Northumberland* (64) and *Alcion* (60) were in every way ready to escort a convoy of merchantmen for Canada. On 29 June the Admiralty learned that at Rochefort four warships, two of them small frigates, were preparing to escort a convoy of merchantmen bound for Martinique. All this information was immediately sent to Warren.[38]

At length, off Cape Ortegal on 21 June 1747, Warren's ships came across four stragglers from the Antilles convoy with its frigate escort, *Etoile*. It was about 6:00 a.m. when Warren signaled *Monmouth, Yarmouth, Defiance, Bristol* (50), *Edinburgh* (64), *Ambuscade*, and *Devonshire* to chase. The French ships tried to take safety in a bay near the Spanish village of Lux. Senior captain Henry Harrison of *Monmouth* ordered the boats to be manned and to row for *Etoile*, under cover of fire from the nearest warship *Ambuscade*, commanded by Capt. Richard Gwynn. *Etoile*'s crew immediately began to abandon ship in great confusion, while *Ambuscade* prepared to come to anchor alongside the prize. Before these orders could be carried out, *Etoile* blew up. Promptly her convoy of trade vessels were captured.[39]

The next day, learning that many coasters had put in at Cedira, Warren sent three small ships under *Viper* into the harbor. The battery at the harbor's entrance was silenced and the defenses destroyed when marines and seamen were landed. Some twenty-eight vessels were burned and six made prizes.

The balance of the cruise witnessed the capture or destruction of a variety of enemy vessels, few of them of any importance. Among these was a fine outward-bound East Indiaman, the 500–ton *Chameau*. Sighted on 7 July she fled toward the Spanish coast. The next day she was found at anchor in Aviles Bay near Cape Pinas on the coast of Galicia by *Ambuscade* in company with *Monmouth* and *Pembroke*. Indeed, *Ambuscade*'s officers were just finishing their midday meal when rounding a point they suddenly came upon the enemy and opened fire. The enemy returned two or three broadsides. So close to the shore was *Ambuscade* that a four-gun battery ashore could not depress its gun barrels to fire on the frigate. Subjected to heavy bombardment, *Chameau* was set on fire; she cut her cables and drifted ashore, whereupon her magazines exploded.[40] Finally on 28 July, *Windsor* took *Saint Antonio*, a 500–ton Compagnie des Indes vessel, mounting sixteen guns and carrying two hundred men, five days out from L'Orient on the Bay of Biscay. She was the first of five ships the Compagnie planned to send singly and without naval escort, as one of her passengers reported.[41] In an attempt to intercept them, Warren ordered *Prince Frederick, Centurion,* and *Augusta* with a frigate to cruise between Belle Isle and Cape Finisterre.[42] In addition, he sent Sandwich's brother, Captain Montagu, in *Bristol* to cruise north of Madeira to intercept outward-bound French East Indiamen and Spanish register ships before calling at Lisbon to escort British trade to England. With no further evidence of a French force preparing for sea, Warren returned to Plymouth and Spithead with the bulk of his squadron.[43]

These were small successes for so large a squadron and consequently disappointed Warren, who perhaps had nurtured excessive expectations. Although Warren had added to his fortune from his squadron's captures, it was clearly an unsatisfactory cruise. "I am heartily sorry," wrote Anson, "your old fortune did not attend you, I am sure if it had the French commerce would have been totally ruined."[44] With sickness spreading among his crews and ill again himself with scurvy, Warren used the excuse of diminishing water and provisions to return to port. "Should the enemy's fleet be ready and put to sea just after we shall be forced to go in for water and provision" the French could "become master (for the shortest interval) of the sea."[45] Yet Warren doubted they would take such bold action "without a very superior force to ours." He suggested that a regular rotation be established of clean ships sent out to replace those at sea in need of cleaning. Moreover, Warren's health was impaired: "You can't imagine how my scurvy disorder increases. I shall want much exercise and a trip to Scarborough, the waters there being proper, I am told, for me."[46]

Warren returned to Plymouth with ten of his ships to learn that on 20 July the Admiralty had named him to sole command of the Western squadron.[47] He was duly grateful to Anson, writing immediately "of the great sense of my obligation to you for the honour done me in my appointment to be your successor in so high a trust as the Western command."[48] His orders listed thirty-six ships placed under his command; some twenty-three ships of the line from fifty to ninety guns, two forty-four gun fifth rates, six frigates ranging from thirty to twenty guns each, three sloops, and two fireships, thus giving him great scope. He was ordered to cruise on whatever station and with whatever size of detachment he might judge necessary and prudent. To protect British trade was his first objective, while to intercept and destroy the enemy's convoys and privateers was his second purpose. Sick with scurvy, he begged for leave ashore to regain his health. He was free to send his ships when foul or sickly into port with orders to their captains to return promptly to the specified rendezvous. He was free also to remain at sea as long as seemed useful and to return to Portsmouth with his second rate, third rate, and fourth rate ships, sending the rest into Plymouth.[49]

His first letter, once he reached Plymouth, begged for "a little respite in port and [medical] advice upon my case."[50] He described it to Anson as "almost a leprosy . . . tho' neither my person nor complexion (to outward appearances) do show the ill habit of my body . . . But I don't therefore see the necessity of letting all the world know of our infirmity."[51] Too ill to go immediately to sea, he recommended that the newly minted rear admiral, Edward Hawke, be appointed his second-in-command and take the squadron out again immediately.[52] He suggested that Hawke be given three capital ships from those Warren had left on station in order to form a suitable squadron. Warren hoped to be fit again by autumn, when the two could cruise together or in separate divisions, "one to cruise upon the Spanish galleons, the other upon the French trade."[53]

The Admiralty consented to both proposals. Leave was granted to Warren and Hawke received his appointment. The Admiralty Board did not question Warren's "zeal for the service than they do your abilities, & that they are very sorry for your indisposition, and that they consent to your staying on shore" for as long a period as he needed to recover his health.[54]

Warren's recommendation of Hawke proved disheartening for the French if brilliant for the Royal Navy. From Hawke's first dispatch to Warren in late August 1747, good fortune seemed married to the skill and spirit he displayed.[55] Sailing from Plymouth with three ships, he had encountered Capt. Harry Norris's detachment within three days, along with Capt. Philip Durell's *Gloucester* (50) and news that Norris had just sent two others—*Bellona* (30) and *Amazon* (24)—to look into Brest. The squadron took its first prize sixteen leagues west of Belle Isle. She was a Compagnie des Indes ship bound for Senegal with pitch, tar, provisions, shot, and gunpowder. From the ship's crew Hawke learned that since late July seven merchantmen owned by the Compagnie had sailed from L'Orient. The first of these, *Saint Antonio*, had been taken by Warren's squadron on 8 July. The rest appeared to have made to sea despite the precautions Warren had taken in the dispositions assigned to his ships. The next piece of good news was the sloop *Viper*'s capture of the French South Sea ship *Hector* en route to France from her last port of call in the Canaries, where she had unloaded 1.6 million pieces of eight.[56] The same day reinforcements from England—*Portland* (50) and *Grand Turk* (20)—joined Hawke. From intelligence he had gathered, Hawke now believed that the French were concentrating their warships at Brest to act as strong escorts for convoys planning to depart from Bordeaux and La Rochelle.[57] These views were seconded by Capt. Samuel Faulkner, who, with *Amazon* (24) flying French colors within reach of the guns defending Brest, had spotted six large warships full-rigged for sea. "I wish, sir, with all my heart you was out," wrote Faulkner to Warren, "for I really believe the ships at Brest are to join three ships of the line at La Rochelle, and that they intend to force a passage for their merchantmen."[58]

Before this news reached Warren in Portsmouth, where he had been pressing forward reinforcements for Hawke, he had asked Anson's permission to visit him in London "to concert measures for the operations of the Western Squadron this fall and winter."[59] Such a meeting seems never to have occurred. Rather, Warren was kept in Portsmouth employing part of his time in entertaining visiting dignitaries, such as the Duke of Richmond. "We were extreamly merry," he informed Anson, "[and] finished my champagne and made a very great hole in your case of charming clarets."[60]

Two days later, with evidence mounting that the French were indeed determined to challenge the British blockade, Warren remained undecided about going to sea himself with the available ships in port. He wrote Anson again, "You know my disorder, which is so bad that I do not believe it possible I can live with it one month at sea. Had the service obliged me to stay out last cruise a fortnight longer I believe I should have died. However sooner than be suspected of want of zeal for the king's service, I will go (at all hazards)" if Anson and the Admiralty Board thought he must take personal command of the Western squadron.[61] He expressed his willingness, for the recovery of his health, to quit the "glorious command" except for the fact that Anson then would have to assume command and go to sea himself.[62]

Two days after writing this he nevertheless went on board his flagship *St. George* (90), determined to put to sea from Spithead the next day in company with *Hampton Court*, *Devonshire*, the sloop *Vulture*, and the

fireships *Vulcan* and *Dolphin* to join Hawke. The same day he learned that
an auxiliary squadron of Dutch warships was ordered to support the Western squadron.[63] Yet when contrary winds prevented him from getting to
sea, he begged Anson's leave to resign the command of the Western squadron on account of his scurvy. Nothing but his illness, he protested, could
have led him so reluctantly to resign the command, both so "very hon-
ourable and profitable."[64] To the Admiralty Board's deputy secretary John
Clevland he explained, "I drink no wine, and eat nothing but white meal
and greens."[65] Three days later he became temporarily bedridden, "The
greatest of my concern, I freely own to you, is the apprehension of dis-
obliging, but when you know my condition, you will judge the necessity of
my acting as I have done."[66] On the same day, 5 September, he made a
formal request to the Admiralty to be relieved of command of the Western
squadron and to be granted leave to recover from "a violent flux." He recommended Captain Savage Mostyn to command the reinforcements he
had, until then, been intent upon taking to sea to join Hawke.[67] Still seriously indisposed two days later, he was not even able to wait upon Admiral
Cornelis Schryver, whose Dutch squadron of four 50–gun ships arrived at
Spithead that day.[68] "I shall follow the advice of my doctors, either by going to Bath, or otherwise as they shall judge proper for me," he wrote when
at last he learned that his resignation had been accepted and leave granted
him.[69]

His health was gradually restored. A week later, from Westbury Manor
he reported to Anson that his doctors disagreed about what action he
should take to recover his health, noting, "My legs are grown a good deal
better, but the other parts of my body, as bad as ever."[70] A month later he
reported to Anson, "My scurvy, except two obstinate large blotches upon
my arm and one on my thighs, [is] going off as fast as can be expected." He
added "There are a good many partridges, but so wild that we bird gunners
can't kill one!"[71]

Once ashore in Hampshire, Warren's thoughts turned immediately to his
family. In April, when plans to send his squadron to North America were
cancelled, he first thought to send for his wife and convey her home in a
merchant vessel. "I beg you will give me your opinion whether, if I was to
desire their Lordships to order a man-of-war from Louisbourg to convoy
her, they would grant me that favour," he asked his old friend and admirer,
Thomas Corbett, the Admiralty's secretary.[72] Upon his return to Portsmouth, he thanked the Duke of Bedford who had assured him through

Anson that a warship would give passage to his wife and children from New York. It was "the only thing that can complete my happiness upon this earth. Mr Anson knows Mrs Warren, and from that knowledge, I daresay, may conclude me miserable as I really am by her and my children's absence."[73] As he told Anson, "All I wish, as to myself, is to have my wife and children conducted in safety to England."[74] The frigate *Scarborough* sailed from Spithead on 5 June bound for New York to convey "my rib and babes" back to England.[75] When on 9 September Warren learned from letters received at Portsmouth that the frigate had not reached New York by the end of June, he feared that some accident "must have befallen her," which made him "exceeding uneasy for my poor family . . . for whose safety I have many anxious hours, and more now than ever, because if she comes late the privateers will all be out," he told Anson.[76] He must have relaxed somewhat when he learned from William Pepperrell that his nephew, Lt. Warren Johnson, departed the Louisbourg garrison "in order to wait on Lady Warren to England."[77] As it turned out, Lady Warren's merchant ship put into Ireland, owing to the activities of privateers. She then crossed Ireland and took the yacht *Dublin* from Dublin to Chester, where she and the children finally landed on 21 November 1747. She then made her way with the children to London and an exciting reunion with the vice admiral.[78]

While recuperating at his Hampshire seat he wrote to Clinton in New York hoping to revive interest in the matter of governorship. He had raised the matter with Anson in September, believing that Clinton planned to come home to England in the spring of 1748. Indeed the Duke of Newcastle had consulted Warren about the best person to head the colony's administration in Clinton's absence, so he had suggested his brother-in-law, Chief Justice James DeLancey. Warren now made it clear to Clinton that if he resigned he would be happy to put in place the terms of the agreement they had been negotiating in 1746.[79]

All such thoughts receded into the background with the welcome news of the convincing victory achieved by Rear Admiral Hawke over a French squadron on 14 October. For the second time in five months, the suitably positioned and well-led Western squadron had defeated a relatively smaller enemy force: 854 guns against 554, 5,890 men against 5,416. Fourteen ships of the line had struck fiercely at eight French ships, five of them larger than anything in the British squadron. Significantly, the two largest French warships, including the flagship, though closely engaged, escaped.

The butcher's bill was not dissimilar on each side as the French suffered 800 casualties, while the British lost 157 killed outright and 577 wounded, several of whom died later as a result of their wounds. "The French must be quite ruined," was Capt. Augustus Keppel's opinion.[80] Newcastle informed the king's son, Frederick, Duke of Cumberland, that "Sir Peter Warren told me this morning that the king had more French ships in his ports than remained now in the ports of France; that we could beat them with their own ships." It was an exaggeration, but a pleasing one to hear.

With this news Warren's leave abruptly ended. He was immediately ordered to Portsmouth to hoist his vice admiral's flag on one of the warships lying at Spithead and to await further orders. He conferred with Hawke in order to hasten the refitting of "the shattered ships of his squadron."[81] This preoccupied them both for the next three weeks; Warren and Hawke were also ordered to recommend suitable responses to petitions from seamen from two ships of the squadron for shore leave. In this matter Warren suggested that Hawke accompany him on board each warship to address the crews on the need for their continued good behavior and punctuality until their ships were at dock, for which the Admiralty would then reward them with leave.[82]

Warren's next task was to preside over the court martial appointed to investigate the behavior of Capt. Thomas Fox of *Kent* in the late battle off Cape Finisterre.[83] The charges against Fox specified that he "did not come properly into the fight, nor do his utmost to engage, distress, and damage the enemy, nor assist his Majesty's ships who did." The charges were serious enough and the possible consequences more so. Two years earlier, after a naval court martial, a second lieutenant of the frigate *Anglesey* (40) had been sentenced to be executed for having surrendered his ship. His captain and first lieutenant had been killed and sixty of the crew killed or wounded in an "obstinate engagement" with the 54–gun privateer *Apollo*.[84] That same year Commodore Cornelius Mitchell was found guilty of cowardice and neglect, mulcted five years' pay, and dismissed the service for failing to engage a squadron of four ships off Hispaniola. Moreover, the House of Commons in March and April 1745 set aside two days a week to inquire into the failure of the fleet to engage the enemy off Toulon. From these deliberations and after long debate, the speaker requested the king to order separate courts martial for the two admirals and six captains concerned. These grave matters had divided the nation and brought ignominy upon the entire naval profession. From the evidence provided, it seemed as though the British fleet, while at sea, was incapable of understanding its own signals, while the commander in chief was so confused that he kept changing those very signals that were actually understood, but all to no effect. Sixty years later the matter still stung, as Beatson noted of Adm. Thomas Mathews, "When it is considered that . . . no signal of which he was possessed, could accomplish his purpose, we may be the more inclined to lay the miscarriage upon the gross negligence or ignorance, which, as would appear, must have pervaded the highest department of naval affairs, than even the flag-officer in this battle."[85]

In his opening address, Warren admitted that he had never presided at so important a court martial. "I shall depend on your candour in excusing my mistakes," he told the court, "and in setting me right when I err." However disconcerting to the members of the court martial, this was characteristic of Warren, whose last thought was to overawe the proceedings with his presence. To Captain Fox he then turned and added,

> How so ever disagreeable the present service enjoined us may be to men of compassionate disposition—for it is my ardent wish that this trial may be the last of the kind known in the British navy—yet what we owe to our king and to our country calls upon us to discharge this our duty, with the utmost faithfulness and impartiality. You may be assured from the honour and candour of the gentlemen who compose this court that, towards you, we will acquit ourselves with a becoming humanity and tenderness. Innocence has nothing to fear, and guilt everything to apprehend. That the first of these is your case is the charitable wish, I dare say, of all your judges. May God direct you in your defence and us in our judgment.[86]

The rest of the court included three rear admirals—Henry Osborne, William Chambers, and John Forbes—and eight captains: Temple West, Merrick de l'Angle, Edward Pratten, Peircy Brett, William Parry, Augustus Keppel, Peter Denis, and Andrew Jelfe. The court sat almost every day for three weeks, between eight in the morning until four in the afternoon. "I am very glad to hear," Warren wrote Anson as the lengthy proceedings drew to a close: "there is a scheme afoot to shorten the proceedings of courts martial." The next year Warren was part of a naval committee that examined the entire matter and proposed a number of reforms, none of them earthshaking.[87]

With the court martial behind him, the Lords of Admiralty required him and a number of other officers from the court martial to give their opinions about modification to warships' breechings. The need for their advice arose as a result of a dangerous incident that had occurred on board Hawke's flagship during the recent sea battle. The breechings holding the engaged guns on the lower deck broke on the recoil after firing at an extreme forward angle when closing upon the French flagship. It is probable that *Devonshire* had a pronounced heel to the disengaged side allowing the guns to recoil downhill.[88] The guns, when recoiling, slewed about so that they were facing fore and aft. This forced Hawke's flagship out of the line of battle for about an hour while repairs were completed to the severed breechings.

Having consulted their best gunners, Admiral Steuart, with Admirals Warren, Osborn, Hawke, Chambers, and Forbes and eight captains, proposed increasing the circumference of breech ropes on 32–pounders and 42–pounders by an inch and on all other guns by a half-inch. The officers did not suggest increasing the actual length of the breechings. They insisted that the rope always be manufactured with the "best hemp, fine yarn and not too much tarr'd."[89] From the master ropemaker at the Portsmouth yard they learned that a seven-and-a-half-inch Board of Ordnance breeching had thirty fewer threads than a six-inch hawser manufactured in the dockyard, the individual yarns in the Ordnance example "being so much larger, consequently the rope so much weaker." They also recommended that thereafter a "timble be fixed properly on the cascable of the gun for the breechings to run through."

It was April 1749 before the committee reconvened.[90] On this occasion it considered the comments made by officers of the Board of Ordnance to the sea officers' 1747 recommendations. The Ordnance officers doubted that an increase in rope size would effect the desired result. The sea officers maintained that a stronger breech rope was needed whether by an increase in size or by improved manufacture. When the Ordnance officers expressed the doubt that a stronger rope would result from a greater number of threads, the sea officers referred the matter to the master ropemakers in all the dockyards and then left the decision to the discretion of the Board of Ordnance. It appears that the breechings were increased in size as advised by the committee, and the problem solved. Certainly in the next war there was no reported incident of the sort that had embarrassed Hawke in October 1747.[91]

Warren anticipated an appointment to the Admiralty Board. Warned by Anson that there was much opposition, Warren was anxious only if it came from the Duke of Bedford. The politics of such naval appointments were clear to everyone who attained the rank of admiral. Whatever one's naval talents, one needed strong political patrons to command at sea. It was the height of his ambition, he told Anson shortly before Christmas, "to serve with his grace's and your lordship's approbation. Should I ever be so unhappy, which I am sure I never can intentionally, as to forfeit his grace's or your favour and good opinion, I would not, under such misfortune, think of serving at sea in any situation."

Nor was Warren immediately reinstated by the Lords of Admiralty to the command of the Western squadron. This he attributed to the opposition of Lord Vere Beauclerk who wrongly believed that Warren was perhaps malingering. Warren admitted that with the arrival of his family from America he had hoped to be "indulged with a fortnight or three weeks' leave to settle them in town." Warren assured Anson that he would venture to say "no man in England is happier in his family nor wishes more to be with them than myself." Yet he was prepared to forsake such company immediately to pursue "the service of my country, and that without any view of profit. For I am quite easy in my fortune, being determined to live within it."[92] Warren had already privately arranged with Hawke, as he explained to Anson, that when he was again appointed to command the squadron Hawke would happily serve under him again.

Thus the Western squadron again went to sea under Hawke in mid-January 1748. This time Hawke's squadron numbered nine ships of the line: two 74–gun ships, three of sixty guns, and four fifty guns. On the last day of the month *Nottingham* (60) and *Portland* (50), after a sharp exchange, took *Magnanime* (74), which lost forty-five men with 105 wounded.[93] She was part of a squadron that had departed Brest on 12 January but had been scattered upon encountering storms. These storms had forced *Arc-en-ciel* (56) back to Brest and *Cumberland* into the safety of Corunna. Only *Alcide* (64) managed to escape into the ocean.[94]

A week after Hawke's departure, Warren was again appointed to the command of the Western squadron. He was then in London temporarily, in a house on Bond Street with his family, and he arrived at Portsmouth only several days later.[95] His instructions specified that he was again to cooperate with a Dutch squadron of four ships of the line and two large frigates under Vice Admiral Schryver, then at anchor at Spithead.[96] As the United Netherlands was not at war with Spain, their auxiliary squadron was not to be used south of Cape Finisterre. While Hawke's squadron of nine ships of the line and four frigates was confined to the Soundings, Warren's instructions allowed him to select the best stations from which to cruise against the trade of France and Spain and to meet either enemy's fleet should it appear.[97] He was prompted, however, to keep a frigate cruising from 41°30′N to 43°N and four ships of the line and a frigate patrolling between Cape St. Vincent and Cape Cantin on the Barbary coast, with three frigates cruising off Cape Clear, some fifty to sixty leagues west of the Soundings.[98]

Warren's squadron was initially to include fourteen ships of the line and four frigates.[99] Yet few of these were immediately ready for sea; consequently, when Warren sailed from Spithead on 5 February he took with him only *Devonshire, Yarmouth, Defiance,* the frigate *Scarborough,* and six Dutch warships.[100] From Plymouth he ordered *Princess Louisa, Edinburgh, Eagle, Windsor,* and *Inverness* to cruise at once between Cape Cantin and Cape St. Vincent.[101] Intelligence reports indicated that there were only about fifteen French privateers at sea—a menace to British trade though rarely to smaller naval warships.[102] One of these privateers Warren promptly captured, and from a recaptured Dutch vessel he learned that two more Spanish warships had reached Cadiz with a convoy late in January. The entire merchant fleet with its powerful escort was expected soon to sail. On 10 February, when he luckily encountered Hawke's force then consisting of *Kent, Centurion, Augusta, Anson,* and the frigate *Tavistock,* he dispatched the rear admiral to join Capt. Thomas Cotes, sending with him four ships of the line and a frigate.[103] If the rendezvous was achieved as now planned, Hawke would have ten warships in his squadron. Should he fail to encounter Cotes, Hawke was ordered to Lisbon to escort home whatever trade was ready to sail.

When Warren learned that six Spanish men-of-war were at Cadiz, he ordered Cotes in *Edinburgh* to take *Eagle, Princess Louisa, Windsor,* and a frigate under his command to join Hawke.[104] If he failed to rendezvous with Hawke's squadron, Cotes was free to add to his force any two ships he came across from Warren's command already at sea.

Hawke and Cotes met, but not in time to effect another great prize haul. Cotes himself was rewarded in a modest way. The expected Spanish convoy was sighted on 7 February, when the squadron was about sixty leagues northwest of Cape Cantin. The Spanish escort was found to consist not of eight warships but nine. While one of these sailed off with the convoy, the other eight formed a line of battle. Heedless of the more powerful enemy force and not waiting to summon his captains to a council of war, Commodore Cotes's squadron attacked, not the escorts of course, but the convoy. His audacity allowed him to make prizes of five of the Spanish stragglers, without the Spanish warships offering any opposition. It was small compensation for what might have developed into a major sea battle had Hawke received his new orders at an earlier moment.[105] Both Hawke and Cotes remained at sea as long as they could before separately heading to the Tagus to revictual. From Lisbon, Hawke sent Cotes to cruise off Cadiz, dispatched the trade home with an escort, and, once he had refitted his remaining ships at Lisbon, he rejoined Warren, who was by this time off Cape Finisterre with the bulk of the Western squadron.[106]

Warren's new target was a large French convoy believed to be sailing from Martinique. Its failure to appear in the sea-lanes to France by mid-March gave Warren reason to suspect that the British squadron in the West Indies had prevented the French convoy from getting to sea.

An alternate target presented itself when Warren learned from Capt. Andrew Jelfe of *Assurance* that four French men-of-war were fitting out at the Spanish port of Corunna, where a fleet of some twenty merchant ships, it was believed, was soon to rendezvous. He thus decided to sail to the Spanish coast along the Bay of Biscay to prevent any attempt by the French convoy to escape into the Atlantic.[107] The Western squadron was thus divided between its station off Cadiz under Hawke and the Bay of Biscay under Warren.

While anticipating the possible appearance of two enemy convoys, Warren also became aware that his squadron was beginning to weaken. He had sent one Dutch ship back to Plymouth as its crew was rapidly sickening. Another Dutch warship, having sprung her bowsprit, he sent to Portsmouth to refit. The Dutch flagship shortly afterwards went to Lisbon for repairs, fresh water, and victuals. By this time, Warren's flagship *Devonshire* had become partly disabled by damage to its rudder, and Warren was determined to shift his flag to the first clean ship that joined his squadron from England.[108] As it turned out, new severe damage to his flagship's rudder forced his immediate return to England for repairs.[109]

At Portsmouth, when he learned from the dockyard's master builder that repairs could be completed without sending *Devonshire* into dry dock, he ordered her hastily refitted, victualed, and completed with sea stores with all possible speed. *Invincible*, which he had intended to make his flagship ever since she had been captured eleven months earlier, was then at Spithead but needed a new foremast. Warren schemed to remove the mainmast from *Duke* to serve as *Invincible*'s foremast, a task that could also be executed without taking her into dry dock.[110]

Thus far, 1748 was proving to be a routine and disappointing season, if glory and profit were the purposes. Three or four enemy privateers had been taken with a number of French prizes of no great value. Warren informed Anson of the "very little success . . . As you know the many disappointments, to which we that go to sea are liable, I flatter myself your lordship will do me the justice to persuade yourself that no pains has been wanting on my part to deserve success, and that is all that mortal can do."[111] He was nevertheless fully aware that the vigilance of the Western squadron had allowed no force from France to penetrate the Atlantic so far that year.

His anxiety again to put quickly to sea sprung from new intelligence supporting his earlier opinion that a strong French escorting squadron was preparing to depart. Also, still anxious about the homeward-bound fleet from Martinique, he hurried the refitting of his ships and the four Dutch ships still with him. "I perfectly agree with their lordships opinion," he wrote to the Admiralty Board's secretary,

> of keeping up at least the whole force now under Sir Edward off Cadiz. I think it would not be an improper step, if at times, when I shall be pretty certain that the motions of the French do not require my remaining in the Bay [of Biscay], I should stretch with my whole force, or the greater part of it, to Sir Edward's station & then back to my own, and that he did the like by stretching from his to mine. For, though by this method there might be a chance of missing something, yet sudden motions of this kind, whereof the enemy could have no knowledge, might produce a very good effect.[112]

This was a novel plan. Underlying it was his hope of delivering a final crushing blow to the French navy and commerce so grave that the enemy would feel obliged to sue for peace.

When Warren again went to sea in mid-April 1748, the Western squadron was still supported by an auxiliary squadron of four Dutch warships.[113] Finally using *Invincible* as his flagship, he was accompanied by *Devonshire*, *Prince Frederick*, and *Culloden*. From Plymouth he was joined by *Gloucester*, *Amazon*, and *Falcon*. He sent orders to Hawke to detach only two light frigates to remain off Cadiz, to send *Princess Louisa* into Lisbon to escort home the trade, and to join him with the rest of his squadron either off Ushant or off Cape Finisterre.[114] He dispatched Captain Mostyn with a force consisting of *Hampton Court*, *Tiger*, *St. Albans*, *Intrepid*, *Salisbury*, and the frigate *Assistance* to cruise off Brest and Rochefort.[115]

Shortly after sailing, the Admiralty informed him that they had learned from sources in Stockholm that Sweden was about to send a force of twelve warships to France, to whom they had been sold; some of these ships were loaded with naval stores of all descriptions. Warren was explicitly ordered to intercept them singly or together.[116] He assured the Admiralty that if should find the Swedes "joined with the enemy, I take it for granted that junction gives us a right to treat them as such."[117] When the Admiralty's orders reached him at sea on 13 May, he immediately sent orders to Hawke also to treat the Swedes as enemies.[118]

Almost simultaneously the Admiralty informed him that recent intelligence indicated that eight warships were actively fitting at Brest and another four at Rochefort "to go and meet a fleet said to be coming from America."[119] By America, the Admiralty must have meant Canada, as ships returning to France departed Quebec in September and October, largely with cargoes of fur. It seems improbable that the purpose of this large French armament, if indeed it was fitting out, was intended to secure the trade of Quebec. More likely the information the Admiralty had received was inaccurate.

The first useful intelligence reached Warren on 3 May. It came from *Ranger*, which on 24 April reported an encounter with three large French frigates at 46°30′N escorting two Indiamen steering west by north. Earlier *Ranger* had captured a small French vessel from Cap François bound to Nantes. From her master, Capt. Anthony Kerly learned that there were at least two hundred sail at the island awaiting escorts.[120] This confirmed what Warren already suspected: that the British blockade in the West Indies was proving effective. Yet a month later, Benjamin Keene, the brilliant and hardworking British ambassador to Portugal, informed Warren that he believed the Martinique fleet had sailed on 4 March, insurance rates being 30 percent if under convoy, otherwise at 45 percent.[121] If this proved to be accurate, Warren had only to maintain his disposition and await the further destruction of French commerce.

When his frigates *Anglesey* and *Falcon* reported only one warship at Brest, while a Portuguese merchantman insisted that there were three frigates there, Warren began to suspect that French warships were already at sea. If this information proved accurate, Warren surmised that their purpose was to escort the outward-bound trade only as far as the Canary Islands before returning to their home port or to some Spanish port.[122] Consequently, in mid-May Warren dispatched *Portland*, *Scarborough*, and *Falmouth* to look into the ports of Corunna and Ferrol before rejoining him off Cape Finisterre.[123] He was able to spare these vessels as he had been joined by Hawke's squadron three days earlier.[124] "It gives me great concern to have had so little success since I have been out, which is likewise Sir Edward's case, & really think it owing to the enemies having so few ships on the sea."[125] He was quite correct, for neither France nor Spain risked sending out their fleets before peace preliminaries were negotiated. British command at least of these seas was now absolute.

It was in this posture that the Western squadron, then off Ushant, on 19 May 1748 learned of the cessation of hostilities with France.[126] Typically the peace treaty came into force at a succession of intervals. By its terms prizes taken in the Channel from the beginning of May were to be restored, as were those taken from the Channel to Cape St. Vincent beginning a month later, and everywhere else from 19 July. As peace preliminaries had been a matter of public discussion before Warren put to sea, he already anticipated an early peace. Anson's letters to Warren at sea confirmed the possibility.[127] Indeed, so unconcerned was Anson when he sent the Western squadron to sea in April for the last time that he took time to marry. His bride was Lord Chancellor Hardwicke's daughter, Lady Elizabeth.[128] As Elizabeth's father had married Pelham's sister, Anson now became securely grafted to the innermost circle of the Pelham administration. Warren took the opportunity to send his congratulations when the news became official.[129]

Upon learning of the signing of the peace preliminaries, Warren directed Capt. Richard Gwynn in *Ambuscade* to intercept the squadron under Commodore Cotes off Cape St. Vincent and convey the news and Warren's new orders. These orders reminded his captains that, if indeed peace with France had been secured, war with Spain still continued.[130]

After consulting Hawke and his remaining captains, Warren decided to shift his squadron to its former station off Cape Finisterre. He thereupon sent *Portland* north to direct all ships coming from Plymouth and Portsmouth to the new rendezvous. As the Dutch republic had never declared war on Spain, their auxiliary squadron was immediately discharged to return home. Warren prepared to send ships as far as the Canaries to intercept both Spanish trade and warships.[131] For the immediate future, he informed Hawke that his rendezvous would be Madeira. Hawke and others were to cruise between Madeira and 36°20'N until 12 July, before sailing for Spithead and a refit.[132]

One interesting incident occurred at this time, when the French frigate *Fidelle* (28) was taken in latitude 32°48'N on 1 July, bound from La Rochelle to St. Domingue. Warren held a council with Hawke and eight captains; although the warship was indeed a "good prize," she carried sealed dispatches that Warren's council correctly believed to contain news of the peace preliminaries to be conveyed to France's West Indies possessions. The council unanimously concluded that to detain the ship might prove injurious to both peace and amity, which were "upon the point of being established between the British and French nations."[133]

The same day the Admiralty Board determined that there was no longer any need to retain two flag officers at sea. Warren was ordered either to come home himself or to order Rear Admiral Hawke to sail for England immediately.[134] Eleven days later the entire Western squadron was ordered home.[135] On 4 August 1748, the vice admiral received permission to strike his flag.[136]

The last order Warren received from the Admiralty had been to detach a single frigate from his force with instructions to put into Brest for provisions. While there her captain was to observe naval matters that would be of use to the Admiralty about the number, size, and condition of warships at anchor.[137]

With this, the ten-year naval war was finally at an end for Warren. Under the terms of the peace treaty, Cape Breton with the fortifications of Louisbourg, rebuilt at the expense of the British taxpayers, was restored to the French. If the conquest was lost, the fortune it had brought Warren had prospered nicely. First invested in the National Debt when the price had been greatly depressed by the Jacobite invasion, Warren's handsome fortune now grew as the stock market revived with the peace.

Half-pay Admiral, 1748–1752

If keeping one's flag flying is necessary to entitle one to an eighth, pray let me know that I may not, without an absolute necessity go so far from Portsmouth as to oblige me to strike mine.[1]

When thwarted in his ambition to become colonial governor—whether in New York or New Jersey—Warren entered Parliament.[2] One of his last letters from Boston in 1746 was addressed to Commodore Knowles who, with Vice Adm. Isaac Townsend's departure from North America, became commander of what remained of the North American squadron. "Remember my advice to you," he cautioned his hot-tempered junior, "to keep your temper and lay up for a rainy day, for if peace come we shall be hanging about the hedges . . . If I don't come abroad in the spring I intend to get into Parliament and perhaps venture to open my mouth there with more temper tho' less eloquence than our friend Mr. Vernon."[3]

When the king dissolved Parliament in 1747, it was agreed between Anson and Bedford that Warren, though at sea in command of the Western squadron, should stand for one of the two seats in the borough of Westminster. With some twelve thousand electors and a male franchise that excluded only the lowest and poorest, Westminster was by far the largest constituency in the realm and among the most democratic. It "invariably returned men of the highest social standing."[4] To stand for Parliament, among other requirements, a prospective candidate had to own land that yielded an income of at least £300 a year. Warren's newly purchased Hampshire estate yielded less than this, but the necessary parliamentary qualification was supplied by Bedford, who sold to him for £4,800 an annuity of exactly £300 a year "issuing out of lands" for Warren's life.[5] This arrangement was identical to one Bedford had arranged for William Pitt two years earlier. Warren's share of the election costs, principally in the form of bribes offered to the electors and gifts of food and drink, came to

£2,200. It thus meant for him an outlay of £7,000 to get into the unre-
formed Parliament.[6] Although polling day saw Warren still at sea, he and
his partner, Viscount Trentham, Bedford's young brother-in-law, achieved
an easy victory for the Whigs.[7] "I heartily congratulate you on your success at Westminster," wrote Anson, "which victory was easily obtained
in comparison with Litchfield where some twenty thousand pounds was
spent to bring in Lord Gower's son and my brother."[8] In reply, Warren
wanted Anson's advice about how he should thank the electors; Warren
suggested an advertisement in the newspapers.[9] In the end, Warren merely
wrote to his stablemate, Lord Trentham, to make in his name whatever
thanks to the electors of Westminster he thought most appropriate.[10]

As a parliamentarian, Warren served on no less than fifty-nine commit-
tees, chairing thirteen of them. On seven occasions he was ordered to bring
in bills and did so on four occasions. Twice he was ordered to bring bills to
the Lords.[11] Most of this work typically focused on local matters in the
home counties surrounding London. These dealt with such matters as
roads, internal commerce, estates and enclosures, taxes and debt recovery,
inland and coastal navigation, harbors, naturalization, parliamentary
privilege, and elections. He was particularly interested in matters affecting
Westminster and actively supported, for instance, a proposal to establish a
fish market there, a scheme in which he also invested. Only when dealing
with trade and the colonies was his committee work reflective of his long
naval experience on the American coast and in the West Indies. He was one
of the best-informed members on American affairs and became actively
involved in plans for Parliament to compensate the colonies for the costs of
the Louisbourg expedition and its garrisoning in 1745–46. He also interested himself in the boundary dispute between New York and New Jersey.

Two of his parliamentary speeches are recorded. They emphasize his
deep suspicions of Bourbon ambitions and his certainty that Britain's
strength rested on her naval power. In the face of the ministry's postwar
austerity, he argued for a strong navy. In November 1749 he unavailingly
argued against a motion to reduce to ten thousand the number of seamen
to be employed the following year. His point was that such a small number
had to be based on the ministry's "assurance of the continuance of the
present tranquillity as long as any of the present generation could remain
alive. I confess, my hopes are far from being so sanguine." Instead he proposed that between fifteen thousand and twenty thousand seamen were
needed "for preserving the respect due to the British flag, and for prevent-
ing our being under a necessity to distress our trade at the breaking out of

a war."[12] He was perhaps also thinking of the dozens of officers who might be relieved from having to survive on half-pay if the government bill was amended to embrace the larger proposal.

In February 1750 he participated in the debate over the French failure to undertake the demolition of the defenses surrounding the harbor of Dunkirk, a provision that had been part of the peace treaties in both 1713 and 1748 but continued to be ignored by France. "We have nothing to do with the continent," he said in part. "We do not stand in need of assistance from any state upon the continent. Let us confine ourselves to our own element, the ocean. There we may still ride triumphant, in defiance of the whole House of Bourbon."[13] Immediately after he sat down, Sir John Hyde Cotton rose to congratulate Warren for reviving "the drooping spirits of the House." He added, "No one knows better than that gentleman our true strength. No one knows better the true use of it. No one has contributed more towards rendering it formidable to our enemies. And, if he can help it, I am sure it will never be allowed to decay."[14]

Despite his wealth, popularity, and parliamentary activity, Warren never gained the office which he sought. Twice he was passed over for a seat on the Admiralty Board. This was extraordinary, for the year earlier Anson expressed his hope that Warren would join him there, while Warren fully expected the appointment. "I beg you will assure his grace the Duke of Bedford, and yourself, that I shall ever upon all occasions adhere with a most firm and unchangeable attachment to his grace's and your interest and service."[15] His first chance came in December 1748 when a recent appointee, James Stanhope, younger brother of the Earl of Chesterfield, unexpectedly died. Warren immediately sought Anson's support, stating that he relied "intirely on your lordship's interest and friendship."[16] Prime Minister Henry Pelham brought two names to the king: Warren's and that of Thomas Villiers, a diplomat and member of Parliament and the son of the Earl of Jersey.[17] Despite Warren's obvious qualifications, the better-connected diplomat was selected.[18] There is no evidence in the political correspondence of such powerful ministers as Newcastle, Hardwicke, or Bedford to hint that Warren lacked devotion to the ministry and his patrons. His unresolved dispute with Governor Clinton of New York might have begun to sour his relations with the Pelhams. Or the dispute over prize money with Sandwich's brother, which will be related later, may equally have cast a shadow over the vice admiral's candidacy, although there is no evidence for this. When a new vacancy occurred six months later upon the resignation of Lord Vere Beauclerk, Warren made no attempt to apply. The position was filled by the youthful, inexperienced, but exceedingly well-connected Viscount Trentham, Warren's parliamentary partner for the borough of Westminster.[19]

That Warren was never again considered for preferment after 1748 would not have surprised him. His political problems stemmed directly from his prominent opposition to one part of the ministry's naval bill, which Anson, as head of the Admiralty Board, had sponsored. The bill, introduced in the House of Commons in February 1749 by way of reform, reduced to one piece of legislation all statutes relating to the navy.[20] However, article thirty-four was an innovation. By it, sea officers on half-pay were now made subject to court martial on grounds similar to those of serving officers.[21] Anson argued that all officers, on half-pay or otherwise, ought to be subject to the same discipline. By contrast, those who objected believed it was an overt challenge to their liberty, as it gave the Admiralty Board unprecedented power over half-pay officers. Professional and political leverage could be exerted over inconvenient or unsatisfactory rivals, they argued, by ordering them to posts known to be disagreeable but which, by virtue of their position of rank and seniority, they would be obliged to decline. Such behavior would thereby subject them to court martial proceedings, which might also entail the loss of half-pay. They argued that half-pay was a reward for past service, not a retainer for the future, and that the clause would give the Admiralty an important new power over sea officers. A pamphlet war ensued.[22]

Warren acted as one of the leading spokesmen of those opposed to the measure and, according to the journal kept by Capt. Augustus Hervey, played a significant role along with Admiral of the Fleet Norris and Vice Adm. Fitzroy Henry Lee.[23] Political support for their position in the Lords came particularly from Egmont, Doneraile, Gage, and Baltimore; in the Commons from Nugent, Colonel Lyttleton, Sir Edmund Thomas, Thomas Pitt, Bone, Bathurst, and Sir John Cust. Discreet support came from Frederick Louis, Prince of Wales, who was quoted by Captain Hervey as saying it was "shameful for Lord Anson and Lord Sandwich to make so many brave men slaves."[24] On 20 February three captains—Hervey, West, and Dutt—appeared before the Lords of Admiralty bearing a petition signed by three admirals and forty-seven captains to urge the Admiralty to remove the offending clause.[25] They complained that the naval bill subjected half-pay officers to a "greater degree of discipline & command" than they already experienced. They argued that during the late war there had been no shortage of half-pay officers willing to serve "king & country." Furthermore, the "methods of compulsion" in the bill "dishonoured the service" and the officer corps. All the offending clause achieved, they believed, was to intimidate those who might already have been reluctant to serve, while tending to "lessen the ardour of the truly gallant & faithful officer, in taking away that liberty which must ever animate him in the defence of his king & country."[26] Sandwich, as First Lord, remarked that a relatively small number of officers had signed the petition, while many other officers, "some at the head of the fleet," had expressed support for the clause.

The next day, the officers were invited to reappear when Sandwich responded in the Admiralty's name. He pointed out that the bill had first to be studied by a parliamentary committee where amendments and additions would be considered. Before summoning the rest of the officers gathered outside, including several admirals, he expressed his concern about the newspaper advertisements that had called "for a body of military men to meet together at a very extraordinary proceeding," a statement he repeated to the whole gathering. He suggested that the "gentlemen of the navy must suffer in the eyes of the public" by their public opposition and divided counsel.[27] Sandwich expressed particular surprise that officers "who had served with honour" should be opposing the bill in this manner. Among them, he undoubtedly included Vice Admiral Warren. Two days later, some ninety-six officers signed a letter of appreciation to thank the Lords of Admiralty for conveying a list of proposed alterations to the bill. Signatories to the counterpetition included nine admirals, sixty-six captains, and two dozen masters and commanders. They assured them that they "never doubted his Majesty's right to our service while we received his pay." Nor did they detect any "hardship or disgrace to our corps," that the king should punish officers by canceling the half-pay of those who refused to serve as ordered.[28]

Captain Hervey and others thereupon formulated a petition to Parliament. Hervey claimed that before the matter was debated by Parliament, Warren "came to me and wanted us to mitigate our resentment to this Article" by substituting an article differently worded "but I would never give way."[29] If true, it would have been very characteristic of Warren to try to find a middle way and thereby avoid irritating Anson and his other well-placed advocates.[30]

A heated parliamentary debate ensued, and the government deleted the offending clause.[31] For his role in this affair, Warren found himself alienated from his principal patrons—Anson, Bedford, and Sandwich. He remained politically estranged from them for the rest of his life.

Besides his life in Parliament, Warren had other interests in retirement. Two months after he struck his flag for what was to prove the last time, he learned of a vacancy to become an Elder Brother of Trinity House. Trinity House was an association concerned with pilot licensing and the construction and maintenance of lighthouses, buoys, and other structures on the coasts of England and Wales. As he had been for many years a Younger Brother, Warren immediately solicited the support of Admiral Anson and the Duke of Bedford.[32] Not only was he overlooked in 1748 but suffered the same humiliation again in 1750 when his former patrons, Bedford and Sandwich, remained resolutely unforgiving and opposed his candidacy. Despite the lack of their support, Warren unwisely attempted to secure the election by attending a meeting of the Elder Brethren and soliciting the votes of each member. His opponent, supported by Sandwich and Bedford, was Mostyn, who was confident of two-thirds of the votes. To ensure Warren's defeat, Sandwich begged Bedford to attend the election, even though he was not a member. Bedford's appearance, Sandwich believed, "will contribute greatly to establish my interest among these people upon such a footing as to give me the direction in their affairs that I can desire to have." He added rather cruelly, "I can promise you as some sort of indemnification for the trouble I am endeavouring to give you that you will see *Don Calascione* make as poor a figure in this affair as he has in most of the other transactions he has been concerned in on shore."[33]

For his part, Warren was grateful that Admiral Anson refused to act against him on this occasion, writing to him to thank him for his public neutrality. His position, he characterized after his defeat, was a "feather which was as little worth the opposition I met with, as it was my while to trouble myself about it."[34] He begged Anson to believe that "however I might have differed in opinion from my friends on a former occasion, that no other motive but principles of honour and self-conviction, however wrong I might be in my judgments, could have induced me to take a part so inconsistent with my own case and private interests."

Like many rebuffed politicians at that time, Warren appears to have gravitated toward Leicester House. We know only that he was listed by the Earl of Egmont as a member of the Admiralty Board in the administration to be formed upon the accession of the Prince of Wales, a plan that came to grief when the prince died in March 1751.[35]

Warren had lobbied effectively for the financial compensation of the American colonies both for their expenses on the Louisbourg expedition and for their costs on the aborted expedition to Canada in 1746. As early as July 1745 Governor Shirley of Massachusetts had raised the matter, but so long as the war lasted nothing was concluded. Warren became involved in the matter in part because he was correctly perceived by colonial officials as a sympathetic friend of the American colonies and also because of his settlement with the Treasury Board of his own accounts arising from the Louisbourg expedition and his time as governor of Cape Breton. In 1747 Warren spent long hours before the Board of Trade and the secretary of war examining and auditing accounts submitted by Massachusetts.[36] Only in 1749 was a parliamentary grant authorized and coin to the value of £179,260 shipped to Boston in the frigate *Mermaid*.[37] In addition, Connecticut received £28,683, New Hampshire £16,355, and Rhode Island £16,322. As Warren had expected and hoped, this unprecedented infusion of specie had a powerful impact on New England paper currencies, which through excessive emissions had led to hyperinflation.[38] The year 1749 marked a turning point in the financial history especially of Massachusetts. Until the eve of the War of Independence, Massachusetts went from having one of the most unstable currencies among the colonies to being favored with one of the most secure.[39] This compensation policy, so successfully pursued by Warren and others in the late 1740s, became established British policy and encouraged colonials in large numbers to participate actively in the successful effort against French power in North America between 1755 and 1763. The reversal of this policy and its substitution for one of imperial taxation in 1764 had consequences in America too well known for comment here.

Leftover business from North America also included the design of two warships, which the Admiralty had obliged the Navy Board to build in New England. The idea had been Warren's, but it had been the Admiralty that had first formally raised the matter in 1742, when Warren was asked to comment on the wisdom of building warships in North America.[40] At the time he believed that ships comparable to those designed to carry up to forty guns could be handled by colonial shipbuilders. He was particularly taken with sloops built in Bermuda and Rhode Island.[41] As captain of the

New York station ship, Warren had been impressed by the shipbuilding skills of New Yorkers, especially those who had outfitted the privateers during the war. Later, when commanding the naval squadron of the Louis-bourg expedition in 1745, the quality of some of the New England vessels also excited him, as we have seen, a reaction also shared by the Admiralty.

As a reward to New Englanders for their participation in the capture of Louisbourg, Warren repeated his suggestions.[42] This time the Admiralty acted, requiring him to let contracts for building four warships, two of forty-four guns and two of twenty-four guns. Copies of contracts were sent to him along with detailed plans.[43] Warren's proposal was to have one each of the larger frigates built in New Hampshire and Massachusetts, and one each of the smaller in New York and Connecticut.[44]

This plan was immediately challenged by the Navy Board, which ignited a serious and, to historians, informative argument about the relative value of English and American timber.[45] The Navy Board believed that American wood could endure no more than for four or five years' use at sea. It feared fraud on the part of colonial shipbuilders, operating at such a vast distance from the Board's overseers. The Board argued that shipbuilding costs would be greater in America than in England; it also doubted that sufficient volunteers could be found in America to man the ships and projected that crews would have to be shipped from England with attendant costs. Shaken by this opposition, the Admiralty pointed out in response that a great part of British trade was already freighted in plantation-built vessels, perhaps as many as one ship in three. If such vessels were so subject to early decay, they wondered, why would merchants use them so readily? In response, the Board raised the serious argument that no plantation-built ships were employed by the East India Company, the Levant Company, the Russia Company, the Eastland Company, the South Sea Company, or in the trade to Portugal and Italy. Such criticism contributed to the Admiralty decision to reduce the scope of its plans. It now limited its orders to building only one 44–gun and one 24–gun frigate.[46]

In the case of each ship, the designs the Navy Board sent to America were not strictly followed. Both Warren and Knowles, after taking advice and using their own experience, suggested altering the length of the ships and thereby added to the cost. Knowles, without consulting either the Admiralty Board or the Navy Board, ordered the builder of the 44–gun frigate in Portsmouth, New Hampshire, to increase its length by six feet, thus adding forty-eight tons. When the Navy Board refused to pay the additional £432, at the contract rate of £9 per ton, Warren was asked to lobby the Admiralty on behalf of the builder.[47]

When required by the Admiralty to explain their behavior, Knowles, always a difficult man with whom to deal, responded brusquely. He stated only that he told the builder to construct "the best ship his capacity would let him."[48] Warren's explanation provided more details. "The unanimous opinion of very good judges in shipbuilding, whom I consulted upon the occasion, and from . . . the experience I have had, that lengthening her would make her a far better sailing vessel . . . This quality is . . . the principal one to be desired in all frigates and light vessels, the best suited for the purpose for which they are most frequently employed."[49] The Navy Board thus appears to have been justified when it feared losing control of the building process once it was contracted in America.

The experiment showed that in another direction the Navy Board was wrong, for ships could be built far more cheaply in America than in England. *America,* the larger ship, cost 19 percent less, while *Boston,* the smaller vessel, cost 40 percent less than equivalent ships constructed in English yards during the 1739–48 war.

Yet the Navy Board was partially correct when it predicted difficulties in manning the new American-built ships. Once the 44-gun ship was ready for sea, her captain experienced enormous difficulty in finding a crew to sail her to England. It seemed that American volunteers would never be forthcoming in adequate numbers to man the newly built warships unless colonial interests were involved. As an example, Warren had experienced no difficulty at Louisbourg in finding volunteers for *Vigilant* when he added her to his line of battle. In wartime the prospect of prize money—the principal inducement to get men to enlist—was very real.

Warren also devoted some of his energies to matters relating to prize money, unsettled at war's end. One of these was somewhat embarrassing as the dispute was with Capt. the Hon. William Montagu, the Earl of Sandwich's younger brother and an officer whose career Warren had deliberately fostered. "Mad" Montagu, as he was known, refused to concede Warren his admiral's eighth share in the net proceeds of the French registered ship *Union,* a rich prize Montagu had taken on 27 February 1748, when under Warren's command.

Montagu for a time had served as a lieutenant on Commodore Warren's *Launceston* off Antigua, where Warren promoted him to the command of the sloop *Mercury.* As a result of a shooting incident that killed a slave,

Montagu was arrested by Commodore Knowles, who denied him a court martial and ordered him home as a prisoner in *Eltham*. When this ship became part of Warren's force off Louisbourg, Montagu was not only released but took post as captain of the frigate *Mermaid*. Warren again favored Montagu by sending him in a vessel to bring news of the capitulation of the garrison to England, for which Montagu was rewarded with £500 by the king.[50] Despite his immediate assignment to another ship and the confirmation of the commission given him by Warren, Montagu remained ungrateful and impossible to manage. His brother said of him: "If this impudent young man has an opinion of anybody it is of Mr. Warren, who might show him the situation he will be in if he loses the only friend in the world."[51] Twice he unsuccessfully petitioned the Admiralty for a court martial to clear his name.[52]

In the matter of the prize money, rather than confront Montagu in the courts, Warren preferred an arbitration by sea officers.[53] Nevertheless he wrote two strongly worded letters to Montagu to assert his claim.[54] When Montagu failed to give way, Warren and Hawke, who by private agreement with Warren had a one-third interest in the admiral's eighth, prepared a full statement of the case which was then submitted to Montagu's counsel.[55] Montagu remained defiant and turned down the chance of an independent arbitration by experienced sea officers, stating to Warren his resolution "to stand the chance of a suit-at-law."[56] How the matter turned out is unclear.

Another dispute occurred over a Spanish prize taken when Warren commanded the Leeward Islands squadron. The captor was Capt. Edward Herbert in *Woolwich*. By agreement with Capt. Charles Knowles, Warren shared half his share of his squadron's prize takings. Warren initiated proceedings in 1749 against Herbert, with half the costs to be borne by Knowles.[57] As late as 1760 Lady Warren and Knowles (then an admiral) were still pursuing what they believed was their share in the prize money.[58]

A third incident related to Warren's role as agent for the captors of the bullion found on board *Notre Dame de la Déliverance*, owned by the Compagnie des Indes and taken off Louisbourg in 1745. By 1748 some of the prize money had been distributed to the captors, but not to the seamen. In mid-October 1748 Warren received at Westbury, his Hampshire seat, a petition forwarded to him by the Admiralty from poor seamen who had yet to receive their shares of the prize money.[59] The prize, first estimated by Warren at £400,000, contained so much bullion that Warren felt obliged to act as agent for that part of her cargo. He kept $100,000 to meet the costs of the garrison that winter, which could not have subsisted otherwise. "I believe my so doing prevented a mutiny in the garrison" of New England volunteers.[60] The money was lodged in the Bank of England, but a partial distribution had been made to the captains, lieutenants, and warrant officers, but none to the petty officers and seamen.[61] Further delay was expected as the whole matter was then tied up in litigation. The appeal was ultimately heard only in May 1750.

As a post captain without a squadron of his own, Warren had done well enough in the matter of prize money. As a commodore of a squadron and later as an admiral he made a fortune, perhaps the largest, next to Anson's, garnered by any sea officer up to the mid-eighteenth century. "Where an admiral was almost certain of a fair fortune," as has been correctly observed, "a captain had to enjoy luck to make one and many never did. Yet when fortune did smile the results could be spectacular."[62] The explanation was found in the method of distribution of the spoils. By common law all prizes were the crown's property, but by an act of Parliament passed in March 1708 both the crown and the Admiralty gave up what right to prize money they had hitherto enjoyed.[63] Thus throughout Warren's naval career and long afterwards, the crown, except in rare circumstances, handed its share to the captors, while the Admiralty, which had formerly used its share to finance its own office together with a number of pension funds, now retained only a few fees.

During the 1739–48 wars with Spain and France three proclamations refined the 1708 act. The first specified that all prizes taken between 10 July and 19 October 1739 would be shared equally, with half paid to the captors and half to indemnify British and colonial merchants who had suffered commercial losses at the hands of Spanish *guardacostas*.[64] By royal proclamation of 19 June 1740 and 29 March 1744, the net value of all prizes was divided into eighths. Three-eighths went to the captain. If in company with other ships, the three-eighths' share was divided equally among the captains involved. If the ships were serving under a commodore's broad pendant or an admiral's flag, one of the captains' eighths went to the commanding sea officer. The fourth eighth was divided equally among the captain of marines, naval lieutenants, and ships' masters. The remaining shares were divided among levels of warrant and petty officers. All but the admirals had to be on board their warships to participate in the sharing of prize money.

An elaborate paper trail was devised. By the first step, as soon as a prize was taken ship commanders had to submit to the Navy Board an appropriate list of their officers and crew, according to the share system. Next, three captains were appointed to verify the lists against the muster books of the ships involved in the captures and to sign a certificate to that effect. The case of the captured merchant vessel or warship then was placed before an Admiralty Court if in England, or a Court of Vice Admiralty if abroad in the colonies. A thorough inventory of the prize ship and cargo was ordered. Once the court had rendered its verdict, the prize and the cargo were sold at public auction, fees were paid to the auctioneer and court, and the net proceeds distributed by the agents of the captors. If the prize was a warship head, money was due the captors and paid by the Navy Board according to the number of officers and crew on board an enemy ship at the time of her capture. The captured warship, if commissioned into the navy, was thereupon evaluated by dockyard officers and the purchase price determined for distribution among the captors. In the matter of merchant vessels, Vice Admiralty Court decisions could be and frequently were appealed to the High Court of Admiralty in London. All papers in such cases had to be printed, which added to the costs and a new set of fees incurred by the captors.[65] Such final judgments thus rendered, usually months or even years later, became part of prize law that in turn modified and elaborated the effect both of statutory law and royal proclamations. Hardship was frequently experienced through long delays in prize money distribution, especially by seamen. In desperation, seamen frequently sold their shares at a discount to lawyers, merchants, dealers, or even to their own officers, who could wait for the final outcome of the cases to realize their profit.

Warren had gained not less than £127,405 in prize money, perhaps 80 percent of it between 1745 and 1747, and continued to benefit after he struck his flag for the last time in 1748.[66] Considerable sums continued to trickle in, especially from the forty-eight prizes and nine recaptured vessels taken by the Western squadron in 1748.[67]

Retirement on half-pay after a long war allowed Peter Warren his first opportunity since 1739 to live a settled family life. Once he had abandoned all hope of a colonial governorship, life in England and Ireland seemed the obvious choice. Yet as late as 1750, in a letter to his brother-in-law, Oliver DeLancey—who acted as Warren's co-agent in New York—Warren remarked: "My view of thinking to go to New York is the more pleasure to me when I think I could be more serviceable to my family and friends with the fortune, with which God has blessed me there than here. Though 'tis not so much as the world imagine nor more than the necessary parade here obliges me to live up to."[68]

Beginning in Christmas 1747 Warren leased for £190 a year a large London house in Cavendish Square, where he, his wife, and three surviving children spent the winter and spring months while Parliament sat.[69] When he was not traveling in Ireland or elsewhere in England, the family lived the balance of the year at Westbury. In fact, he had little time for travel. We know that in 1751 he took his family to Scarborough for some weeks for the benefit of the waters, as his health, which had been impaired by his winter at Louisbourg in 1745–46 and had forced him to give up his command of the Western squadron in 1747, was now again a cause of concern. He made at least two visits to Ireland. The first occurred in 1750, seventeen years after his last visit in 1733.[70] His 1752 trip to Ireland proved fatal, for he died on 29 July 1752 after a four-day battle with an infection, perhaps incurred from drinking the waters of the River Liffey, where he had been fishing.[71]

When he quit North America for the last time in October 1746, he did not add to his American land holdings.[72] By then his property was principally located in the colony of New York, especially on Manhattan Island and on the south bank of the Mohawk River. On Manhattan, Warren's most impressive holdings were three contiguous farms amounting to some three hundred acres in what was to become Greenwich Village and at the careening facilities at Turtle Bay, now the site of the United Nations building. In the Mohawk valley at Warrensbush he extended and supported a settlement on a 16,200–acre tract, which he placed under the care of two of his Irish nephews.[73] One of these—William Johnson—emerged as unquestionably the most interesting and influential European personality on the New York colonial frontier.[74]

Warren's wealth encouraged him to add to his Hampshire holdings and to extend his investments in Irish land. In Hampshire in 1750–52 he purchased five more farms in a conspicuous attempt to establish a large estate. He was deeply engaged in further land deals in the Meon valley when his sudden death ended negotiations, his widow having no desire to pursue them.[75] In Ireland, prize money allowed him not only to pay off the mortgage on his 433–acre ancestral property at Warrenstown in County Meath but also to purchase in 1750 the portion alienated in 1723 by his elder brother, the long-deceased naval lieutenant Oliver Warren. Between 1750 and his death two years later, Warren purchased another 1,049 acres of farmland in County Meath. His last land arrangement was concluded only three weeks before his death, when he was still actively negotiating a large deal to include a spacious house in Dublin and an extensive estate in County Wicklow to the south, the property of the late Sir Richard Kennedy.[76]

One odd contribution made by Warren to his "corps" was in the design of officers' uniforms. We learn from a letter of Anson's that Warren's 1747 proposal "about rank and uniform for sea officers" had been sent forward by Anson to Admirals Norris and Martin. Anson wrote: "I find all the officers of rank of flag and above as well raise objections in order to stop the thing we propose, but I will join you in it with the officers below us, and push in spite of all opposition."[77] Warren could not understand "what reasonable objection our seniors can have to a uniform and rank, as proposed in the instruments I sent you, but that it is a scheme of ours."[78] In particular, Warren put down objections made by Admiral Norris—a man "whom gratitude obliges me to love, honour and wish well"—to his being "sower'd with disappointments."

The following November the Admiralty Board submitted a memorial to the king to suggest the military equivalents for naval rank: thus, a vice admiral held rank with a lieutenant general, a rear admiral with a major general, a commodore with a broad pendant with a brigadier general, and so on. To match this, suitable uniforms needed to be designed to distinguish the rank of each officer, both commissioned and warrant. The proposal then came from admirals Sir Chaloner Ogle, James Steuart, Edward Boscawen, Warren, twenty-six captains, and fifty-four lieutenants.[79] The Board, of which Anson was a member, chose to do nothing at the time in the matter of uniforms.

Like many men of means Warren became something of a philanthropist. His charity was distinguished more by its variety than by its sheer size. His largest act of philanthropy occurred in New England. In 1749, for helping the New England colonial governments secure compensation for their wartime military expenditures—especially in 1745–46, Warren received a £900 commission. Not wanting any reward for his services, he hoped it to be put to some "public use" in Massachusetts.[80] At first he thought to apply it to the erection of a new town hall in Cambridge. In the end, he used £150 to buy and ship two stallions to Boston to improve the breeding of horses throughout New England. The matter was discussed between Warren and Pepperrell when this first American baronet visited

England.[81] The horses were shipped on the same vessel that carried Pepperrell home to Kittery.[82] With the balance of £750 Warren established a trust for the education of native children. This seemed to him a perfect blending of religion and practical politics. On the one hand, it would bring the children to a "knowledge of and subjection to the Glorious Redeemer of the world," and, on the other, it would attach them to the "British interest, and the American colonies in particular."[83] So enthusiastic did Warren become about this education project that he intended to organize a subscription in England, Ireland, and perhaps also in the colonies to increase the capital; his untimely death in 1752 suspended his plans before they matured.[84] The Warren fund lay unused until 1761 when Eleazar Wheelock, a Congregationalist minister, received permission from the Massachusetts general court to use the income for his school for natives at Lebanon, Connecticut.[85] The capital had not grown during the decade since Warren had established it, the interest being absorbed into the general revenues of the colony. Ultimately, the fund seems to have been misappropriated and used in 1772 to help fund Dartmouth College, of which Wheelock was the founder. For this Peter Warren has yet to be acknowledged.

Other donations are worth mentioning. Warren's gifts extended to such items as a set of silver service and a handsome pair of pistols, which he gave Pepperrell.[86] This perhaps occurred in 1750 when Pepperrell made his only trip to England. He also donated a reflecting telescope to Harvard College in 1749.[87] (It appears to have been destroyed by the great fire there in 1760.) In addition, Warren also subscribed sums for the building of churches in New York and Boston. These included St. George's chapel in New York, King's chapel in Boston, and a new Anglican church in Cambridge, Massachusetts.[88]

In England he was particularly interested in hospitals; he served for several years both as vice president of the Middlesex Hospital, founded in 1745, and as steward of the London Hospital, founded in 1740. He subscribed small sums in London to St. Bartholomew's, the Westminster Infirmary, the Lock Hospital, and the Hampshire County Hospital at Winchester.[89] In Ireland he was concerned with the Incorporated Society for Promoting Protestant Working Schools. As early as 1743 he donated £179.13.9. to the society.[90]

Peter Warren drew up his will three days before his death. Foremost it displayed his deep affection for Susannah, his wife since 1732, and the trust he placed in her. He wrote of her in the first few sentences as "my most dear and well-beloved wife . . . my most entirely beloved wife . . . my second self."[91] Wherever she is mentioned in his correspondence he refers to her with the same fondness. Even in his account books there can be found loving references to her. His will gave her the use for life of one-third of the income from his property; he appointed her guardian of their four daughters—the youngest, Catherine, was but four months old—thus giving her access to all his income until the girls came of age or married.

John Campbell wrote of Warren that he "had not only the singular happiness of being universally courted, esteemed, and beloved; but had the additional consolation of having passed through life without making, as far as we can investigate, a single enemy."[92] Our account differs somewhat from this assessment for it is plain that Charles Knowles retained a professional jealousy of him and that George Clinton suspected him of conspiring against him, while blaming Warren for many of his difficulties that were brought about principally by his own ineffectual behavior as New York's governor. We are also aware that the ungrateful "Mad" Montagu cut him, that Sandwich and Bedford shunned him even as they accepted his advice, and that Anson, if on one occasion doubted his judgment, remained his friend. Warren appears to have had a sharp disagreement with Pepperrell, but soon enough the general was completely won over once he was able to gauge the extent of Warren's sympathy for the New Englanders.

There are few tangible traces of Warren's existence and none of them well known. Halifax, whose settlement he had advocated in Nova Scotia, while naming streets after Shirley, Vernon, and Pepperrell, continues to ignore Warren. Yet New York, Charleston, Louisbourg, and London named streets after him. London unwittingly affixed his name to an underground station, when the Victoria Line, with its different symbols at each station, failed to assign a naval anchor to Warren Street Station but instead rather lamely produced something incomprehensible to symbolize a rabbit warren. Best known is the large and unlovely marble monument of him in the east transept of Westminster Abbey, carved by Louis François Roubiliac, the most popular sculptor of the mid-century. Hercules, on the left bearing up the admiral, is balanced by a woman thought to be Susannah, his darling wife. There is a bust of Admiral Warren, also by Roubiliac and obviously made for Lady Warren, which is now owned by the Huntington Library and Art Collections in San Marino, California.

There are portraits of him by the American John Smibert done in Boston in 1746, at the height of his power and popularity in the northern colonies.[93] There are three copies of another portrait by Thomas Hudson, completed in 1751, by which time he appears to have acquired a consider-able paunch. They are now found in the National Gallery, London, the National Maritime Museum, Greenwich, and a third in Heveningham House, Halesworth, Suffolk. Additionally, a gift of silver given to Warren by the Corporation of the City of London is now in the Dupont family museum in Virginia, and a silver service and handsome pair of pistols, given to Sir William Pepperrell by Warren in 1750, is still in the Pepperrell house in Kittery, Maine.

Conclusion

When Peter Warren joined the navy at Dublin in 1716 it was led by a "professional corps of commissioned sea officers."[1] Unlike the army where commissions were purchased, to be promoted sea officers had to pass an examination. In 1729 the minimum sea service required to be examined for promotion to lieutenant was raised from four to six years. Furthermore, by 1713 all commissioned ranks were entitled to half-pay and officers could now take post as captains in the lowest rated ships, the sixth-rate frigate carrying at least twenty great guns. Beyond the rank of captain lay only that of admiral, where no examination was required. Rather, one needed timely and enduring patronage, good luck, and professional longevity. Proven talent in command of warships, as the career of George Clinton demonstrated, could be unnecessary.

Perhaps owing to low pay, ship commanders were notorious in "falsifying muster books, mistreating servants, profiteering on refitting expenses, slop clothes, and victuals—in short, contravening regulations and instructions that had been assembled in cold clear print" when *Regulations and Instructions Relating to His Majesty's Service at Sea* was first published in 1731.[2] If the corps was honorable, as Warren often wrote of it, it was also largely dishonest in money matters. An occasional officer was cashiered for such behavior.

There is not the slightest evidence in Warren's record that he was corrupt in this way. Still, an incident in the Leeward Islands involving Charles Knowles is worth noting. Knowles was prosecuted for having pressed men from a privateer in the West Indies, contrary to statutes. Convicted of this offence, he was heavily fined and, unable to pay, imprisoned. Finding him in this condition, Warren, then commodore of the Leeward Islands squadron, on his own initiative commissioned into the navy one of the prize vessels valued at £2,666 and used Knowles's share of the prize money to release his colleague.[3] In defending this action, Warren explained to the Admiralty that Britain would have suffered more by Knowles's imprisonment and the consequent neglect of the work on the English Harbour fortifications and careening yard than "twice the value of that vessel."[4] Typical of Warren, this effort had been taken not in the shadows but openly. His actions certainly drew heavy Admiralty criticism but had no lasting impact on his career.

There is evidence that Warren dabbled in trade while abroad, especially before the outbreak of war in 1739, but none to suggest that he ever carried trade goods on board the warships he commanded. Besides those items he ordered to be shipped from England for the Mohawk valley settlements, he traded on his own account. He employed Peter Faneuil of Boston, for instance, in an apparently clandestine export trade to Louisbourg in 1737.[5] From his early West Indies experience Warren dealt in spirits and wine and in slaves from South Carolina. "I left my brother [-in-law] James DeLancey twenty dozen of rum in a wooden case," he noted in an early account book, "100 gallons of brandy in the hands of John Hamilton of [Perth] Amboy . . . Stephen Bayard was to have . . . a pipe of brandy containing 160 gallons, 100 of which he was to pay Col Gilbert for a negro I bought off him, the remainder he was to be accountable to me." Some of these items might have been gifts as we know was the case when, in September 1743, he paid to send a pipe of Madeira to Adm. Sir John Norris.[6]

Warren was a slave owner and held the contracts for white indentured servants, some of whom he sent to his nephew, William Johnson, to work his land along the Mohawk River. In 1732 his accounts refer to Scarborough and Barbados, the names by which two black slaves were known, "not yet sold but left to be hired" to Governor Cosby of New York. He also left in the hands of David Smith at New York "a negro boy named Cambridge." Another he left with his brother-in-law, Peter DeLancey, "a negro called Pompey . . . I likewise left a negro boy named Cezar to be sold."[7] It seems that his interest in buying slaves began in Charleston where he found "a negro man . . . left to be sold by [Capt. George] Anson."[8] That slave Warren had valued at SC£200 (or £28 10s.). Another entry reads: "I have left my attorneys a bill of sale from Mr. D'Hariet for three negroes . . . which I have as security for the payment of the SC£849.9.9."[9] In September 1737 he listed eight slaves he then owned and a ninth, named Albany, whom he exported from Boston to Jamaica.[10] How common a practice this was among sea officers who served abroad for extended intervals is unclear. A reading of both French and British naval correspondence indicates that it was widespread among sea officers as well as among masters of merchant vessels of both France and Britain. The scale of Warren's dealings in the 1730s was possibly unusually large. Thereafter it vanishes, though he kept a slave at Louisbourg in 1745 and in Boston in 1746, who was skilled at music.

The corps of sea officers also had its litigious members. Charles Knowles was one of the most notorious. In 1748 a controversial sea action involved Knowles in a spate of bitter courts martial. Warren, by contrast, was involved only twice, and in both cases the issue was prize money and not honor. The first case, with Knowles as co-plaintiff, was over Captain Herbert's unwillingness to share his prize money. The second suit dealt with the same topic and involved Captain Montagu.[11] Typically, Warren had made great efforts to resolve both disputes before going to court. No aspect of his naval career was ever subjected to a court martial. Indeed, his personality was that of a diplomat who attempted to smooth over differences between brother officers or to find a peaceful solution. Dr. William Douglass of Boston, when contrasting the rash behavior of Knowles, who had ignited an impressment riot in Boston in 1747, wrote of Warren's "universally acknowledged good character . . . a gentleman of paternal estate, naturally good and human, always friendly to trade, benevolent and beloved by his officers and common sailors, assiduous and constant, therefore successful and fortunate."[12] This was not far from the truth.

Many sea officers fought duels with each other or with those they encountered ashore when their honor appeared to be in question. The same violent and bitter quarrels over the behavior of Knowles and his captains in 1748 resulted in several duels. Knowles himself received no fewer than four challenges on that occasion.[13] Warren never placed himself in a situation that might have led to such a symbolic piece of folly.

Like so many of his fellow officers, Warren was no literary giant. Of his formal education we know nothing, although as a member of a gentry family he was presumably not taught in an Irish hedge school. Before he entered the navy at thirteen he had acquired a weak hold on no more than phonetic spelling and seemed to have been largely ignorant of classical learning. The form of his correspondence reflected poorly both on him and on the secretaries he later selected. They seemed to have been chosen more for their calligraphy than for their orthography. This contrasts with the education offered to Knowles, the illegitimate offspring of a father who called himself Earl of Banbury—an unrecognized title—and a French lady of quality; when he joined the navy at fourteen he was already well grounded in mathematics, mechanics, and French. His correspondence on occasion had a suitable sprinkling of poetical allusions, both classical and contemporary, something that never characterized Warren's letters. In all of this, Warren was closer to the norm displayed by his contemporary sea officers than was Knowles.

From Warren's accounts may be reconstructed something of the contents of his library: publications purchased in the last five years of his life. There were current pamphlets, like Onno Zweir van Haren's *The Sentiments of a Dutch Patriot, being the Speech of *** in an August Assembly on the Present State of Affairs* (1746) and material concerned with the courts martial relating to the Mathews-Lestock impasse off Toulon in 1744, such as *An Impartial View of the Conduct of Admirals M——ws and L——k, in the Late Engagement in the Mediterranean* (1745), and of the courts martial of his friends including Captains Richard Norris and John Ambrose.[14] There were histories, naval and local: Thomas Lediard's *The Naval History of England in all its Branches, from the Norman Conquest, 1066 to the Conclusion of 1734* (1735) in two volumes; *The History of the Mediterranean Fleet from 1741 to 1744 with Original Letters, &c. that Passed between Admirals Mathews and Lestock. . .* (1745); *The History of the Rise, Progress, and Tendency of Patriotism* (1747) by a Freeholder; a *Parliamentary History* in eight volumes; Pierre Charlevoix's *Histoire et description générale de la Nouvelle France, avec le journal historique d'un voyage fait par ordre du Roi dans l'Amérique septentrionale* (1744) in three volumes; *Memoirs of Exeter;* and Rev. Griffith Hughes's *The Natural History of Barbados* (1750). There were encyclopedias and dictionaries, notably Pierre Bayle's *Dictionnaire historique et critique* (1740) in four folio volumes; Ephraim Chambers's *Cyclopaedia, or an Universal Dictionary of Arts and Sciences* (1741) in two folio volumes; Abel Boyer's *Dictionnaire royal, françois-anglois, et anglois-françois* (1727); Pedro Pineda's *Nuevo Dicionario Espanol e Ingles e Ingles y Espanol* (1740). Lighter reading included *The Pleasures of Imagination. A Poem in Three Books* (1744) and *The Comedies of Plautus* in English translation.[15] He must also have owned George Anson's *Voyage Round the World*, first published in 1748, and perhaps Josiah Burchett's *A Complete History of the Most Remarkable Transactions At Sea, from the Earliest Accounts of Time to the Conclusion of the Last War with France* (1720) as Warren had regularly corresponded with the former secretary to the Admiralty Board until his retirement in 1742.

Such purchases, beyond those concerned with the sea, collectively resemble those made by a successful if unread businessman, who having acquired his fortune, sets himself the task of quickly accumulating some well-packaged learning and the more rounded manifestations of a gentleman. There was nothing very light or uplifting of the human spirit, it seems, in Warren's library either at Cavendish Square or at Westbury Manor. Where are the novels, the books of poetry, and the works of philosophy? After all, Fielding's *The History of Tom Jones, a Foundling* appeared in 1748, the year that Warren was in a book-buying mode and the same period Hume published *Enquiry Concerning Human Understanding*. Where are the works of Pope or that great Anglo-Irishman, Jonathan Swift? Perhaps all these titles were purchased and noted in account books now lost to the historian.

The most striking aspect of his life and career was his remarkable rise. Through a lucrative career in a relatively new profession—the navy—his social position was transformed from that of the youngest son of an indebted and declining Irish Catholic gentry family to that of an English gentleman and member of Parliament for the most democratically elected constituency in the land. Crucial to this was the decision to abandon Catholicism and to conform instead to the established church. Significantly important in aiding his career was the presence of powerful patrons, especially Irish ones, who themselves had made very successful careers in the Royal Navy. Later when he had reached flag rank, his English patrons Anson, Bedford, Sandwich, and Newcastle, proved to be too politically narrow for Warren's taste. In 1749 a chasm suddenly emerged to separate them from him. His hopes to become a Lord of Admiralty evaporated when he led a faction in 1749 that opposed one clause of the Navy Bill, whose general purposes Warren supported. In an instant he lost his powerful political patrons, who then in turn humiliated him. For this independent act he was never forgiven, never trusted, and effectively isolated from any influence.

He could not even secure a colonial governorship in America where he maintained wide connections, both family and business, and where he had such extensive experience. There his principal ambition was to become governor of New York. His negotiations for the governorship led nowhere when his brother-in-law, James DeLancey, opposed the governor, who was himself tied by marriage to the Pelhams. Had Warren not died so soon after he fell from political grace he might have been forgiven and restored to favor as Knowles was after he had been reprimanded by a court martial in 1749 and then appointed governor of Jamaica three years later.

Prize money at Louisbourg and from the activities of the Western squadron made Warren a rich man. To his extensive land holdings in New York he had added an estate in Hampshire within easy reach of Portsmouth and a large estate in Ireland, some of it embracing his ancestral home. While on a land-purchasing foray in Ireland he died suddenly in July 1752, leaving a widow and four young daughters. The eldest two married into the English aristocracy and the daughter and only child of the third married into the Irish aristocracy. From the vantage point of Dublin, where Warren entered the navy in 1716, his was an extraordinary transformation.

Warren's lasting monuments were two: his remarkably perceptive comments on the future course of Anglo-American and Anglo-French relations in North America and his considerable fortune, traces of which survive even today among his descendants through his daughters' marriages.

Warren's career as a sea officer is unusually interesting, especially owing to its connections with the American colonies. With an American wife, American-born children, and extensive family and business connections from Boston to Charleston, he was well placed to become an advocate for American hopes and ambitions.

The establishment of the North American squadron, the garrisoning of British regulars at Louisbourg, the large parliamentary subsidies paid to the New England colonies to diminish their war debts, the settlement of Nova Scotia with Protestants, and the fortification of the town of Halifax in Chebucto harbor—all of which Warren either advocated or supported—positioned Great Britain to undertake the conquest of France's possessions in Canada. The capture of New France by 1760 and its retention under the terms of the subsequent peace treaty entirely vindicated Warren's strategic vision, unmatched by any other naval or military figure of his day. If the language of his dispatches was unremarkable, the message, for a sea officer, was altogether exceptional. The year Fortress Louisbourg was captured few sea officers had much experience of North American waters. Yet by 1775 very few did not—such was the transformation in the disposition of the fleet within a single generation. Warren's ideas and his achievements as a sea officer had much to do with the start of this process and helped to expand Britain's American vision beyond the fishing grounds off Newfoundland and the tobacco plantations of Virginia and Maryland.

His understanding of the prospects for British America in general, and New England in particular, was also rare. "A vulgar notion has prevailed with many," he wrote to Anson as he made his way from Antigua to Cape Breton in April 1745, "that the colonies should be kept poor in order to be [kept] humble, upon a supposition that in time they may be in a condition and desirous of throwing off that parental yoke." He had no doubt that the colonies with time would be so placed that this could transpire. Rather than retain policies that might lessen their affection for the mother country, he suggested a different approach: let the colonies develop their manufactures, especially those currently derived from foreign imports into Britain, which then were re-exported to the colonies.[16]

There is no doubt that Warren helped make North America, for the first time, a place of permanent importance in British policy. From 1745 onwards the British government was prepared to invest heavily in men and materials, not only to secure its North American colonies but, under Pitt— one of Warren's converts—to despoil France of her North American possessions in the next war and thereby raise the possibility of opening the old English colonies in America to independence, something on which Warren himself commented.

New Englanders he knew were very proud of their accomplishments at Louisbourg. His recommendation to the ministry to honor their commander, William Pepperrell, was founded on the belief that, when a call went out from the mother country to raise troops in America, the response would again be positive. "At any time 30,000 men may be procured by any gentleman in whom they have confidence," Warren informed the Duke of Newcastle immediately after Louisbourg had fallen. He then sagely observed, "As they have the highest notions of the rights and liberties of Englishmen, and indeed are almost Levellers, they must know when, where, how and what service they are going upon, and be treated in a manner that few military-bred gentlemen would condescend to." Yet he wisely suggested: "If they do the work in which they are engaged, every other ceremony should . . . be winked at."[17] What enabled Warren to plumb the depths of this aspect of the New England psyche? Was it merely a shrewd conclusion based on observing the New Englanders preparing to risk their lives? Was it something he heard while dining with Pepperrell and his officers? Or, did it derive from his own sense of separation and insecurity, springing first from his Catholic upbringing, his Irishness, and the fact that he had married an urban American from a family with wide international business connections, yet who, a generation earlier, had been refugees themselves? Anson, despite having circumnavigated the world and served in South Carolina, probably understood none of this. Newcastle, who quailed at the mere prospect of a trans-Channel crossing and who only recently had discovered that Cape Breton was indeed an island, would have supposed that Warren was writing in a mystical new language quite beyond the understanding of a plainspoken, if neurotic, English duke. As it turned out neither Anson nor Newcastle was roused sufficiently to respond to Warren's observations, perhaps the most significant of his public life.

Notes

Preface

1. Crick and Almon, *Guide to Manuscripts Relating to America in Great Britain and Ireland.*

2. Gwyn, *Enterprising Admiral.*

3. Gwyn, ed., *The Warren Papers, 1736–52.*

4. By Thomas A. Janvier and Horace Lyman Weeks. Their notes are found respectively in the Houghton Library at Harvard and in the New York Public Library.

5. Williams, *The Whig Supremacy, 1714–1760.*

6. The most notable exceptions are Richmond, *Navy in the War of 1739–1748,* and MacKay, *Admiral Hawke.* Warren was not included in Le Fevre and Harding, *Precursors of Nelson.* See Thomas, *Battles and Honours of the Royal Navy.*

7. *The Naval Chronicle: or, Voyages, Travel, Expeditions, . . . of the Most Celebrated English . . . Sea-Commanders* 3:162–67.

8. Charnock, *Biographia Navalis,* 6 vols., 4:184–92.

9. Clarke *et al.,* eds., *Naval Chronicle* 4:516–24.

10. By Laughton, 59:876–77. Sedgwick, *History of Parliament. House of Commons* 2:522–23.

11. Thomas A. Janvier, a noted historian of New York City, published *In Old New York.*

12. Horace Lyman Weeks.

13. For enthusiastic mythology, see Chapin, *Greenwich Village,* especially her chapter, "The Gallant Career of Sir Peter Warren."

14. Rogers, "Vice-Admiral Peter Warren, 1703–52," *Dictionary of American Biography,* a much more useful entry than in the earlier *Dictionary of National Biography.* I have written the entry for Warren in the forthcoming *New Oxford Dictionary of National Biography.*

15. Katz, *Newcastle's New York,* and Tully, *Forming American Politics.*

16. Typical is Parsons, *William Pepperrell.*

17. Bourinot, *Historical Account of Cape Breton,* and Gow, *Cape Breton Illustrated.*

18. McLennan, *Louisbourg, from Its Foundation to Its Fall*.

19. The papers of Marshal Richard Warren, as far as I know still unexamined by scholars, are in the *Archives départementales de Morbihan*, at Vannes, in Brittany, where I discovered them in 1969. Among other notable accomplishments, Richard Warren commanded the squadron that rescued Bonnie Prince Charles when he fled to France after his army's rout at Culloden.

Chapter 1. Early Life and Connections, 1703–1730

1. Warren, *A History and Genealogy of the Warren Family*, 186.

2. They appeared on 7 March and 4 May 1663. See appendix to the *19th Report of the Deputy Keeper of the Public Records of Ireland*, 46, 52.

3. "An Abstract of the Title of the Late Sir Peter Warren's Estate in Ireland," ESRO, Gage papers, G/Ir/2 (68), 1, and "A List of Deeds belonging to the late Sir Peter Warren, Knight of the Bath," ESRO, Gage papers, G/Ha/37.

4. Simms, ed., "Irish Jacobite Lists from Trinity College Dublin MS, N.1.3.," 104.

5. See Aylmer, *The Aylmers of Ireland*.

6, PRO ADM33/307; for his lieutenant's commission, 8 Dec. 1719. ADM6/12, 184; Aldridge, "Admiral Sir John Norris," 173–83. Norris himself may have been Irish-born. Aldridge appears to have added nothing new in his chapter on Norris in Le Fevre and Harding, eds., *Precursors of Nelson*, 129–50.

7. For further references to Oliver's naval career see PRO ADM6/12, 184; PRO ADM25/81, 28, 33.

8. ESRO, Gage papers, G/Ir/2 (68), 8.

9. Warren, *A History and Genealogy of the Warren Family*, 187–88.

10. Gwyn, "William Johnson, c.1717–74," 394–95.

11. Sampson, "Peter Warren Dease, 1788–1863," 196–99.

12. ESRO, Gage papers, G/Ir/2 (68), 8.

13. See "List of Converts and Protestant Settlers in Ireland," BL. Egerton MSS, 77.

14. "Survey of Forfeited Estates in Counties Meath and Louth," BL. ADD MSS 41159, f. 112b.

15. Cogan, *The Diocese of Meath* 2:351–52.

16. Though the muster books of his first ship *Rye*, are missing, the ship's pay books show that he entered 18 April 1716, PRO ADM33/307. In 1743 Warren wrote that he had served in the navy for twenty-eight years, indicating that he had joined in 1715.

17. Aylmer, *The Aylmers of Ireland*, 168–95. Matthew, first Baron Aylmer (1650–1720), though of Roman Catholic parents, adhered early on to Protestantism and served first in the household of the second Duke of Buckingham, later for the Prince of Orange as an ensign, then became a sea officer stationed at Tangier. In 1688 he played some part in bringing the navy over to William's side. He saw action at Bantry Bay in 1689, Beachy Head in 1690, and La Hogue in 1692. In 1698 he commanded the Mediterranean fleet and was in retirement from 1702 to 1709, when the

Whigs appointed him commander in chief and admiral of the fleet, commissions he was forced to vacate when the Tories formed the government, only to be restored after the accession of George I.

18. *Rye* was a fifth rate of twenty-eight guns, increased to thirty in February 1716 and normally carried a crew of 100 but increased to 125 in April 1716.

19. Field's earlier commands had been *Jolly* in 1709, *Ormonde* in 1711, and *Ludlow Castle* in 1712.

20. NMM ADM/L/R, 369.

21. Warren's warrant is dated 5 Feb. 1718: "Mr Peter Warren, within the age [16], to be a Voluntr in the *Rose*." PRO ADM6/12, 114.

22. Rogers, *A Cruising Voyage Round the World.*

23. Details sent to Burchett, 29 April 1719, PRO ADM1/1597. The vessels were the sloops *Drake* from Rhode Island (John Draper, master), *Ulster* from New York (John Fred, master), *Eagle* from Rhode Island (Robert Browne, master), *Dove* from South Carolina (William Harris, master), and *St. Martin* from Bordeaux (Joseph Allegro, master).

24. Vernon to Burchett, 21 April 1721, PRO ADM1/2624.

25. The United Nations building now occupies the site.

26. NMM ADM/L/R, 212.

27. This comment was interposed between two of the copied letters, all of which were sent to Burchett, 28 Jan. 1720, PRO ADM1/1597.

28. Whitney to Admiralty, 6 April 1721, PRO ADM1/2650.

29. Whitney to Admiralty, 13 Oct. 1721, PRO ADM1/2650.

30. The examiners were captains Thomas Swanton, William Clevland, and Stephen Vincent, PRO ADM107/3, 112.

31. Aldridge, "Admiral Sir John Norris."

32. For monthly lists of warship deployment see NMM Sergison MSS and PRO ADM8.

33. An account of their voyage was published by Atkins, *Voyage to Guinea, Brazil and the West Indies.*

34. Admiralty to Percy, 11 July 1722, PRO ADM2/50, 541.

35. Percy to Burchett, 31 Oct. and 25 Nov. 1722, PRO ADM1/2282.

36. Lawrence, *Trade Castles and Forts of West Africa*, 41.

37. One example is Phillips, *A Journal of a Voyage Made in the Hannibal of London, 1693, 1694.*

38. The lieutenants' logs agree; the master's log has vanished for the period 28 Oct. 1722 to 10 April 1723, NMM ADM/L/G, 176.

39. *Guernsey*'s pay book, PRO ADM33/308.

40. Percy to Burchett, 4 Jan. 1723, PRO ADM1/2282.

41. See Percy's letters, PRO ADM1/2283.

42. National Library of Scotland, MS 7111, 8 Feb. 1741, Hay papers, Yester collection. There are no other manuscripts to explain why Dixon made that statement at

the time. The document is published *in extenso* in Gwyn, "An Incident on West Africa's Grain Coast, 1722."

43. For an excellent contemporary description of the West African coast see Bosman, *A New and Accurate Description of the Coast of Guinea.* See also Lawrence, *Trade Castles and Forts of West Africa.*

44. NMM ADM/L/G, 179.

45. Harris to Burchett, 2 Aug. 1722 and 20 Jan. 1723, PRO ADM1/1880; Admiralty to Harris, 13 April 1723, PRO ADM2/50, 612.

46. Admiralty to Harris, 10 Oct. 1721, PRO ADM2/50, 445.

47. Admiralty to Harris, 13 April 1723, PRO ADM2/50, 612.

48. Portland to Board of Trade, 22 March 1723. See Cundall, *Governors of Jamaica in the First Half of the Eighteenth Century,* 110.

49. Ibid., 111.

50. See Carswell, *The South Sea Bubble,* 195ff.

51. See Warren's log, NMM ADM/L/F, 14.

52. See *Falkland's* pay book, PRO ADM33/289.

53. Aylmer, *The Aylmers of Ireland.*

54. See *Griffin's* muster book, PRO ADM36/1369 and pay book, PRO ADM33/314.

55. All of Vernon's biographers have missed this point and believe he continued in command of *Grafton.* Vernon reached London on 29 June 1727. Vernon to Burchett, 4 Aug. 1727, PRO ADM1/2624.

56. Lewis, *The Navy in Transition,* 132.

57. Warren to Burchett, 24 April 1728, PRO ADM1/2650; St. Lo to Burchett, 8 and 24 June 1728, PRO ADM1/230. St. Lo died at Port Royal on 22 April 1729.

58. Warren's log, NMM ADM/L/S, 305.

59. Thompson, "George Anson in the Province of South Carolina," 279–80.

60. Warren carried Anson's letter to Burchett, dated 1 Jan. 1729, and Arnold's of 10 Jan. 1729, PRO ADM1/1438.

61. Warren to Burchett, 14 Feb. 1729, PRO ADM1/1438.

62. 10 June 1729, PRO ADM2/52, 407.

63. Ibid.

64. 5 Sept. 1729, PRO ADM2/52, 500.

65. 11 Dec. 1729, PRO ADM2/52, 520.

66. Baugh, *British Naval Administration in the Age of Walpole,* 93–146.

Chapter 2. North America: First Taste of War, 1730–1740

1. ESRO, Gage papers, G/Ir/2 (68), 8.

2. Details from Warren's log, NMM ADM/L/S, 303.

3. Warren to Burchett, 27 June 1730, PRO ADM1/2651.

4. 11 Feb. 1731, *Minutes of the Common Council of the City of New York 1675–1776* 4:44. The same day Stephen DeLancey's eldest son, James, received the same honor, along with James Alexander, William Jamison, William Smith, and John

Avery. The Museum of the City of New York has DeLancey's original certificate. De Lancey papers, 40.190.10.

5. The contract was completed on 20 July 1731, a copy of which is in NYHS, John E. Stillwell collection.

6. Warren to Burchett, 17 May 1732, PRO ADM1/2651.

7. The number of seamen voted annually by Parliament from 1715 to 1762, as well as the funds voted for other naval expenses, is in Clowes, *The Royal Navy: a History from the Earliest Times to the Present* 3:5.

8. Warren's log. NMM ADM/L/S, 404. Tyrrell's log is found in ADM/L/S, 198.

9. Katz, *Newcastle's New York,* chapters 4–5.

10. Fox, *Land Speculation in the Mohawk Country,* 47.

11. *The Letters and Papers of Cadwallader Colden* 2:152.

12. Susannah Warren called Mrs. Boydell her "best friend at Boston" in a letter to Mrs. Boydell, 18 Feb. 1740. MHS, Misc. Bound Collection. See Warren's letter to John Payne of Boston on Boydell's death, 8 Sept. 1740. MHS, Misc. Bound Collection.

13. Norris to Warren, 24 Feb. 1737, PRO ADM1/2216.

14. For details, see Warren's log, NMM ADM/L/S, 404 and that of Lieutenant Bladwell in ADM/L/S, 198.

15. The account book, begun in 1731 and concluded 29 March 1737, with the remark "I don't owe a farthing in this place." ESRO, Gage papers, G/Am/12.

16. Warren to Burchett, 27 March 1737, PRO ADM1/2652. Warren communicated Norris's orders to the governor and council of Massachusetts and left his station with their approval.

17. New York State Archives, Land papers, XII, 79; *Calendar of New York Manuscripts: Endorsed Land Papers in the Office of the Secretary of State of New York,* 168–69.

18. Fairchild, *Messrs. William Pepperrell,* passim.

19. George was born on 4 June 1739 and the salute fired on 29 August 1739.

20. Flemming, *The Canso Islands: An 18th Century Fishing Station.*

21. In 1715, they forced Cyprian Southack to abandon his two houses at Port Roseway, while Cape Sable Mi'kmaq seized twenty-seven fishing vessels, released only after negotiations with Massachusetts officials. Dickason, "La guerre navale: des Micmacs contre les Britanniques, 1713–1763," 233–48.

22, PRO CO217/2, f. 250; Massachusetts Council Minutes, 18 Oct. and 3 Nov. 1718, PRO CO5/792, f. 221–22, 225–26. Though called a pirate, Capt. Thomas Smart was acquitted of all wrongdoing in 1722. Browne, "Thomas Smart, d. 1722," 601–10.

23, PRO ADM1/1598; PRO ADM1/2453; Admiralty minutes, 9 March 1723, PRO ADM3/35.

24. Gwyn, "The Royal Navy in North America, 1712–1776," 129–47.

25. For 1721, 1723–26, 1730: PRO CO217/4, f. 44, 278, 294, 299v–301v; CO217/5, f. 6, 231v–32v; CO221/28, f. 13–4. There were only fifty ships listed at Canso in 1739, all from New England. CO217/6, f. 340–45, when Capt. Peter Warren de-

scribed the "English fishery at Canso is much decayed . . . within these ten years past." Gwyn, ed., *The Warren Papers, 1736–1752*, 12.

26. Durell in *Seahorse* first called at Canso in 1721 on his passage to Boston, PRO ADM1/1694–5.

27. Warren to Burchett, 9 July 1739, PRO ADM1/2652. There is also a copy in the Library of Congress, Vernon-Wager papers.

28. William Johnson to Warren, 10 May 1739. See Warren to Johnson, 20 Nov. 1738; Hamilton, ed., *The Papers of Sir William Johnson* 13:1–3.

29. Warren's log, NMM ADM/L/S, 404.

30. George Townshend to Burchett, 15 Aug. 1739, PRO ADM1/2578.

31. Warren to Burchett, 10 Aug. 1739, PRO ADM1/2652.

32. Wood, *Black Majority: Negroes in Colonial South Carolina from 1670 through the Stono Rebellion*.

33. Warren to Bull, 12 and 14 Sept. 1739; Bull to Warren, 13 and 15 Sept. 1739, PRO ADM1/2652.

34. A copy of the council of war has not been located.

35. Oglethorpe to Georgia Trustees, 1 Feb. 1740, PRO CO5/640, f. 453; Capt. Charles Fanshawe to Burchett, 6 Dec. 1739, PRO ADM1/1780.

36. PRO CO5/654, f. 225, 229–30.

37. Oglethorpe to Georgia Trustees, 16 Nov. 1739, received 10 March 1740, PRO CO5/640, f. 415–6.

38. Enclosures in Pearse's letter to Burchett, 20 Feb. 1740, PRO ADM1/2284. For the South Carolina contribution to the expedition, see Killpatrick, *An Impartial Account of the Late Expedition against St. Augustine under General Oglethorpe*, and Lanning, *The St. Augustine Expedition of 1740*.

39. Pearse to Burchett, 14 April 1740, PRO ADM1/2284.

40. George Smith, perhaps a native New Englander, who had joined the ship in Boston only on 10 April 1739. See *Squirrel*'s pay book, NMM ADM/L/S, 404.

41. Pearse to Burchett, 6 May 1740, PRO ADM1/2284; Warren's log, PRO ADM/L/S, 404.

42. *Flamborough*'s log, sent to Burchett at the end of the siege, PRO ADM1/2284. The document recording the council's full statement has not survived. Warren was not in attendance.

43. See Capt. John McIntosh's letters to his kinsman, Alexander McIntosh of Lothbury, 1 May and 20 June 1741, PRO CO5/654, f. 347.

44. *Flamborough* 's log, PRO ADM1/2284.

45. Council of war, 24 June 1740, signed by Pearse, Peyton, Warren, Laws, Townshend, and Dandridge, PRO ADM1/2284.

46. Pearse to Oglethorpe, 26 June 1740, PRO ADM1/2284.

47. The council was attended by Pearse, Warren, Laws, Fanshawe, Townshend, and Dandridge, 3 July 1740, PRO ADM1/2284.

48. Oglethorpe to Pearse, 5 July 1740, PRO ADM1/2284.

49. Oglethorpe to Newcastle, 19 July 1740, PRO CO5/654, f. 397–98; received 31 Oct. 1740.

50. Information from a merchant, a prisoner of the Spanish, reached Oglethorpe in January 1741, PRO CO5/654, f. 318–19.

51. Vandussen to Pearse, 8 June 1740, PRO ADM1/2284.

52. Pearse to Burchett, 28 July 1740, PRO ADM1/2284; received 31 Oct. 1740.

53. Warren to Burchett, 28 Aug. 1740, PRO ADM1/2652.

54. Warren to Messrs. Baker, 5 March 1741, ESRO, Gage papers, G/Am/21.

Chapter 3. War 1740–1744: The West Indies and New York

1. *Astrea,* captured at Portobelo, was fitted out as a mastship capable of carrying masts for warships of seventy guns. The New England timber supply to Jamaica is considered in Crewe, *Yellow Jack and the Worm,* 263–83.

2. Vernon to Warren, Feb. 1740; Ranft, *Vernon Papers,* 68; Warren to Burchett, 28 Aug. 1740, PRO ADM1/2652. On a second trip to New England, *Astrea* caught fire and was destroyed at Piscataqua, Swanton to Ogle, 20 June 1743, PRO ADM1/233.

3. 10 May 1711, PRO ADM106/2889.

4. Vernon to Sir Charles Wager, 18–31 Jan. 1740; Ranft, *Vernon Papers,* 60; Malone, *Pine Trees and Politics,* 48.

5. Ranft, *Vernon Papers,* 10. See also Wilson, "Empire, Trade, and Popular Politics in Mid-Hanoverian Britain: The Case of Admiral Vernon," 74–109.

6. This analysis follows Harding, *Amphibious Warfare in the Eighteenth Century.*

7. 30 April–1 May, 1741, NMM ADM/L/S, 404; see Michael Tyrrell to William Johnson, 28 May 1741; Hamilton, ed., *The Papers of Sir William Johnson* 1:10–14.

8. Vernon to Warren, 30 Jan. 1741; Ranft, *Vernon Papers,* 169–70.

9. Ranft, *Vernon Papers,* 180.

10. Hartmann, *The Angry Admiral: The Later Career of Edward Vernon, Admiral of the White,* 64. See also Harding, *Amphibious Warfare in the Eighteenth Century.*

11. William Johnson to Susannah Warren, 11 May 1741; Hamilton, ed., *The Papers of Sir William Johnson* 13:5–6. The original draft is in the Gratz collection, Historical Society of Pennsylvania.

12. See "List of Bonds and Security's belonging to the Estates of Lady Warren & Sir Peter Warren," prepared by Oliver DeLancey, 10 April 1772, ESRO, Gage papers, G/Am/134.

13. Benjamin Colman to William Pepperrell, 21 Sept. 1745. MHS, Belknap papers, 61.B.

14. Warren to Corbett, 8 Jan. 1742, PRO ADM1/2653.

15. Warren to Corbett, 1 Dec. 1741, PRO ADM1/2653.

16. Prepared on 19 March 1741 and sent the next day, PRO ADM1/2653.

17. These orders are fully reproduced in Richmond, *Navy in the War of 1739–1848* 3:276–78.

18. Warren to Corbett, 20 May 1742 (with details of each prize), PRO ADM1/2653.

19. Warren to Corbett, 26 April 1742, PRO ADM1/2653.

20. Warren to Corbett, 21 June 1742, PRO ADM1/2653.

21. Elizabeth DeLancey (née Colden) to her mother, 9 Sept. 1742, Museum of the City of New York, DeLancey papers, doc. 49.48.73.

22. On 4 August, Warren had written to Corbett to remind him of his earlier memorandum and if it was to be adopted, that he would have to make haste, as the season advanced rapidly. PRO ADM1/2653.

23. Warren to Clinton, 22 Aug. 1742, WLCL, Clinton papers, box 1.

24. Clinton to Warren, 9 April 1743, WLCL, George Clinton papers, box 1.

25. Clinton to Newcastle, 18 Nov. 1743; Katz, *Newcastle's New York*, 167.

26. The board of trade made its decision on 27 Jan. 1744, WLCL, George Clinton papers, box 1. Reference to the mandamus is in O'Callaghan, ed., *Documents Relative to the Colonial History of the State of New York* 6:165.

27. His only surviving son, Sir Henry Clinton, commanded the British army against rebel America from 1778 to 1782.

28. Baugh, *British Naval Administration in the Age of Walpole*, 120.

29. Fisher, "The Expeditionary Force Designed for the West Indies in 1740."

30. Katz, *Newcastle's New York*, 34, and Henretta, "*Salutary Neglect.*"

31. Warren to Clinton, 26 Oct. 1742, WLCL, George Clinton papers, box 1.

32. Warren to Corbett, 2 Nov. 1742, PRO ADM1/2653.

33. Capt. Edward Hawke, whom Warren met at Barbados, carried two of Warren's dispatches to London, those of 1 and 2 Dec. 1743, PRO ADM1/2653. It was perhaps their first meeting since Hawke served on *Leopard* as third lieutenant for a month in December 1729.

34. Richmond, *Navy in the War of 1739–1748* 1:249–50.

35. Warren to Corbett, 6 Feb. 1743, public letter, PRO ADM1/2653.

36. Warren to Corbett, 6 Feb. 1743, private letter, PRO ADM1/2653.

37. His appointment was dated 4 Oct. 1743, PRO ADM1/480, 3.

38. Warren's log, NMM ADM/L/L, 46.

39. *Loo,* under Capt. Ashley Litting, went ashore on the Florida coast and became a total loss. May, "The Wreck of the *Loo*," 139–42.

40. Katz, *Newcastle's New York*, 167.

41. Warren already had three children. I have not yet been able to discover when his son Peter was born. It could have been anytime from 1739 onwards. This next child, Susannah, was born on 28 March 1744. ESRO, Gage papers, G/Ir/2 (68), 43.

42. Baugh, *British Naval Administration in the Age of Walpole*, 352. For his sketch of the development of English Harbour, see 352–55. See also *Romance of English Harbour* and Crewe, *Yellow Jack and the Worm*, 232–37.

43. MacKay, *Admiral Hawke*, 18; Lisle to Corbett, 24 Oct. 1742, PRO ADM1/2041; Warren to Corbett, 18 Dec. 1742, PRO ADM1/2653.

44. Warren to Corbett, 9 April 1744, PRO ADM1/2654.

45. Warren to Corbett, 17 April 1744, PRO ADM1/2654.

46. Warren to Corbett, 22 April 1744, received 18 June 1744, PRO ADM1/2654.

47. Warren to Mathew, 20 April 1744, PRO ADM1/2654.

48. Warren to Mathew, 5 and 8 May 1744; Mathew to Warren, 7 May 1744, PRO ADM1/2654.

49. NMM ADM/L/L, 46.

50. Ibid.

51. Warren to Corbett, at sea, 5 June 1744, PRO ADM1/2654.

52. Lydon, "The Great Capture of 1744," 257.

53. Prize money was distributed to the crew on 13 and 22 Sept. 1744. NMM ADM/L/L, 46.

54. Susannah Warren to William Johnson, 21 April 1744. Hamilton, ed., *The Papers of Sir William Johnson* 1:21–22.

55. Warren to Pepperrell, 12 July 1751. Maine Historical Society, Fogg collection; reproduced with errors in Parsons, *Life of Sir William Pepperrell,* 237–38, 246.

56. Warren to Clinton, 6 July 1744, WLCL, George Clinton papers, box 1; Clinton to Admiralty Board, 8 July 1744, WLCL, George Clinton papers, box 1; Corbett to Clinton, 2 Jan. 1745, WLCL, George Clinton papers, box 2; Newcastle to Clinton, 3 Jan. 1744/5, WLCL, George Clinton papers, box 1.

57. Warren to Clinton, 6 July 1744, WLCL, George Clinton papers, box 1.

58. Clinton addressed the assembly on 18 July 1744 and again on 12 March 1745 on the same subject. Lincoln, ed., *State of New York Messages from the Governors* 1:320–21, 332–33.

59. Rawlyk, *Yankees at Louisbourg.*

60. Warren to Corbett, 6 Feb. 1743, private letter, PRO ADM1/2653.

61. This letter, not located, may have been written in the summer of 1743, as all Warren's official and private letters to Corbett from Feb. 1743 to April 1744 are missing.

62. PRO ADM1/2653.

63. Warren to Corbett, 8 Sept. 1744, PRO ADM1/2654.

64. Warren to Clinton, 27 Sept. and 26 Oct. 1744, WLCL, George Clinton papers, box 1; Warren to Corbett, 27 Sept. and 5 Oct. 1744, PRO ADM1/2654.

65. Warren's letter to Shirley and the governor's reply have not survived. Shirley's feelings were later expressed in a letter to Henry Pelham, 27 Sept. 1745, The Huntington Library and Art Collections, HM9707.

66. Warren's other personal success that month took place on 28 December, when *Lièvre,* (Nicholas Goquit, master) a Martinique privateer with a crew of 106, ten carriage guns, and sixteen swivel, was taken. Warren to Corbett, 4 and 13 Dec. 1744 and 30 Dec. 1744, PRO ADM1/2654.

67. Warren to Corbett, 22 Dec. 1744, PRO ADM1/2654.

68. Warren to Corbett, 4 and 13 Dec. 1744, PRO ADM1/2654.

69. Warren to Heyliger, 28 Jan. 1744/5, PRO ADM1/2654.

70. Pieter to Warren, 13 Feb. 1745, PRO ADM1/2654.

71. Warren himself, shortly afterwards, had to purchase eighty bushels of powder from Curaçao, 7 Feb. 1745, PRO ADM1/2654.

72. Warren to Corbett, 9 and 25 Feb. 1745, PRO ADM1/2654.

73. Warren to Corbett, 7 Feb. 1745, PRO ADM1/2654.

74. Warren to Corbett, 9 and 25 Feb. 1745, PRO ADM1/2654.

75. May, "The Wreck of the *Weymouth*," 207–15.

76. Warren to Corbett, 9 and 25 Feb. 1745, PRO ADM1/2654.

77. "When or where ever I have it in my power, he shall not want my friendship nor favour." Warren to Corbett, 9 and 27 Feb. 1745, PRO ADM1/2654.

78. Calmady joined the navy as a volunteer in 1726; he had been promoted lieutenant only in 1739 and captain, by Knowles, in 1743.

79. The consultation took place on 23 Feb. 1745, PRO ADM1/2654.

80. Warren to Corbett, 9 and 23 Feb. 1745, PRO ADM1/2654.

81. Reference to the commission is in PRO ADM1/480, 3; Corbett to Warren, 4 Jan. 1745, ADM2/486. See also ADM2/63, 55; Newcastle to Clinton, 3 Jan. 1745, WLCL, George Clinton papers, box 2, and Lincoln, ed., *Correspondence of William Shirley* 1:155–56.

82. Warren to Knowles, 8 March 1745, PRO ADM1/2007.

83. Warren's response to them, 11 March 1745, PRO ADM1/2007.

84. Knowles to Mathew, 8 March 1745, PRO ADM1/2007. Antigua council to Warren, 10 March 1745. ADM1/2007. See the complaints addressed to the king by the councils of Montserrat, St. Christopher's, and Antigua, PRO ADM1/4114.

85. Knowles to Warren, 8 March 1745, PRO ADM1/2007; Knowles to Warren, 9 March 1745. ADM1/2007.

86. Warren to Knowles, 8 March 1745 [second letter], PRO ADM1/2007. Warren to Knowles, 9 March 1745. ADM1/2007. "I find there is no end of this disagreeable subject; 'tis the first of the kind I have ever entered into, and hope it will be the last."

87. Warren to Corbett, 10 March 1745, PRO ADM1/2654; for his letter of complaint see Knowles to Corbett, 20 March 1745, PRO ADM1/2207.

88. Warren to Corbett, 6 Feb. 1743, public letter, PRO ADM1/2653.

89. Warren to Corbett, 9 April 1744, PRO ADM1/2654.

90. Warren to Corbett, 22 April 1744, PRO ADM1/2654.

91. Warren to Corbett, 24 May 1744, PRO ADM1/2654.

92. Warren to Corbett, 9 and 25 Feb. 1745, PRO ADM1/26554.

93. Warren to Corbett, 10 March 1745, PRO ADM1/2654.

94. PRO ADM1/2654.

Chapter 4. The Siege of Louisbourg, 1745

1. Warren to Anson, 2 April 1745, BL, ADD MSS 15957. Anson papers, 147. See also Warren to Corbett, 8 Sept. 1744 and 10 March 1744/5, PRO ADM1/2654.

2. Rawlyk, *Yankees at Louisbourg*, 33.

3. Rawlyk, *Yankees at Louisbourg*, 35.

4. Ibid.

5. Shirley to Newcastle, 15 Jan. 1745; Lincoln, ed., *Correspondence of William Shirley* 1:163.

6. Rawlyk, *Yankees at Louisbourg,* 174n. 30.

7. Elizabeth DeLancey to her father, Cadwallader Colden, 13 April 1745, New York State Archives, DePeyster papers, folder 12, item 16. On 22 April *Boston Evening News* reported that she had arrived the Thursday before.

8. Fairchild, "Sir William Pepperrell, 1696–1759," 505–9 and his *Messrs. William Pepperrell.*

9. Shirley to Pepperrell, 10 April 1745, MHS, Belknap papers, 1744–45.

10. Shirley to Pepperrell, 22 April 1745, MHS, Belknap papers, 1744–45.

11. *Molineux* (12–12 swivel), 150 men under Capt. Joseph Snelling, hired by the Massachusetts government; *Caesar* (14), 80 men under Capt. John Griffith was a Rhode Island brigantine; *Shirley* (24), 180 men under Capt. John Rous, hired by the Massachusetts government; *Prince of Orange* (14), 80 men under Capt. Joseph Smedhurst, owned by the Massachusetts government; *Boston Packet* (12–2), 100 men under Capt. William Fletcher was a brigantine, also owned by the Massachusetts government; *Massachusetts* (20–2), 150 men under Capt. Edward Tyng, hired by the Massachusetts government; *Fame* (20–4), 150 men under Capt. Thomas Thompson, hired by the Massachusetts government; *Tartar* (12–12), 95 men under Capt. Daniel Fones, a 115–ton Connecticut cruiser; *Defence,* under Capt. John Prentice was the Connecticut guard sloop; *Bonetta,* under Captain Beckett; *Lucetania,* under Capt. Joseph Giddings.

12. There are several good accounts of the 1745 siege: Gwyn and Moore, eds., *La Chute de Louisbourg,* 15–51; Douglas, "Nova Scotia and the Royal Navy, 1713–1766," chapter 3; Rawlyk, *Yankees at Louisbourg,* chapters 7–11; McLennan, *Louisbourg from Its Foundation to Its Fall,* 147–80; Gow, *Cape Breton Illustrated,* chapters 6–8.

13. Some 762 in Louisbourg itself and 138 in the Island battery, AN, Fonds des colonies, F3, vol. 50, 407.

14. Maurepas to St.-Ovide, le 10 mai 1735, AN, Fonds des colonies, B63, 561–62.

15. Adams, "Jean-Baptiste-Louis Le Prévost Duquesnel, d. 1744," 392–93.

16. *Capitulation de Canso, le 24 mai 1745* in *Collection de manuscrits* 3:201–2.

17. Especially successful among the New England privateers were Edward Tyng and John Rous. See Douglas, "John Rous, d. 1760," 572–73.

18. Greer, "Mutiny at Louisbourg, December 1744," 305–36.

19. *Collection de manuscrits,* 3:237.

20. Duchambon and Bigot to Maurepas, le 20 novembre 1744, AN, Fonds des colonies, C11B, 26:40–43.

21. Warren to Pepperrell, 23 April 1745, NYHS, Misc. MSS Louisbourg.

22. Warren to Pepperrell, 23 April 1745, MHS, Pepperrell papers, 71.A.

23. Warren to Pepperrell, 25 April 1745, NYHS, Misc. MSS Louisbourg.

24. NYHS, Misc. MSS Louisbourg.

25. Warren to Pepperrell, 1 May 1745, MHS, Belknap papers, 61.B.

26. Warren to Pepperrell, 4 May 1745, MHS, Belknap papers, 61.B.

27. 29 April 1745, MHS, Belknap papers, 1744–45.

28. Warren to Pepperrell, 27 April 1745, MHS, Pepperrell papers, 71.A.

29. Crowley and Pothier, "Louis DuPont Duchambon, 1679–1775," 246–49.

30. Gwyn and Moore, *La Chute de Louisbourg,* 66.

31. Duchambon stated sixty men formed the party. *Collection de manuscrits* 3:237–57, put the figure at 240; Duchambon to Maurepas, le 2 septembre 1745, AN, Fonds des colonies, F3, 50:368–82; Bigot claimed only forty. Bigot, "Relation du siège de Louisbourg et de sa capitulation, le 19 août 1745," mémoire 218; Lacroix-Girard states forty-five. Gwyn and Moore, *La Chute de Louisbourg,* 67.

32. Duchambon's figures. *Collection de manuscrits* 3:240; while Lacroix-Girard states only fifty. Gwyn and Moore, *La Chute de Louisbourg,* 69.

33. Chassin de Thierry [commander at the Grand battery] to Duchambon, le 11 mai 1745; Duchambon to Chassin de Thierry, same date, AN, Fonds des colonies, F3, 50:300–303; Pothier, "François-Nicolas de Chassin de Thierry, d. 1755," 115–16. Wrong, ed., *Louisbourg in 1745,* 38–39; Gwyn and Moore, *La Chute de Louisbourg,* 71–72.

34. Warren to Pepperrell, 2 May 1745, NYHS, Misc. MSS Louisbourg.

35. Pepperrell to Warren, 4 May 1745, MHS, Pepperrell papers, 71.A.

36. Warren to Pepperrell, 4 May 1745, NYHS, Misc. MSS Louisbourg. Signed also by Durell, Calmady, Douglass, Tiddeman, and the New Englander, Edward Tyng.

37. NYHS, Misc. MSS Louisbourg.

38. Warren and Pepperrell to Duchambon, 6 May 1745, *Collection de manuscrits* 3:220; Duchambon to Warren and Pepperrell, le 18 mai 1745, *Collection de manuscripts* 3:221.

39. For an account of Warren's alleged behavior on the evening of 9 May, see DeForest, ed., *Louisbourg Journals 1745,* 15. The decision of the council is in MHS, *Collections,* sixth series, 10:17.

40. The New Englanders lost seven men killed and thirty wounded. Pepperrell to Warren, 31 May 1745, Connecticut Historical Society *Collections* 9:301. The French admitted to ten or twelve killed and twenty wounded or taken prisoner. Duchambon to Maurepas, le 2 septembre 1745, *Collection de manuscrits* 3:248; Bigot to Maurepas, 1 août 1745, AN, Fonds des colonies, F3, 50:377v.

41. Warren to Pepperrell, 13 May 1745, MHS, Belknap papers, 61.B.

42. Warren to Pepperrell, 16 May 1745, MHS, Belknap papers, 61.B.

43. Warren to Pepperrell, 16 May 1745, MHS, Belknap papers, 1744–45. If the plan was adopted and carried to execution after *Princess Mary* and *Hector* had arrived, an additional three hundred men would have been available. Warren to Pepperrell, 17 May 1745, MHS, Belknap papers, 1744–45. When Douglass and Tyng were shown the plan, they expressed their agreement.

44. Pepperrell to Warren, 17 May 1745, MHS, Pepperrell papers, 71.A.

45. Warren to Pepperrell, 18 May 1745, NYHS, Misc. MSS Louisbourg. Warren's

orders of the same date are in MHS, Belknap papers, 61.B. Pepperrell said he was "much pleas'd" with them, to Warren, MHS, Pepperrell papers, 71.A.

46. "Probably the fastest frigate of her day." Gardiner, *The First Frigates,* 11.

47. *Renommée* was taken by *Dover* (44) in a single ship battle in 1747.

48. *Mars* (64) was taken by *Nottingham* later in 1745 and was commissioned into the British fleet. She foundered on her first entry into Halifax harbor, when her pilot drove her onto a rock, thereafter known as "Mars Rock." The pilot was put in chains by Vice Admiral Boscawen. Her captain was John Ambrose.

49. Maurepas to la Maisonfort, le 21 avril 1745, AN, Fonds des colonies, B, vol. 82, 111. The captain, once released, was never again employed at sea. Taillemite, "Alexandre de la Maisonfort du Boisdecourt, Marquis de la Maisonfort," 345–46.

50. Warren to Pepperrell, MHS, Belknap papers, 61.B.

51. This account has been reconstructed from the captains' logs of the warships involved.

52. La Maisonfort to Duchambon, 18 juin 1745; Duchambon to la Maisonfort, 19 juin 1745, *Collection de manuscrits* 3:229–31.

53. Pepperrell to Warren, 21 May 1745, MHS, Pepperrell papers, 71.A.

54. Some 40,320 lbs. of bread, 5,040 gallons of wine, 5,760 pieces each of beef and pork, 180 bushels peas, 270 bushels oatmeal, 4,320 lbs butter. Warren to Corbett, 3 June 1747, PRO ADM1/88.

55. Warren to Pepperrell, 20 May 1745, NYHS, Misc. MSS Louisbourg.

56. Shirley to Pepperrell, 5 May 1745, MHS, Belknap papers, 1744–45.

57. Douglas, "Joshua Loring, 1716–81," 486–88.

58. Warren to Pepperrell, 23 May 1745, MHS, Misc. MSS Louisbourg.

59. Warren to Pepperrell, 24 May 1745, MHS, Belknap papers, 61.B. The plan is found in NYHS, Louisbourg MSS, VI.

60. NYHS, Louisbourg MSS, VI.

61. Pepperrell to Warren, 28 May 1745, NYHS, Louisbourg MSS, V. Lacroix-Girard stated that three hundred or four hundred were killed among the attackers and ninety taken prisoner, while the French suffered but three killed and four wounded. Bigot to Maurepas, 1 août 1745, AN, Fonds des colonies. F3, 50:376; Gwyn and Moore, *La Chute de Louisbourg,* 87–88. Duchambon later reported 119 taken prisoner. *Collection de manuscrits* 3:250. Rawlyk believed that some sixty were killed or died later of their wounds. Rawlyk, *Yankees at Louisbourg,* 130.

62. There were about six hundred men searching for the two enemy parties, leaving only fifteen hundred effectives in front of the town (Rawlyk).

63. For the council's decisions see Rawlyk, *Yankees at Louisbourg,* 128–29.

64. Warren to Pepperrell, 29 May 1745, NYHS, Louisbourg MSS, VI.

65. Douglas, "Philip Durell, 1707–66," 208–10.

66. Ibid.

67. Waldo to Pepperrell, 27 May 1745, MHS, *Collections,* sixth series, 10:223–26.

68. Warren to Pepperrell, 30 May 1745, MHS, Belknap papers, 61.B.

69. Warren to Pepperrell, 31 May 1745, MHS, Belknap papers, 61.B.

70. Present at the council of war were Warren, Calmady, Cornwall, Douglass, Durell, Edwards, Montagu, and Tiddeman. NYHS, Louisbourg MSS, VI.

71. Warren to Pepperrell, 3 June 1745, MHS, Belknap papers, 61.B.

72. The resolutions of the council are in MHS, *Collections*, sixth series, 250–51; Pepperrell to Shirley, 5 June 1745, MHS, *Collections*, sixth series, 260–63.

73. Warren to Pepperrell, 1 June 1745, NYHS, Louisbourg MSS, VI.

74. Warren to la Maisonfort, 6 June 1745, NYHS, Louisbourg MSS, VI. Pepperrell read both Warren's letter and la Maisonfort's before sending Captain Macdonald into Louisbourg with them.

75. A transcript of the original is in NYHS, Louisbourg MSS, VI.

76. Warren to Pepperrell, 9 June 1745, MHS, Belknap papers, 61.B.

77. Warren to Pepperrell, 3 June 1745, MHS, Belknap papers, 61.B.

78. Pepperrell to Warren, 10 June 1745, NYHS, Louisbourg MSS, V.

79. For details of the plan, see Warren to Pepperrell, 10 and 11 June 1745; Warren's memorandum, 11 June 1745; Warren's orders to his squadron, 12 June 1745; all of which may be found in MHS, Belknap papers, 61.B.

80. Consultation of captains, 14 June 1745, PRO ADM1/2655.

81. Warren to Pepperrell, 14 June 1745, MHS, Belknap papers, 61.B.

82. DeForest, *Louisbourg Journals 1745*, 26.

83. From Dudley Bradstreet's diary, Green, ed., *Three Military Diaries Kept by Groton Soldiers in Different Wars*, 25.

84. Ibid.

85. Verrier to Duchambon, le 26 juin 1745, AN, Fonds des colonies, F3, 50:319.

86. Allard de Sainte-Marie to Duchambon, le 26 juin 1745, AN, Fonds des colonies, F3, 50:319v–20.

87. Bigot, "Relation du siège de Louisbourg, le 19 août 1745," mémoire, 218.

88. Duchambon to Warren and Pepperrell, le 26 juin 1745, *Collection de manuscrits*, 234.

89. Duchambon to Warren and Pepperrell, le 27 juin 1745, AN, Fonds des colonies, F3, 50:328–32v.

90. Bastide to Warren, 4 June 1745, MHS, *Collections*, sixth series 10:256.

91. *Collection de manuscrits* 3:224–25.

92. *Collection de manuscrits* 3:22. For the final terms see Lincoln, ed., *Correspondence of William Shirley*, 1:239n–241n.

93. Pepperrell to Duchambon, 17 June 1745. "Letters Relating to the Expedition to Cape Breton," in MHS *Collections*, first series, 1:46.

94. Pepperrell to Duchambon, 17 June 1745, *Collection de manuscrits* 3:226.

95. Warren to Pepperrell, 17 June 1745, MHS, Pepperrell papers, 71.A.

96. Warren to Pepperrell, 16 June 1745, MHS, Pepperrell papers, 71.A.

97. Warren to Duchambon, *Collection de manuscrits* 3:223.

98. Warren to Pepperrell, 20 June 1745, MHS, Belknap papers, 61.B.

99. "Directions for an Alarm," partly in Warren's hand, undated. MHS, Belknap papers, 1744–45.

100. Warren to Corbett, 22 June 1745, PRO ADM1/2655.

101. Warren to all governors, 24 June 1745. Copy in PRO ADM1/2655.

102. Warren to Pepperrell, 26 June 1745, MHS, Belknap papers, 61.B.

103. Warren to Pepperrell, 27 June 1745, MHS, Belknap papers, 61.B.

104. Warren and Pepperrell to Newcastle, 18 June 1745, MHS, *Collections*, first series, 1:48–49.

105. Warren to Pepperrell, 20 June 1745, MHS, Belknap papers, 61.B.

106. Warren to Corbett, 18 June 1745, PRO ADM1/2655.

107. Warren and Pepperrell to Newcastle, 18 June 1745, MHS, Belknap papers, 61.C.

Chapter 5. Cape Breton and the Conquest of Canada, 1745–1746

1. Rev. Benjamin Colman to Warren, 17 Aug. 1747, Boston Public Library, Chamberlain collection, Ch.A.2.83.

2. Not until 19 Sept. 1745 was *Launceston* freed to return to England, carrying almost three hundred released English seamen. Warren to Corbett, 4 July 1745, PRO ADM1/2655. See also Capt. Robert Mann's log, NMM ADM/L/L, 45.

3. This summary is drawn from the Louisbourg fuel accounts, 1745–46, WLCL, Warren papers, vol. 2. The total fuel bill that winter was £3,702 13s., of which £1,086 9s. was for coal at thirty shillings a chauldron. Hard or green wood cost twenty shillings a cord and dry wood ten shillings. John Bradstreet was the principal supplier, earning £1,393 16s. See also Warren and Pepperrell to Waldo, 19 Dec. 1745, MHS, Pepperrell papers, 71.A.

4. Warren to Pepperrell, 16 July 1745, MHS, *Collections*, sixth series, 10:327–29.

5. Pepperrell to Warren, 18 July 1745, MHS, *Collections*, sixth series, 10:333–35.

6. This summary is drawn from Warren's voucher books. WLCL, Warren papers, I–II; Bastide to Warren, 28 June 1745, PRO ADM1/2655; Bastide to Warren and Pepperrell, 22 July 1745, MHS, Pepperrell papers, 71.A.

7. Clinton to Warren, 24 and 29 June 1745, and Warren to Clinton, 1 Aug. 1745, WLCL, George Clinton papers, II.

8. Some 250 tons with 100,200 pieces of eight on board. Warren commissioned her as fireship *Louisbourg*. NMM ADM/L/L, 45.

9. Her cargo included 111,348 lbs. of pepper.

10. Warren to Corbett, 25 July 1745, PRO ADM1/2655.

11. Some 500 tons and 118 men, with a cargo of 250,847 lbs of pepper.

12. Warren to Corbett, 1 Aug. 1745, PRO ADM1/5655.

13. Also known as cinchona bark, containing quinine and used as a febrifuge. She had on board 972,000 pieces of eight, 13,278 gold double doubloons, 291.5 lbs. of virgin silver, 65.5 lbs. in gold bars. Warren to Corbett, 8 Aug. 1745, PRO ADM1/5655.

14. William Waldron to Richard Waldron, 24–26 July 1745, WLCL, Louisbourg Manuscripts.

15. Warren to Corbett, 8 Aug. 1745, PRO ADM1/2655.

16. Warren to Anson, 2 April 1745, a second letter, Anson papers, BL, ADD MSS 15957, f. 152–54.

17. Ibid.

18. Warren to Clinton, 28 Aug. 1745, WLCL, George Clinton papers, II.

19. Harrington to Bedford, 14/15 Aug. 1745, Bedford Manuscript Letters, 10:39.

20. See Sosin, "Louisbourg and the Peace of Aix-la-Chapelle, 1748," 518–22.

21. Pitt to Bedford, 2 Aug. 1745, Bedford Manuscript Letters, 10:33.

22. Pitt to Pelham, 17 Aug. 1745, Department of Manuscripts, University of Nottingham, Newcastle MSS, 447.

23. Chesterfield to Robert Trevor, 13 Aug. 1745, Buckinghamshire Record Office, Trevor MSS, D/MH/50.

24. Samuel and William Baker to Warren, 1 Aug. 1745, WLCL, Warren papers, I.

25. 9 Aug. 1745. Warren was the last of four flags made in 1745; Lord Vere Beauclerk, after twenty-four years as a post captain, and his old companion, Perry Mayne, after twenty years, had received their flags in April; John Byng was made a rear admiral eighteen years to the day after his commission as post captain on 8 August.

26. Warren to Bedford, 4 Oct. 1745, Bedford Manuscript Letters, 10:94.

27. Shirley to Pelham, 27 Sept. 1745, The Huntington Library and Art Collections, HM9707.

28. Warren to Corbett, 25 July 1745, PRO ADM1/2655.

29. Warren to Corbett, 23 Nov. 1745, PRO ADM1/2655.

30. Warren to Corbett, 18 Jan. 1745/6, PRO ADM1/480.

31. Warren to Corbett, 23 Nov. 1745, PRO ADM1/2655.

32. "At a Consultation held on board his Majesty's Ship *Superbe,*" 30 Sept. 1745, PRO ADM1/2655.

33. Graham, ed., *The Walker Expedition to Quebec, 1711.*

34. Warren to Corbett, 18 June 1745, PRO ADM1/2655.

35. Knowles to Newcastle, 9 July 1746, PRO CO5/44, f. 136–46.

36. Warren to Knowles, 2 June 1746, PRO CO5/44, f. 33–37; Warren to Corbett, 2 June 1746, PRO ADM1/480; Warren to Newcastle, 3 Oct. 1745, PRO CO5/44, f. 95–7.

37. Admiralty to NB, 2 Nov. 1745, PRO ADM2/208, 39.

38. Corbett to Warren, 9 Aug. 1745, PRO ADM2/490, 4–10.

39. Warren to Corbett, 3 Oct. 1745, PRO ADM1/480.

40. Shirley to Board of Trade, 10 July 1745; Lincoln, ed., *Correspondence of William Shirley* 1:246; Armytage, *The Free Port System in the West Indies.*

41. Warren, Clarke, and Bollan to Newcastle, 17 Jan. 1747, Sandwich Papers.

42. Warren to Newcastle, 23 Nov. 1745, PRO CO5/44, f. 105–14; Warren to Corbett, 23 Oct. 1745, PRO ADM1/480.

43. Warren to Corbett, 18 Jan. 1746, PRO ADM1/480.

44. This advice the Admiralty followed, for when Messrs. Baker received the contract to victual and pay the garrison they employed Warren's brother-in-law,

Oliver DeLancey, and his partner John Watts of New York, as well as the New England partners Thomas Hancock and Charles Apthorp.

45. Bedford to Warren, 30 Oct. 1745, Bedford Manuscript Letters 10:118.

46. Sandwich to Bedford, 4 March 1746, Bedford Manuscript Letters 11:27.

47. Signed by Warren, undated, probably mid-May, Maine Historical Society, Fogg Autograph collection.

48. From various account books in the WLCL, Warren papers, II.

49. Corbett to Warren, 14 March 1746, PRO ADM2/496.

50. There were two meetings of the council on 6 June. A third took place the following day after Warren had departed for Boston. Those attending included Townsend, Warren, Pepperrell, Knowles, Colonel Warburton as lieutenant governor, Lieutenant Colonel Hopson, Horseman, and Ellison, PRO ADM1/480.

51. Warren to Corbett, 6 June 1746, PRO ADM1/480.

52. Warren to Norris, 7 June 1746, ESRO, Gage Papers, G/Am/6.

53. Owen, *The Rise of the Pelhams*. Chapter 7 provides a detailed analysis of English politics between 1744 and 1746.

54. Sandwich to Bedford, 4 March 1746, Bedford Manuscript Letters 11:27.

55. Bedford to Newcastle, 24 March 1746, PRO CO42/13, f. 108–19.

56. Bedford, General Wade, and General St. Clair to Newcastle, 30 March 1746, Bedford Manuscript Letters 11:27.

57. An earlier detailed account of the political background and implications in England of the Canada expedition was based only on published sources and transcripts of English manuscripts available in the United States at the time. Buffinton, "The Canada Expedition of 1746. Its Relation to British Politics," 552–80.

58. Warren's orders from Newcastle were dated 7 April 1746; those from Corbett, 9 April 1746, PRO SP42/30.

59. By then he had raised 770 men for his own regiment (400 in Massachusetts, 150 each in Pennsylvania and at Louisbourg, 70 in New York and New Jersey). Pepperrell had raised 370 (300 at Louisbourg, 50 in Connecticut, 20 in New York and New Jersey). Shirley to Pelham, 15 May 1746, The Huntington Library and Art Collections, HM9709.

60. Warren to Corbett, 6 June 1746, PRO ADM1/480.

61. Warren and Shirley to Benning Wentworth, governor of New Hampshire, 25 Aug. 1746, MHS, Belknap papers, 61.C.

62. Warren to Townsend, 8 Aug. 1746, PRO ADM1/480.

63. Warren and Shirley to Wentworth, 25 Aug. 1746, MHS, Belknap papers, 61.C.

64. Warren to Clinton, 8 Sept. 1745, Clinton to Warren, 4 Oct. 1746, WLCL, George Clinton papers, IV.

65. Anson to Bedford, 24 Aug. 1746, Bedford Manuscript Letters 13:29.

66. Pritchard, *Anatomy of a Naval Disaster*. I follow Pritchard in the spelling of d'Enville's name, hitherto d'Anville.

67. Taillemite, "Constantin-Louis d'Estourmel, 1691–1765," 213–14.

68. Taillemite, "Jacques-Pierre de Taffanel de la Jonquière. Marquis de la Jonquière, 1685–1752," 609–12.

69. Townsend to Warren, 6 July 1746, PRO ADM1/480.

70. Warren and Shirley to Townsend, 8 July 1746, PRO ADM1/480.

71. Moody, "A Just and Disinterested Man: The Nova Scotia Career of Paul Mascarene, 1710–1752"; Sutherland, "Paul Mascarene, c. 1684–1760," 435–40.

72. Shirley and Warren to Townsend, 3 Sept. 1746, PRO ADM1/480.

73. Townsend and Knowles to Warren and Shirley, 11 Sept. 1746, PRO ADM1/480.

74. Warren and Shirley to Townsend, 12 Sept. 1746, PRO ADM1/480.

75. Warren to Knowles, 6 Oct. 1746, ESRO, Gage papers, G/Am/6.

76. Townsend to Shirley and Warren, 17 Sept. 1746, PRO ADM1/480.

77. Warren to Corbett, 23 Sept. 1746, PRO ADM1/480.

78. Warren to Spry, 21 Sept. 1746, ESRO, Gage papers, G/Am/6.

79. Warren to Douglass, 1 Oct. 1746, ESRO, Gage papers, G/Am/6.

80. Warren to Corbett, 23 Sept. 1746, ESRO, Gage papers, G/Am/6.

81. Warren to Corbett, 2 June 1745; Warren to Norris, 2 and 7 June 1745; Warren to Newcastle, 7 June 1745; all in ESRO, Gage papers, G/Am/6.

82. Warren to Messrs. Baker, 7 June 1746, ESRO, Gage papers, G/Am/6.

83. Warren to Corbett, private letter, 10 Oct. 1746, ESRO, Gage papers, G/Am/6.

84. Warren to Clinton, 28 Aug. 1745, WLCL, George Clinton papers, II.

85. Clinton's memorandum: "A scheme how to get home," WLCL, George Clinton papers, II.

86. Warren to Clinton, 11 Oct. 1745, WLCL, George Clinton papers, II.

87. Clinton to Warren, 24 and 27 April 1746, WLCL, George Clinton papers, III.

88. Warren to Clinton, 24 June 1746, WLCL, George Clinton papers, III.

89. Clinton to Warren [July or Aug. 1746], WLCL, George Clinton papers, III.

90. Warren to Clinton, 8 Sept. 1746, WLCL. George Clinton papers, III. It was a friendly letter of congratulations on Clinton's successful negotiations with the Iroquois. "The last letter your excellency will have receiv'd from me on the subject of the government should have gone by the express some time ago to Albany but it was unluckily left behind."

91. Warren to Clinton, 20 Oct. 1746, and Clinton to Warren, 4 Oct. 1746, WLCL, George Clinton papers, III.

92. Warren to Clinton, 18 Oct. 1747, ESRO, Gage Papers, G/Am/6; Warren to Clinton, Dec. 1747, extract quoted in Clinton to Cadwallader Colden, New York's lieutenant governor, 11 March 1748, *The Letters and Papers of Cadwallader Colden* 3:364.

93. Varga, "Robert Charles: New York Agent, 1748–1770," 211–35.

Chapter 6. The Western Squadron, 1747–1748

1. Beatson, *Naval and Military Memoirs of Great Britain from 1727 to 1783* 1:414.

2. 12 Jan. 1747, PRO CO5/901, f. 50–56.

3. Gwyn, ed., *The Warren Papers, 1736–1752*, 378.

4. Admiralty to Warren, 5 March 1747, PRO ADM2/69, 178.

5. Warren to Wickham, 21 March 1747, PRO ADM1/88.

6. Warren to Clevland, 18 March 1747, PRO ADM1/88. In her place Warren was assigned his old ship, *Launceston*. Admiralty to Warren, PRO ADM2/504, 371.

7. Gwyn, ed., *The Warren Papers, 1736–1752*, 387.

8. Ibid., 207. See original Warren to Anson, 18 Jan. 1746, BL, ADD MSS 15957, Anson papers, f. 170–71.

9. Admiralty to Anson, 30 March 1747, PRO ADM2/69, 267–68.

10. Admiralty to Warren, 31 March 1747, PRO ADM2/69, 269; Warren to Corbett, 2 April 1747, PRO ADM1/88.

11. Warren to Anson, 23 April 1747, BL, ADD MSS 15957, Anson papers, f. 172–73.

12. Anson to Corbett, 11 May 1747, PRO ADM1/87.

13. As distinct from sailing close-hauled, or by the wind; hence the term "by and large."

14. La Jonquière to Maurepas, Portsmouth, 17 May 1747, Archives Nationales (Paris), Marine B4/61, f. 105–10 [at 108].

15. L'Abbadie to Maurepas, 19 May 1747, Archives Nationales (Paris), Marine B4/61, f. 168–69.

16. Extracts from la Jonquière's journal, Archives Nationales (Paris), Marine B4/61, f. 148–49.

17. McCarthy to Maurepas, 23 May 1747, Archives Nationales (Paris), Marine B4/61, f. 160–61.

18. Prévost to Maurepas, 17 May 1747, Archives Nationales (Paris), Marine B4/61, f. 171–75.

19. A letter from an officer, who was an eyewitness. *The Naval Chronicle or, Voyages, Travels, Expeditions, Remarkable Exploits and Achievements, of the Most Celebrated English Navigators, Travellers, and Sea-Commanders, from the Earliest Accounts to the End of the Year 1759* 3:167.

20. Warren to Bedford, 18 May 1747, Bedford Manuscript Letters, box 16, 105.

21. Warren to Anson, BL, ADD MSS 15957, Anson papers, f. 174–75.

22. Total prize yield amounted to £755,896, of which the flag's share was £95,487. Of this, one-third went to Warren and two-thirds to Anson. BL, ADD MSS 15957, Anson papers.

23. Pepperrell to Warren, 10 Sept. 1747, in Parsons, *The Life of Sir William Pepperrell*, 166.

24. Willard to Warren, 19 Sept. 1747, Massachusetts Archives, vol. 53, f. 277–78. Sent in *Scarborough*.

25. Colden to Warren, 26 Sept. 1747, in *The Letters and Papers of Cadwallader Colden 1743–1747* 3:425.

26. Law to Warren, 22 Nov. 1747, in *Papers of Jonathan Law, Governor of Connecticut, 1741–1750* 13:106–7.

27. "If no more ships are to be sent to the Mediterranean, why might I not have the *Princessa* to hoist my flag in 'till the *Invincible* can be got ready?" Warren to Anson, Portsmouth, 19 May 1747, BL, ADD MSS 15957, Anson papers, f. 176–78. "I hope that the *Invincible* may be fitted for me . . . and as I want no decorations, but that she may be fitted to encounter the sea and enemy I believe it can't take much time." Warren to Clevland, 18 Aug. 1747, PRO ADM1/88.

28. Warren to Anson, 19 May 1747, BL, ADD MSS 15957, Anson papers, f. 176–78.

29. Captain Boscawen's wife had it on good authority in March that he "will certainly agree with Mrs. Cavendish about the villa. I envy her, and expect and require you, dear Sir, to provide me with some such agreeable villa. For this I empower you to draw on the French for such sums as you shall want." Fanny Boscawen to Boscawen, 24 March 1747, in Aspinall-Oglander, *Admiral's Wife*, 31.

30. Warren to Anson, 31 May 1747, BL, ADD MSS 15957, Anson papers, f. 193.

31. Gwyn, *Enterprising Admiral*, 145–46.

32. Warren to Anson, 19 May 1747, BL, ADD MSS 15957, Anson papers, f. 179–80. Two days later Warren wrote him, "I hope you will struggle for my having a vice flag, and a main for yourself. You should strike while things are warm, for I know by experience that good works are soon forgot by great talks. You have it now in your power, therefore, my dear sir, make use of it." Warren to Anson, 21 May 1747, BL, ADD MSS 15957, Anson papers, f. 191–92.

33. Corbett to Warren, 19 May 1747, PRO ADM2/504, 291–92.

34. "Such is my own anxiety for the service of my country, and the approbation of their lordships, that tho' my private affairs may suffer in the highest degree by my sudden sailing, yet, if they think my going to sea necessary, I will immediately proceed with as few, or as many, ships, as they shall judge proper for the service expected to be done." Warren to Corbett, 20 May 1747, PRO ADM1/88.

35. Warren to Anson, 20 May 1747, BL, ADD MSS 15957, Anson papers, f. 188–89.

36. Warren to Anson, 1 June 1747, BL, ADD MSS 15957, Anson papers, 195.

37. Corbett to Warren, 13 June 1747, PRO ADM2/504, 469–70. This intelligence was repeated in July. Clevland to Warren, 7 July 1747, sent by *Weazle*, PRO ADM2/505, 13–14.

38. Corbett to Warren, 29 June 1747, PRO ADM2/504, 554–55. Warren subsequently was informed that the order for an armed escort had been countermanded. Clevland to Warren, 4 July 1747, PRO ADM2/505, 4.

39. Captain Gwynn's testimony, PRO HCA30/666.

40, PRO HCA30/666.

41. Warren to Anson, off Plymouth Sound, 1 Aug. 1747, PRO ADM1/88.

42. Warren to Capt. Harry Norris, 28 and 30 July 1747, NMM, Hawke papers, In-letterbook, 1747–59, 36–38.

43. He also sent *Ambuscade* to search for a French privateer reported to the west of the Isles of Scilly. Warren to Corbett, 3 Aug. 1747, PRO ADM1/88.

44. Anson to Warren, 23 July 1747, Staffordshire Record Office, Anson papers, U/3/1.

45. Warren to Anson, 5 July 1747, BL, ADD MSS 15957, Anson papers, f. 200–203.

46. Ibid.

47. Clevland to Warren, 3 Aug. 1747, PRO ADM2/505, 129–30.

48. Warren to Anson, 3 Aug. 1747, BL, ADD MSS 15957, Anson papers, f. 204.

49. Admiralty Board to Warren, 20 July 1747, PRO ADM2/70, 125.

50. Warren to Corbett, 3 Aug. 1747, PRO ADM1/88.

51. Warren to Anson, 3 Aug. 1747, BL, ADD MSS 15957, Anson papers, f. 204–5.

52. The Admiralty agreed and Warren issued his order to Hawke, 8 Aug. 1747, NMM, Hawke papers, In-letterbook, 1747–59, 30–32.

53. Warren to Anson, 3 Aug. 1747, BL, ADD MSS 15957, Anson papers, f. 205. In the matter of prize money, Warren told Anson that he would manage matters with Hawke, "as we did."

54. Clevland to Warren, 5 Aug 1747, PRO ADM2/505, 136–37.

55. MacKay, *Admiral Hawke.*

56. *Hector* was above five hundred tons, mounted twenty-eight guns, and had a crew of sixty. Captain Hay, *Viper*'s captain, was killed in the action. Hawke to Warren, *Windsor* at sea, 20 Aug. 1747, PRO ADM1/88.

57. Hawke to Warren, 21 and 29 Aug. 1747, PRO ADM1/88.

58. Faulkner to Warren, Falmouth, 25 Aug. 1747, PRO ADM1/88. At the same time the Admiralty learned that there were actually eight or nine French warships ready to sail from Brest bound initially for Rochefort. Clevland to Warren, 26 and 27 Aug. 1747, PRO ADM2/505, 264–65, 267–68.

59. Warren to Anson, 25 Aug. 1747, BL, ADD MSS 15957, Anson papers, f. 219.

60. Warren to Anson, Portsmouth, 26 Aug. 1747, BL, ADD MSS 15957, Anson papers, f. 222.

61. Warren to Anson, Portsmouth, 28 Aug. 1747, BL, ADD MSS 15957, Anson papers, f. 223–24.

62. Warren to Anson, 29 Aug. 1747, BL, ADD MSS 15957, Anson papers, f. 232–33. These sentiments he repeated to the Admiralty secretary. Warren to Clevland, 28 Aug. 1747, PRO ADM1/88.

63. Warren to Clevland, 30 and 31 Aug. 1747, PRO ADM1/88.

64. Warren to Anson, 1 Sept. 1747, BL, ADD MSS 15957, Anson papers, f. 236–37. He added "I hope I shall have the pleasure of spending many pleasant days with you at Soberton and Westbury when retired." Six days later he noted "the blo[tches] about me grew red, angry, and larger every day. My flux is abated, but a slow fever still continues." Warren to Anson, 7 Sept. 1747, BL, ADD MSS 15957, Anson papers, f. 248–49.

65. Warren to Clevland, 2 Sept. 1747, PRO ADM1/88.

66. Warren to Anson, off St. Helen's, 5 Sept. 1747, BL, ADD MSS 15957, Anson papers, f. 246.

67. Warren to Clevland, 5 Sept. 1747, PRO ADM1/88. He now suggested that it was too late in the season to send such a large ship as *St. George* to sea. The Admiralty order to resign was sent 7 Sept. 1747, PRO ADM2/70, 253.

68. Warren to Clevland, 7 Sept. 1747, PRO ADM1/88.

69. Warren to Clevland, *St. George* off St. Helen's, 9 Sept. 1747, PRO ADM1/88.

70. Warren to Anson, 16 Sept. 1747, BL, ADD MSS 15957, Anson papers, f. 354.

71. Warren to Anson, Westbury, 16 Oct. 1747, BL, ADD MSS 15957, Anson papers, f. 156–57.

72. Warren to Corbett, 3 April 1747, PRO ADM1/88.

73. Warren to Bedford, 18 May 1747, Bedford Manuscript Letters, box 16, 105.

74. Warren to Anson, 19 May 1747, Anson papers, BL, ADD MSS 15957, f. 179–80.

75. Warren to Anson, 31 May 1747, BL, ADD MSS 15957, Anson papers, f. 193–94.

76. Warren to Anson, 9 Sept. 1747, BL, ADD MSS 15957, Anson papers, f. 250.

77. Pepperrell to Warren, 10 Sept. 1747, original not located; printed in Parsons, *Life of Pepperrell,* 166–68.

78. Warren to Anson, 26 Nov. 1747, BL, ADD MSS 15957, Anson papers, f. 258. He told Anson that by December they had joined him in Portsmouth where he was busy presiding over a court martial. Warren to Anson, 2 Dec. 1747, BL, ADD MSS 15957, Anson papers, f. 260. Fanny Boscawen noted, "I have also visited Lady Warren, Sir Peter's lady, on her arrival, being desirous to pay all due respect to your profession." 11 Jan. 1748, in Aspinall-Oglander, *Admiral's Wife,* 74.

79. Warren to Clinton, 18 Oct. 1747, ESRO, Gage papers, G/Am/6.

80. Keppel to Anson, 26 Oct. 1747, BL, ADD MSS 15955, Anson papers.

81. Corbett to Warren, 2 Nov. 1747, PRO ADM2/506, 22–23.

82. Warren to Clevland, 4 Nov. 1747, PRO ADM1/88.

83. Admiralty Board to Warren, 31 Oct. 1747, PRO ADM2/70, 426; Corbett to Warren, 31 Oct. 1747, PRO ADM2/506, 21.

84. Beatson, *Naval and Military Memoirs* 1:297, 321.

85. Ibid., 1:221.

86. The court sat on seventeen separate days between 25 Nov. and 21 Dec. 1747, PRO ADM1/5291.

87. "Observations on the rules proposed for the more orderly proceedings at courts martial in the sea service" with the minutes of 1 Feb. 1748 meeting at Admiral Steuart's lodgings. The committee, including Steuart, consisted of Warren and captains Roger Martin, John Pritchard, Peircy Brett, John Bentley, and William Parry, PRO ADM1/917.

88. This point is made in Creswell, *Britain's Admirals of the Eighteenth Century,* 86. Creswell was unaware that the matter was immediately taken up by the Admiralty.

89. Steuart et al. to Corbett, Portsmouth, 2 Dec. 1747, PRO ADM1/916.

90. The Admiralty ordered the committee to reconvene 20 March 1749.

91. Lavery, *The Arming and Fitting of English Ships of War 1600–1815*, 139–41.

92. Warren to Anson, 2 Dec. 1747, BL, ADD MSS 15957, Anson papers, f. 260–62.

93. "'Tis a happy event and greatly so as it must in all probability disappoint them in their grand schemes to the East Indies." Warren to Anson, 22 Feb. 1748, BL, ADD MSS 15759, Anson papers, f. 276.

94. Richmond, *The Navy in the War of 1739–1748* 3:229.

95. Warren to Corbett, Portsmouth, 29 Jan. 1748, PRO ADM1/88.

96. *Haarlem* (76), *De Burgh van Leyden* (52), *Leuvenhorst* (52), *Assendelft* (52), *Maarsen* (44), *Middleburg* (44).

97. Warren to Hawke, 28 Jan. 1748, NMM, Hawke papers, In-letterbook, 1747–59, 65.

98. Admiralty to Warren, 22 Jan. 1748, PRO ADM2/71, 140–43.

99. "List of Ships appointed," 25 Jan. 1748, NMM, Hawke papers, In-letterbook, 1747–59, 66.

100. Warren to Clevland, 5 and 6 Feb. 1748, PRO ADM1/88. He sent the Admiralty a copy of the agreement he and Admiral Schryver had reached over the distribution of prize money. Warren to Clevland, off Plymouth Sound, 6 Feb. 1748, ADM1/88; Admiralty to Newcastle, 11 Feb. 1748, PRO ADM2/370, 241–42.

101. Rear Admiral Chambers to Warren, 29 Jan. 1748, PRO ADM1/88; Warren to Corbett, 30 Jan. 1748, PRO ADM1/88; Warren to Anson, 30 Jan. 1748, BL, ADD MSS 15957, Anson papers, f. 270–71.

102. List of French privateers at sea, 27 Jan. 1748, PRO ADM1/88.

103. Warren to Corbett, 12 Feb. 1748, 46°N, about one hundred leagues westward of Belle Isle, PRO ADM1/88.

104. Warren to Cotes, 2 Feb. 1748, NMM, Hawke papers, In-letterbook, 1747–59, 71; Warren to Clevland, 2 Feb. 1748, PRO ADM1/88. On 10 Feb. 1748 he notified Hawke of these plans. Warren to Hawke, NMM, Hawke papers, In-letterbook, 1747–59, 67–68.

105. News of this limited success did not reach Warren at Portsmouth for almost two months. "The success would have been complete if Capt. Cotes and Sir Edward Hawke had been joined." Warren to Clevland, 4 April 1748, PRO ADM1/88. "Had he been joined by Sir Edward, it would have been a glorious thing." Warren to Anson, 4 April 1748, BL, ADD MSS 15957, Anson papers, f. 290.

106. Hawke to Warren, 7 April 1748. NMM, Hawke papers, Out-letterbook, 1747–58.

107. Warren to Corbett, 18 March 1748, and Warren to Hawke, 19 March 1748, PRO ADM1/88.

108. Warren to Corbett, 26 March 1748, 47°12′N, ninety leagues from Belle Isle, PRO ADM1/88.

109. Warren to Corbett, off the Lizard, 28 March 1748, PRO ADM1/88; Warren to Anson, 28 March 1748, BL, ADD MSS 15957, Anson papers, f. 280–81.

110. Warren to Corbett, Spithead, 31 March 1748, PRO ADM1/88.

111. Warren to Anson, 26 March 1748, Anson papers, BL, ADD MSS 15957, f. 278–79.

112. Warren to Corbett, 31 March 1748, PRO ADM1/88.

113. *De Burg van Leyden, Maarsen, Middleburg,* and *Leuvenhorst.* The crew of *Assendelft* was still so sickly that the ship could not sail. Warren to Clevland, 16 April 1748, PRO ADM1/88.

114. Warren to Hawke, 6 April 1748, received 25 April, NMM, Hawke papers, In-letterbook, 1747–1759, 78–79.

115. Warren to Clevland, 6 April 1748, PRO ADM1/88.

116. Admiralty Board to Warren, 14 April 1748, PRO ADM2/71, 422–23. Before this order reached him, Warren learned this from the British consul at Oporto.

117. Warren to Clevland, 3 May 1748, 45°15′N, with Ushant distant ninety-four leagues, PRO ADM1/88.

118. Warren to Hawke, 13 May 1748. NMM, Hawke papers. In-letterbook, 1747–59, 83.

119. Clevland to Warren, 18 April 1748, PRO ADM2/507, 401.

120. Anthony Kerly to Warren, 24 April 1748, PRO ADM1/88.

121. Keene to Warren, 14 May 1748, BL, ADD MSS 32812, f. 146. Called "an ambassador of rare talent." Woodfine, *Britannia's Glories: The Walpole Ministry and the 1739 War with Spain,* 27.

122. Warren to Consul Parker, 6 May 1748, and Warren to Clevland, 16 May 1748, PRO ADM1/88.

123. Warren to Clevland, 16 May 1748, PRO ADM1/88.

124. Hawke then commanded only *Kent, Anson, Tavistock,* and *Amazon.* Warren to Clevland, 16 May 1748, PRO ADM1/88.

125. Warren to Clevland, 16 May 1748, PRO ADM1/88.

126. Corbett to Warren, 3 May 1748, PRO ADM2/507, 505–6. From Captain Wickham in *Panther* with a convoy bound for Newfoundland. Preliminaries signed 19 April 1748. Proclamation, 5 May 1748, forwarded by the Admiralty on 8 May 1748, PRO HCA30/666.

127. Warren to Anson, 16 May 1748, Anson papers, BL, ADD MSS 15957, f. 304–5.

128. Barrow, *The Life of Lord Anson,* 205–9.

129. Warren to Anson, 16 May 1748, BL, ADD MSS 15957, Anson papers, f. 305.

130. Thereafter *Ambuscade* was to make for Lisbon and escort the homeward-bound trade, PRO HCA30/666.

131. Warren to Clevland, 25 May 1748, PRO ADM1/88.

132. Warren to Hawke, 7 June 1748, NMM, Hawke papers, In-letterbook 1747–59, 86; Warren to Mostyn, 7 June 1748, PRO ADM1/2106; Warren to Keppel, 13 June 1748, to make for Lisbon and escort the homeward-bound trade, PRO ADM1/2008.

133. Consultation aboard *Invincible,* 1 July 1748, PRO ADM1/88. Warren out-

lined the episode to Corbett, 23 July 1748. His letter was minuted on 26 July 1748, "Acquaint him the lords are so extremely well-satisfied with his conduct in this affair, that they have directed the whole to be laid before the lords justices of the kingdom." PRO ADM1/88. Clevland to Warren, 26 July 1748, PRO ADM2/508, 239; Admiralty to Bedford, 26 July 1748, PRO ADM2/370, 283.

134. Admiralty Board to Warren, 1 July 1748, PRO ADM2/72, 89.

135. Admiralty Board to Warren, 11 July 1748, PRO ADM2/72, 116.

136. Warren to Clevland, *Invincible* at Spithead, 29 July & 12 Aug. 1748, PRO ADM1/88.

137. Clevland to Warren, 12 July 1748, PRO ADM2/508, 194–96.

Chapter 7. Half-pay Admiral, 1748–1752

1. Warren to Anson, *Devonshire* at sea, 26 March 1748, BL, ADD MSS 15957, Anson papers, f. 279.

2. As late as June 1748 Jonathan Belcher, governor of New Jersey, to whom Warren had loaned £800 in February 1747 wrote to him of his colony as "represented to me before my arrival a very lean, thin government. I suppose of the least profit to a governor of almost any in the king's gift." He estimated it to be worth no more than NJ£1,210 [or £654], including house rent and perquisites. Belcher found it though "an obscure part of the world . . . very expensive." Belcher to Warren, 27 June 1748, MHS, Belcher letterbook, 1747–48, 388.

3. Warren to Knowles, 10 Nov. 1746, ESRO, Gage papers, G/Am/6.

4. Namier and Brooke, eds., *The History of Parliament: The House of Commons, 1754–1790* 2:336.

5. Bedford to Anson, 20 June 1747, BL, ADD MSS 15955, Anson papers, f. 141.

6. Warren to Anson, 26 Aug. 1747, BL, ADD MSS 15957, Anson papers, f. 222. Bedford to Warren, 23 Aug. 1747, asked Anson to write to Warren to "remit immediately to my agent, Mr. Butcher, £2,200 in order to provide payment of the victualler and others who have bills directed to Mr. Butcher," BL, ADD MSS 15955, Anson papers, f. 149.

7. Warren received 2,858 votes, Trentham 2,873, and their two opponents 544 and 514 votes respectively. *Gentleman's Magazine* 1747, 307. For Trentham, see Namier and Brooke, eds., *History of Parliament* 3:38–39.

8. Anson to Warren, 23 July 1747, Staffordshire Record Office, Anson papers, U/3/1.

9. Warren to Anson, 3 Aug. 1747, BL, ADD MSS 15957, Anson papers, f. 204–9.

10. Warren to Anson, BL, ADD MSS 15957, Anson papers, f. 212.

11. Details are taken from *Journals of the House of Commons*, vols. 25–26. For a brief account of Warren's parliamentary career, where none of these details appear, see Sedgwick, ed., *The History of Parliament: The House of Commons 1715–1754* 2:522–23.

12. Cobbett, ed., *Parliamentary History* 14:613.

13. Ibid., 14:713.

14. Ibid., 14:713.

15. Warren to Anson, 3 Aug. 1747, BL, ADD MSS 15957, Anson papers, f. 204–9.

16. Warren to Anson, Cavendish Square, 3 Dec. 1748, WLCL, Warren papers, box 1.

17. Walpole to Horace Mann, 26 Dec. 1748, in Lewis, ed., *Horace Walpole's Correspondence* 20:16–17.

18. Letters patent for the new Admiralty Board, 24 Dec. 1748, PRO ADM4/25.

19. Letters patent for the new Admiralty Board, 18 Nov. 1749, PRO ADM4/26.

20. *Journals of the House of Commons* 25:708.

21. The article from the proposed statute called *A Bill for amending, explaining and reducing into one act of Parliament, the laws relating to the government of his Majesty's ships, vessels, and forces by sea* read: "All half-pay officers belonging to his Majesty's fleet shall be equally subject to discipline, and to be commanded whenever the good of his Majesty's service shall require their attendance, as if they were actually upon full pay." Read 1 Feb. 1749.

22. Titles of some of these—all published in London in 1749—were: Augustus Hervey, *Objections to the Thirty-Fourth Article of the Navy Bill*, London, 1749; Augustus Hervey, *A Letter from a friend . . . in relation to three Additional Articles of War*, London, 1749; Lord Barrington, *Considerations on the Navy Bill*, London, 1749; Rear Adm. Temple West, *An Examination and Refutation of the Late Pamphlet . . . over Half-pay Officers*, London, 1749.

23. Erskine, ed., *Augustus Hervey's Journal*, 80.

24. Ibid., 81.

25. Signed by Admirals Norris, Warren, Lee, and one other admiral, with forty-seven captains. Barrow, *Life of Lord Anson*, 219.

26. Admiralty minutes, 20 Feb. 1749, PRO ADM3/60.

27. Admiralty minutes, 21 Feb. 1749, PRO ADM3/60.

28. 23 Feb. 1749, PRO ADM1/578. For the list of those supporting the administration, see Baugh, ed., *Naval Administration 1715–1750*, 86–87.

29. Erskine, ed., *Augustus Hervey's Journal*, 83.

30. Hervey claimed that both the Duke of Cumberland and Anson were "very angry with me." Erskine, ed., *Augustus Hervey's Journal*, 83.

31. PRO HCA30/524, 22 Geo. II. c.33.

32. Warren to Anson, 9 Oct. 1748, Anson papers, BL, ADD MSS 15957, f. 310; Sandwich to Anson, 11 Aug. 1750, BL, ADD MSS 15955, Anson papers, f. 99; Sandwich to Bedford, 23 Sept. 1750, Bedford Letters, vol. 26, item 68; Warren to Bedford, 7 Oct. 1750, BL, ADD MSS 15957, Anson papers, f. 312.

33. Sandwich to Bedford, *Hinchinbroke*, 23 Sept. 1750, Bedford Letters, vol. 26, item 68. In Gaetano Latilla's comic opera entitled *La Finta Cameriera* (1738), the role is that of a silly, pompous, and grotesque suitor to Erosmina, whose father urges her to accept Don Calascione's proposal. The outcome is not what Calascione had hoped.

34. Warren to Anson, 7 Oct. 1750, BL, ADD MSS 15957, Anson papers, f. 312.

35. Newman, ed., "Leicester House Politics, 1750–60," 145.

36. Willard to Warren, 28 Aug. 1747, Massachusetts Archives, vol. 53, f. 272–73.

37. The parliamentary grant amounted to £183,649, but various fees and commissions reduced the amount. Details are found in Warren and Bollan to Willard, Portsmouth, 12 Aug. 1749, Massachusetts Archives, vol. 20, f. 554–57.

38. Warren to Pepperrell, 13 Aug. 1749, in Parsons, *The Life of Sir William Pepperrell*, 207.

39. Gwyn, "Financial Revolution in Massachusetts," 59–77; Davis, *Currency and Banking in the Province of the Massachusetts Bay.*

40. Warren to Clinton, 4 Aug. 1742, PRO ADM1/2653.

41. Warren to Corbett, 6 July 1744, PRO ADM1/2654.

42. Warren to Corbett, 23 Nov. 1745, PRO ADM1/480.

43. Corbett to Warren, 10 Sept. 1746, PRO ADM2/500, 117–18.

44. Warren to Corbett, 26 June 1746, PRO ADM1/480.

45. Gwyn, "Shipbuilding for the Royal Navy in Colonial New England," 22–30. See Pool, *Navy Board Contracts 1660–1832*, 84–85.

46. Corbett to Warren, 24 Sept. 1746, PRO ADM2/500, 340–41.

47. Nathaniel Meserve to Warren, 18 Nov. 1748, PRO ADM1/88.

48. Knowles to Cleveland, 12 July 1750, PRO ADM1/234; His words had been "I enclose a paragraph of my letter I sent to the Admiralty, just after I had discoursed with you upon this subject before, so that I think you will be very safe in building the ship to your own mind. You may be sure if she turns out a good ship you will be commended." Knowles to Meserve, Louisbourg, 16 Aug. 1747, PRO ADM1/88.

49. Corbett to Warren, 31 May 1750, WLCL, Warren papers, box 4; Warren to Corbett, 4 June 1750, PRO ADM1/579.

50. Shaw, ed., *Calendar of Treasury Books and Papers, 1742–1745*, 820.

51. Sandwich to Anson, 14 April 1747, BL, ADD MSS 15957, Anson papers.

52. Aug. 1745, PRO ADM1/2100; Oct. 1746, PRO ADM1/3103.

53. Warren to Anson, 9 Oct. 1748, BL, ADD MSS 15957, Anson papers, f. 310–11.

54. Warren to Montagu [April 1748?] and [August 1748?], WLCL, Warren papers, box 4.

55. Warren and Hawke to Montagu's prize agent, 9 Feb. 1749, and Warren and Hawke to Montagu, 24 Feb. 1749, WLCL, Warren papers, box 4.

56. Montagu to Warren, 5 March 1749. Warren responded with a final appeal to Montagu's good sense. Warren to Montagu, March 1749. See Dr. Lee's opinion of the case, 4 March 1748, WLCL, Warren papers, box 4.

57. 20 June 1749, account book, 1749–52, WLCL, Warren papers.

58. Knowles to Cleveland, 15 June, 26 July, 4 and 6 Aug. 1760, PRO ADM1/578; Cleveland to Knowles, 22 July 1760, PRO ADM2/529, 111; Cleveland to Sir Peircy Brett, 5 Aug. 1760, PRO ADM2/529, 163.

59. The New England vessels laid an elaborate claim to a share in the rich prizes taken at Louisbourg. MHS, Belknap papers, 61.C.

60. Warren to Corbett, 16 Oct. 1748, in Gwyn, ed., *The Warren Papers, 1736–1752*, 397.

61. Carried by warships from Louisbourg, it amounted to $1,024,941, with $16,041 in two chests of double doubloons, two chests of gold bars, seven pigs of virgin silver weighing 282 lbs, eighteen bars of gold weighing 65.5 lbs, gold and silver rings, chains, ornaments, jewelry, and plate. The captains typically would have been paid at least 2 percent freight to carry the coin. See receipts signed by Captains Hore, Calmady, Brett, and Edwards, 4 Oct. 1745, WLCL, Warren papers, box 1.

62. Lewis, *A Social History of the Navy, 1793–1815*, 321.

63. For copies of this statute, see PRO and the one in January 1740 entitled *"For the more effectual securing and encouraging trade of his Majesty's British subjects to America, and for the encouragement of seamen to enter his Majesty's service,"* PRO HCA30/524.

64. On 10 July orders were first given to make reprisals on Spanish shipping, while 10 Oct. saw the formal declaration of war against Spain.

65. This was the case of *Notre Dame de la Déliverance*. See her prize appeal papers, 3 May 1750. New York Public Library, Manuscript Division, *KC+++p.v.20.

66. He acquired at least £53,500 at Louisbourg in 1745 and another £48,100 in 1747. For some details, see Gwyn, *Enterprising Admiral*, 18–20, 212–13.

67. PRO HCA30/377, I.

68. Warren to DeLancey, Westbury, 11 Aug. 1750, NYHS, Warren papers, 37.

69. From a Mr. Long; 18 Jan. 1850, account book, 1749–52, WLCL, Warren papers.

70. Requested leave. Warren to Corbett, 5 July 1750, PRO ADM1/578.

71. Request for leave to go to Ireland "for a short time." Warren to Clevland, Cavendish Square, 18 June 1752, PRO ADM1/578.

72. It should be noted that as late as the summer of 1751 he expressed interest in an estate in New Jersey. Jonathan Belcher to Warren, Perth Amboy, 8 June 1751, MHS, Belcher letterbook, 1750–52, 153–54; George Thomas to Warren, 11 June 1751, WLCL, Warren papers, box 4.

73. Gwyn, *Enterprising Admiral*, chapters 3–4, 29–93.

74. Gwyn, "Sir William Johnson, c. 1717–74," 394–98.

75. Gwyn, *Enterprising Admiral*, 147–50.

76. Ibid., 132–34.

77. Anson to Warren, 23 July 1747, Staffordshire Record Office, Anson papers, U/3/1.

78. Warren to Anson, 3 Aug. 1747, BL, ADD MSS 15957, Anson papers, f. 208–9.

79. 13 Nov. 1747, PRO ADM7/340, 331–38.

80. Warren to Josiah Willard, 12 Aug. 1749, Massachusetts Archives, vol. 20, f. 559–60; Warren to Willard, 30 March 1751, Massachusetts Archives, vol. 13, f. 245.

81. On 22 Feb. 1751 the Massachusetts House of Representatives appointed a committee "to take care of the horses lately sent as present to the province by Sir Peter Warren," and to receive funds paid for their use. The matter had been sent to them in January by the Massachusetts Council. Massachusetts Archives, vol. 1, f.

213, 230; Warren to Willard, 27 March 1750, Massachusetts Archives, vol. 53, f. 502–3; Pepperrell to Warren, Spring Garden, 31 July 1750, in Parsons, *Life of Pepperrell*, 227.

82. Pepperrell to Warren, 19 Oct. 1750. Parsons, *Life of Pepperrell*, 224–5; Pepperrell to Lt. Gov. Spencer Phipps, 28 Jan. 1751. Read in Council, 29 Jan. 1751, Massachusetts Archives, vol. 1, f. 296–98; WLCL, Warren accounts, 1749–52.

83. Warren to Willard, 30 March and 26 April 1751, Massachusetts Archives, vol. 13, f. 245–9.

84. Warren to Pepperrell, Scarborough, 12 July 1751, Maine Historical Society, Fogg collection; Warren to Willard, 22 March 1752, Massachusetts Archives, vol. 13, f. 143–44.

85. McCallum, *Eleazar Wheelock*, 143–44.

86. Trafton, "Louisbourg and the Pepperrell Silver," 366–67. I saw these items when I visited Pepperrell's home at Kittery Point, Maine, in 1966.

87. 30 Nov. 1749, WLCL, Warren accounts, 1749–52; acknowledged 28 Feb. 1750, Harvard College minutes, *Publication of the Colonial Society of Massachusetts* 16:813.

88. Henry Caner and John Gibbons to Warren, 29 Jan. 1749; Foote, *Annals of King's Chapel* 2:50–51, 63; Dix, *A History of the Parish of Trinity Church in the City of New York* 1:258; Oliver DeLancey to Thomas Hancock, 28 Nov. 1763, Boston Public Library, MSS. B.11.94; 3 June 1762, Chamberlain Collection of Hancock Manuscripts, Boston Public Library, Ch.M.1.10.

89. Dalton, *A Sermon Preached . . . before the Governors of Middlesex Hospital . . .*, 10–11. These amounted to £171. See Warren accounts, 1749–52, WLCL, Warren papers.

90. Accounts with Edward Jasper, 1742–44, WLCL, Warren papers.

91. Manuscript copies in New York State Archives. Deed book 19, 277–78 and NYHS. Warren papers; printed in Hamilton, ed., *The Papers of Sir William Johnson*, vol. 13, 19–22.

92. Campbell, *The Naval History of Great Britain*, vol. 4, 523–4.

93. A copy is held by The Athenaeum, Portsmouth, New Hampshire.

Chapter 8. Conclusion

1. Baugh, ed., *Naval Administration 1715–1750*, 35.

2. Ibid., 40.

3. Warren to Corbett, 24 May 1744, PRO ADM1/2654; Corbett to Warren, 17 Sept. 1744, PRO ADM2/484, 397–8.

4. Warren to Corbett, 9 & 29 Feb. 1745, PRO ADM1/2654.

5. Peter Faneuil to Warren, 19 Sept. 1737. Harvard University, Baker Library. Peter Faneuil letterbook, 1737–39, F-4.

6. Account with Messrs Baker, 1738–45. WLCL. Warren papers.

7. Account book, 1729–38. ESRO. Gage papers. G/Am/13, 13–14.

8. Account book, 1731–37. ESRO. Gage papers. G/Am/12, 18.

9. Or £121 7s., account book, 1731–37. ESRO. Gage papers. G/Am/12, 18; account book, 1729–38. ESRO. Gage papers. G/Am/13, 18.

10. Warren's account book, 1729–38. ESRO. Gage papers. G/Am/13, 5.

11. Account book, 1749–52, 20 June 1749. WLCL. Warren papers.

12. Douglass, *A Summary, Historical and Political, and Present State of the British Settlements in North America*, vol. 1, 236–7. Incidentally, the description of Knowles proved so offensive that Douglass was sued by Knowles. The offending passages were expurgated when the second edition appeared in 1760.

13. Baugh, ed., *Naval Administration 1715–1750*, 330.

14. As examples, see Norris, *Capt. Richard, fl. 1735–1745, defendant. Minutes taken at a court-martial, assembled on board His Majesty's ship Torbay. Began the 28th of January, 1744. And ended the 5th of February following. Being an enquiry into the conduct of Captain Richard Norris, in the engagement between the English fleet, under the command of Admiral Mathews, and the united fleet of French and Spaniards in the Mediterranean, on the 11th of February, 1743*. London, W. Webb, 1745. With *An appendix to the Minutes taken at a court-martial . . .*, London, 1745.

15. His account with Josiah Graham, 23 Jan. to 25 May 1747, ESRO, Gage papers, G/Am/3; account book, 1749–52, WLCL. Warren papers.

16. Warren to Anson, 2 April 1745, BL, ADD MSS 15957, Anson papers, f. 147–51.

17. Warren to Newcastle, 18 June 1745, PRO CO5/44, f. 53–54v.

Glossary

Admiral. A flag rank, attained through seniority from among serving captains, for those in command of a squadron or fleet.

Ballast. Additional weight added to a ship, usually in the form of stones or iron, placed in the ship's hold to give it greater stability by increasing her draught.

Base. A facility where expendable stores were replenished, where damaged or worn masts, yards, spars, rigging and sails were replaced, where careening occurred, and all but the most radical repairs carried out.

Beam. The width of the ship.

Breechings. When a gun was fired using a normal charge on a level gun platform it would recoil too far into the crowded gun deck, unless the backward movement of the gun was restrained. This was effected by means of breech ropes, known as breechings. Each end of a thick rope was made fast by an eye-splice to ringbolts attached to the ship's side. The rope passed through eyebolts on each side of the gun carriage and then through a ring above the cascabel. The breechings were normally three times the length of the gun, the heavier the gun the greater the circumference of the breechings.

Careen. To heave a vessel over on her side by applying cables to the upper masts, in order to clean, caulk, or repair the exposed side of her bottom.

Cascabel. The part of the gun beyond the closed end, known as the breech. It was around the neck of the cascabel that the breechings were looped.

Caulker. An artificer whose special tools make a seam watertight between two planks, either on a ship's bottom or deck planking, by forcing in strips of hot tarred rope fibers or oakum, before paying with pitch.

Chaser, bow. Cannon situated in the forepart of a ship to fire upon any object ahead of her.

Chaser, stern. Cannon placed in the afterpart of a ship, pointing astern, and intended to strike any ship that chases her or any other object astern.

Clean. The process of freeing vessels of weeds, barnacles, and anything else that might contribute to rot or slower sailing.

Commodore. A captain in command of a detached squadron, with the right to fly a broad pendant.

Convoy. A group of merchant ships, transports, naval storeships etc., escorted by warships; sometimes also used to denote the escorting warship.

Covertway. Path on top of the counterscarp protected by a parapet formed from the crest of the glacis; outer line of defense.

Dry dock. An excavated area in a yard often referred to as a graving dock, separated from water by watertight gates, into which a ship was floated. The water was then pumped out in order to inspect, clean, and repair the ship. When a new hull or hull repairs were completed water was then admitted to float the hull and tow it out.

Escort. A warship sailing with and protecting a convoy.

Foremast. The mast nearest the bow, in a vessel with more than one mast.

Half-pay. Portion of pay, received by statutory right by sea officers, and by Admiralty regulations by pilots on warships during periods when not actively engaged in the naval service.

Guardacostas. Spanish custom-house cutters; vessels employed to clear the coasts of smugglers or other marauders.

Letter-of-marque. Either a commissioned private vessel or the commission authorizing a private vessel to operate against enemy vessels, at its own risk, while still carrying freight.

Magazine. Place where ammunition is stored either on board a warship, or on a specially designated vessel in harbor, or in a purpose-built structure ashore.

Mainmast. The middle mast in a three-masted ship; the aftermast in a two-masted vessel.

Marines. Soldiers serving aboard ships, raised especially for sea duty.

Impressment. A statutory system of compulsory service by seamen, and later by landsmen, to man the fleet.

Press. Force to serve in the navy; thus a press gang was a group of men employed to press men into involuntary service.

Paying. To smear a ship's bottom with pitch and tar, known as "black stuff" in the ratio of two parts pitch to one part tar, or with oil, rosin and brimstone, known as "white stuff."

Privateer. A privately owned vessel, heavily armed and crewed, with a government commission to sail against enemy shipping.

Prize. A captured enemy warship or merchant vessel, later condemned by a vice admiralty court.

Prize money. The net proceeds accruing to the captors from the process of bringing a capture before a vice admiralty court, distributed by shares determined by parliamentary statute if the capturing vessel was a warship, or by contractual agreement if a privateer or letter-of-marque ship.

Riding. When expressed of a ship, it is the state of being retained in a particular station, by means of one or more cables with their anchors, which for this purpose are sunk into the bottom of the sea in order to prevent the vessel from being driven at the mercy of the wind or current.

Sailing large. To sail with the wind near or abaft the beam, as distinct from sailing close-hauled, or by the wind; hence the term "by and large."

Sloop. A small warship, armed on a single deck, with usually sixteen or eighteen light cannon.

Sticks. Naval jargon for masts, bowsprits, topmasts, yards, and spars.

Swivel gun. A light easily handled cannon on a nonrecoiling swivel mount, firing a projectile as light as a half pound, and mounted on a ship's bulwarks or in the tops.

Tops. Platform located high on a mast, manned in action by seamen and marines armed with muskets or swivel guns to fire down onto the enemy's crowded deck.

Transport. A vessel converted to convey soldiers and their officers, refugees, or others.

Victualer. A ship, owned or hired by the Victualing Board, to carry barreled provisions, provided by contractors, principally of bread and biscuit, beef and pork, beer and butter, and peas, for the use of ships in commission.

Wharf. A substantial structure, in this era, built of timber, earth, and stone secured with pilings, built usually at right angles to the shore to enable ships to lie alongside to load, unload, or careen.

Bibliography

Manuscript Sources

Great Britain

Bedford Estate Office, London
    Bedford Manuscript Letters, boxes 6, 11, 16, 26.
British Library, London
    Anson papers: ADD MSS, 15955, 15957.
    ADD MSS, 32812, 41159.
    Egerton MSS, 77.
Buckinghamshire Record Office
    Trevor MSS, D/MH/50.
East Sussex Record Office, Lewes
    Gage papers: G/Am/1; G/Am/3; G/Am/6; G/Am/12; G/Am/13; G/Am/21; G/
    Am/134; G/Ir/2; G/Ha/37.
National Library of Scotland, Edinburgh
    Hay papers, Yester collection, MS 7111.
National Maritime Museum, Greenwich
    ADM/L/F, 14; ADM/L/G, 179; ADM/L/L, 45–46; ADM/L/R, 212, 369; ADM/L/
    S, 198, 303, 305, 404.
    Hawke papers, In-letterbook, 1747–59, Out-letterbook, 1747–58.
    Sergison MSS.
Nottingham University Library
    Newcastle MSS, 447.
Public Record Office, Kew
    Admiralty: ADM1/88, 230, 233, 234, 480, 578–79, 916, 1438, 1597–99, 1780,
    1880, 2007–8, 2041, 2100, 2106, 2216, 2282–84, 2453, 2624, 2652–55, 3103, 4114,
    5291, 5655; ADM2/50, 52, 63, 69, 70–72, 208, 370, 486, 496, 500, 504–6, 508, 529;
    ADM3/35; ADM6/12; ADM7/340; ADM/8; ADM25/81; ADM33/289, 307–8,
    314; ADM36/1369; ADM106/2889; ADM107/3.
    Colonial Office: CO5/44, 640, 654, 792, 901; CO42/13; CO217/2, 4–6; CO221/28.

High Court of Admiralty: HCA30/377, 524, 666.
State Papers: SP42/30.
Staffordshire Record Office, Stafford
    Anson papers, U/3/1.

United States

Boston Public Library
    Chamberlain Collection of Hancock Manuscripts, Ch.A.2.83, Ch.M.1.10.
    MSS. B.11.94.
Harvard University, Baker Library, Cambridge, Mass.
    Peter Faneuil letterbook, 1737–39, F-4.
Harvard University, Houghton Library, Cambridge, Mass.
    Thomas A. Janvier MSS.
Historical Society of Pennsylvania
    Gratz collection.
The Huntington Library and Art Collections, San Marino, Calif.
    Henry Pelham papers, HM9707, HM9709.
Library of Congress
    Vernon-Wager papers, MS, 46018–19.
Maine Historical Society, Portland
    Belcher letterbook, 1750–52.
    Fogg Autograph collection.
    Miscellaneous Bound Collection.
Massachusetts Archives, Boston
    Vols. 1, 13, 20, 53.
    Massachusetts Council Minutes.
Massachusetts Historical Society, Boston
    Belknap papers, 61.B, 61.C, 1744–5.
    Pepperrell papers, 71.A.
Museum of the City of New York
    DeLancey papers, 40.190.10, 49.48.73.
New-York Historical Society
    John E. Stillwell collection.
    Louisbourg MSS, V, VI.
    Misc. MSS, Louisbourg.
    Warren papers.
New York Public Library
    Horace Lyman Weeks MSS.
    Manuscript Division, *KC+++p.v.20.
New York State Archives, Albany
    Deed book 19.
    DePeyster Family papers, folder 12.

Land papers, 12.
New York Council Minutes.
William L. Clements Library, Ann Arbor, Mich.
George Clinton papers, vols. I–IV.
Louisbourg Manuscripts.
Warren papers, boxes 1–4.

France

Archives Nationales, Paris
Fonds de la marine: B4/61.
Fonds des colonies: B 82–110; B 63, 561–62; F3, vols. 50, 57; C11B 23 A 26.
Section outremer. Dépôt des fortifications des colonies, Amérique septentrionale.
Bigot. "Relation du siège de Louisbourg, *le 19 août 1745,*" mémoire 218.

Printed Sources

Primary

Atkins, J. A. *Voyage to Guinea, Brazil and the West Indies.* London, 1735.
Barrington, Lord. *Considerations on the Navy Bill for the Better Government of the Navy by a sea-officer; Remarks on a Pamphlet called Considerations on the Bill for the Better Government of the Navy.* London, 1749.
Baugh, Daniel A., ed. *Naval Administration 1715–1750.* Vol. 120. London: Navy Records Society, 1977.
Bosman, William. *A New and Accurate Description of the Coast of Guinea.* London, 1705.
Calendar of New York Manuscripts: Endorsed Land Papers in the Office of the Secretary of State of New York. Albany, 1864.
Collection de manuscrits contenant lettres, mémoires, et autres documents historiques relatifs à la Nouvelle France, recueillis aux archives de la Province de Québec ou copiés à l'étranger. 4 vols. Québec: Demers, 1883–85.
Dalton, John. *A Sermon Preached . . . before the Governors of Middlesex Hospital.* London, 1751.
DeForest, Louis Effingham, ed. *Louisbourg Journals 1745.* New York: Society of Colonial Wars in the State of New York, 1932.
Douglass, William. A *Summary, Historical and Political, and Present State of the British Settlements in North America.* 2 vols. Boston: Rogers and Fowle, 1749.
Erskine, David, ed. *Augustus Hervey's Journal, being the Intimate Account of the Life of a Captain in the Royal Navy Ashore and Afloat, 1746–1759.* London: William Kimber, 1953.
Gentleman's Magazine. 1747.
Green, S. A., ed. *Three Military Diaries Kept by Groton Soldiers in Different Wars.* Groton, 1901.

Gwyn, Julian, ed. *The Royal Navy and North America. The Warren Papers, 1736–1752.* Vol. 118. London: Navy Records Society, 1973.

Gwyn, Julian, and Christopher Moore, eds. *La Chute de Louisbourg. Le journal du 1ᵉ siège de Louisbourg du 25 mars au 17 juillet 1745 par Gilles Lacroix-Girard.* Editions de l'Université d'Ottawa, 1978.

Hamilton, Milton W., James Sullivan, and Alexander C. Flick, eds. *The Papers of Sir William Johnson.* 14 vols. Albany: University of the State of New York, 1921–65.

Harvard College Minutes. *Publication of the Colonial Society of Massachusetts* XVI. Boston, 1825.

Hervey, Augustus. *A Letter from a friend to Will's Coffee House in relation to three Additional Articles of War.* London, 1749.

———. *Objections to the Thirty-Fourth Article of the Navy Bill.* London, 1749.

Journals of the House of Commons. Vols. 25–26.

Killpatrick, James. *An Impartial Account of the Late Expedition against St. Augustine under General Oglethorpe.* London, 1742.

Lanning, John Tate, ed. *The St. Augustine Expedition of 1740: A Report of the South Carolina General Assembly.* Columbia: University of South Carolina Press, 1954.

The Letters and Papers of Cadwallader Colden. 9 vols. New York: New-York Historical Society Collections, 1917–35.

Lincoln, C. H., ed. *Correspondence of William Shirley Governor of Massachusetts and Military Commander in North America, 1731–1760.* 2 vols. New York: Macmillan, 1912.

Lincoln, Charles Z., ed. *State of New York Messages from the Governors. . . .* 11 vols. Albany: Lyon, 1909.

Massachusetts Historical Society. *The Pepperrell Papers. Collections,* sixth series, X, Boston, 1899.

———. "Letters Relating to the Expedition to Cape Breton." *Collections,* first series, I, Boston, 1806.

Minutes of the Common Council of the City of New York, 1675–1776. 8 vols. New York, 1905.

The Naval Chronicle or, Voyages, Travels, Expeditions, Remarkable Exploits and Achievements of the Most Celebrated English Navigators, Travellers, and Sea-Commanders, from the Earliest Accounts to the End of the Year 1759. 3 vols. London: J. Fuller, 1760.

Newman, Aubrey N., ed. "Leicester House Politics, 1750–1760, from the Papers of John, Second Earl of Egmont." *Camden Miscellany,* vol. 23. *Camden Fourth Series.* London: Royal Historical Society, vol. 7, 1969.

19th Report of the Deputy Keeper Public Records of Ireland. Dublin, 1887.

O'Callaghan, E. B., ed. *Documents Relative to the Colonial History of the State of New York.* 15 vols. Albany: Weed, Parsons, 1855–87.

Papers of Jonathan Law, Governor of Connecticut, 1741–1750. Hartford: Connecticut Historical Society Collections, 1912, XIII.

Phillips, Thomas. *A Journal of a Voyage made in the* Hannibal *of London, 1693, 1694, from England to Cape Monseradoc, in Africa and thence along the Coast of Guiney to Whidaw. . . .* London, 1732.

Ranft, B. McL., ed. *The Vernon Papers.* Vol. 99. London: Navy Records Society, 1958.

Rogers, Woodes. *A Cruising Voyage Round the World.* London, 1712.

Shaw, William A., ed. *Calendar of Treasury Books and Papers, 1742–1745 in the Public Record Office.* London: HMSO, 1903.

West, Rear Adm. Temple. *An Examination and Refutation of a Late Pamphlet Intitled Considerations on the Navy Bill Wherein the Present Power of the Lords Commissioners of the Admiralty over Half-pay Officers is shewn to be fully sufficient to answer every Good End and useful Purpose. By a Real Sea Officer.* London, 1749.

Wrong, George M., ed. *Louisbourg in 1745: The Anonymous Lettre d'un habitant de Louisbourg (Cape Breton), Containing a narrative by an eye-witness of the siege of 1745.* Toronto, 1897.

Secondary

Adams, Blaine. "Jean-Baptiste-Louis Le Prévost Duquesnel, d. 1744." *Dictionary of Canadian Biography* IV. Toronto: University of Toronto Press, 1974, 392–93.

Aldridge, D. D. "Admiral Sir John Norris, 1670 [or 1671]–1749: His Birth and Early Service, His Marriage and His Death." *Mariner's Mirror* 51 (1965): 173–83.

———. "Sir John Norris, 1660?–1749." Peter Le Fevre and Richard Harding, eds. *Precursors of Nelson. British Admirals of the Eighteenth Century.* London: Chatham, 2000, 101–28.

Armytage, Frances. *The Free Port System in the West Indies: A Study in Commercial Policy 1766–1822.* London: Longmans, Green, 1953.

Aspinall-Oglander, Cecil. *Admiral's Wife. Being the Life and Letters of The Hon. Mrs. Edward Boscawen from 1719 to 1761.* London: Longmans, Green, 1940.

Aylmer, Sir Fenton J. *The Aylmers of Ireland.* London: Mitchel, Hughes, and Clarke, 1931.

Barrow, Sir John. *The Life of Lord Anson, Admiral of the Fleet.* London, 1839.

Baugh, Daniel A. *British Naval Administration in the Age of Walpole.* Princeton, N.J.: Princeton University Press, 1965.

Beatson, Robert. *Naval and Military Memoirs of Great Britain from 1727 to 1783.* London: Longmans 1804.

Bourinot, J. G. *Historical Account of Cape Breton.* Montreal: Brown, 1892.

Browne, G. P. "Thomas Smart, d. 1722." *Dictionary of Canadian Biography* II. Toronto: University of Toronto Press, 1969.

Buffinton, Arthur H. "The Canada Expedition of 1746. Its Relation to British Politics." *American Historical Review* 45 (1940): 552–80.

Campbell, John. *The Naval History of Great Britain . . . including the History and Lives of the British Admirals.* Vol. 4. London, 1818.

Carswell, John. *The South Sea Bubble.* London: The Cresset Press, 1961.

Chapin, Anna Alice. *Greenwich Village.* New York: Dodd, Mead and Company, 1917.

Charnock, John. *Biographia Navalis; or, Impartial memoirs of the lives and characters of officers of the navy of Great Britain, from the year 1660 to the present time . . . With portraits and other engravings, by Bartolozzi, &c.* 6 vols. London: R. Faulder, 1794–98.

Clarke, James Stanier, et al., eds. *The Naval Chronicle. (Containing a general and biographical history of the Royal Navy of the United Kingdom; with a variety of original papers on nautical subjects).* 2nd edition. 40 vols. London, 1799–1818, vol. 4, 516–24.

Clowes, Sir William Laird. *The Royal Navy: A History from the Earliest Times to the Present.* 7 vols. London: Sampson, Low, Marston, and Co., 1897.

Cobbett, William, ed. *The Parliamentary History of England from the Earliest Period to the Year 1803 . . . .* London: Longmans & Company, 1806–12.

Cogan, Anthony. *The Diocese of Meath, Ancient and Modern.* 3 vols. Dublin: Fowler, 1862–70.

Creswell, John. *Britain's Admirals of the Eighteenth Century.* London: Allen and Unwin, 1972.

Crewe, Duncan. *Yellow Jack and the Worm. British Naval Administration in the West Indies, 1739–1748.* Liverpool: University of Liverpool Press, 1993.

Crick, B. R., and Miriam Almon. *Guide to Manuscripts Relating to America in Great Britain and Ireland.* London: Oxford University Press, 1961.

Crowley T. A., and Bernard Pothier. "Louis Du Pont Duchambon, 1679–1775." *Dictionary of Canadian Biography* IV. Toronto: University of Toronto Press, 1979, 246–49.

Cundall, Frank. *The Governors of Jamaica in the First Half of the Eighteenth Century.* London: The West India Committee, 1937.

Davis, Andrew McFarland. *Currency and Banking in the Province of the Massachusetts Bay.* 2 vols. New York: Kelley, reprint edition, 1970.

Dickason, Olive P. "La guerre navale: des Micmacs contre les Britanniques, 1713–1763." Ed. Charles Martijn. *Les Micmacs et la mer.* Montréal: Recherches amérindiennes au Québec, 1986.

Dix, Morgan. *A History of the Parish of Trinity Church in the City of New York.* New York: Putnam, 1898.

Douglas, W. A. B. "Joshua Loring, 1716–81." *Dictionary of Canadian Biography* IV. Toronto: University of Toronto Press, 1979, 486–88.

———. "Philip Durell, 1707–66." *Dictionary of Canadian Biography* III. Toronto: University of Toronto Press, 1974, 208–10.

———. "John Rous, d. 1760." *Dictionary of Canadian Biography* III. Toronto: University of Toronto Press, 1974, 572–73.

———. "Nova Scotia and the Royal Navy, 1713–1766." Ph.D. thesis. Queen's University, 1973.

Fairchild, Byron. *Messrs. William Pepperrell. Merchants at Piscataqua.* Ithaca: Cornell University Press, 1954.

————. "Sir William Pepperrell, 1696–1759." *Dictionary of Canadian Biography* III. Toronto: University of Toronto Press, 1974, 505–9.

Fisher, J. Lawrence. "The Expeditionary Force Designed for the West Indies in 1740." Masters thesis. University of Ottawa, 1970.

Flemming, David B. *The Canso Islands: An 18th Century Fishing Station.* Ottawa: National Historical Sites Service. Manuscript Report 308, 1977.

Foote, Henry Wilder. *Annals of King's Chapel from the Puritan Age of New England to the Present Day.* 3 vols. Boston: Little, Brown and Company, 1896–1900.

Fox, Edith. *Land Speculation in the Mohawk Country.* Ithaca: Cornell University Press, 1949.

Gardiner, Robert. *The First Frigates. Nine-pounder and Twelve-pounder Frigates, 1748–1815.* London: Conway, 1992.

Gow, John M. *Cape Breton Illustrated. Historic, Picturesque, and Descriptive.* Toronto: Briggs, 1893.

Graham, Gerald S., ed. *The Walker Expedition to Quebec, 1711.* Vol. 94. London: Navy Records Society, 1953.

Greer, Allan. "Mutiny at Louisbourg, December 1744." *Histoire sociale-Social History* 10 (1977): 305–36.

Gwyn, Julian. *The Enterprising Admiral. The Personal Fortune of Admiral Sir Peter Warren.* Montréal: McGill-Queen's University Press, 1974.

————. "Financial Revolution in Massachusetts. Public Credit and Taxation, 1692–1774." *Histoire sociale-Social History* 17 (1984): 59–77.

————. "An Incident on West Africa's Grain Coast, 1722." *Mariner's Mirror* 56 (1970): 315–25.

————"The Royal Navy in North America, 1712–1776." Jeremy Black and Philip Woodfine, eds. *British Navy and the Use of Naval Power in the Eighteenth Century.* Leicester: Leicester University Press, 1988, 129–47.

————. "Shipbuilding for the Royal Navy in Colonial New England." *The American Neptune* 48 (Winter 1988): 22–30.

————. "William Johnson, c. 1717–74." *Dictionary of Canadian Biography* IV. Toronto: University of Toronto Press, 1979, 394–98.

Harding, Richard. *Amphibious Warfare in the Eighteenth Century: The British Expedition to the West Indies, 1740–1742.* Woodbridge: Royal Historical Society, 1991.

Hartmann, Cyril Hughes. *The Angry Admiral: The Later Career of Edward Vernon, Admiral of the White.* London: Heinemann, 1953.

Henretta, James A. *"Salutary Neglect": Colonial Administration under the Duke of Newcastle.* Princeton, N.J.: Princeton University Press, 1972.

Janvier, Thomas A. *In Old New York.* New York: Janvier, 1894.

Katz, Stanley Nider. *Newcastle's New York. Anglo-American Politics, 1732–1753.* Cambridge: Harvard University Press, 1968.

Lavery, Brian. *The Arming and Fitting of English Ships of War 1600–1815.* London: Conway Maritime Press, 1987.

Laughton. J. K. "Vice-Admiral Sir Peter Warren." *Dictionary of National Biography*. 63 vols. London: Oxford University Press, 1921–22, vol. 59, 876–77.

Lawrence, A. W. *Trade Castles and Forts of West Africa*. London: Jonathan Cape, 1963.

Le Fevre, Peter, and Richard Harding, eds. *Precursors of Nelson. British Admirals of the Eighteenth Century*. London: Chatham Press, 2000.

Lewis, Michael Arthur. *The Navy in Transition, a Social History, 1814–1864*. London: Hodder and Stoughton, 1965.

———. *A Social History of the Navy, 1793–1815*. London: Allen and Unwin, 1960.

Lewis, W. S., ed. *Horace Walpole's Correspondence*. New Haven: Yale University Press, 1960.

Lydon, James G. "The Great Capture of 1744." *The New-York Historical Society Quarterly* 53 (1968): 255–69.

Malone, Joseph J. *Pine Trees and Politics. The Naval Stores and Forest Policy in Colonial New England 1691–1775*. Seattle: University of Washington Press, 1964.

MacKay, Ruddock F. *Admiral Hawke*. Oxford: Clarendon Press, 1965.

May, W. E. "The Wreck of the Loo." *Mariner's Mirror* 47 (1961): 139–42.

———. "The Wreck of the Weymouth." *Mariner's Mirror* 48 (1962): 207–15.

McCallum, James Dow. *Eleazar Wheelock. Founder of Dartmouth College*. Hanover: Dartmouth College Press, 1939.

McLennan, J. S. *Louisbourg from its Foundation to its Fall*. London: Macmillan, 1918.

Moody, Barry M. "A Just and Disinterested Man: The Nova Scotia Career of Paul Mascarene, 1710–1752." Ph.D. thesis. Queen's University, 1976.

Namier, Lewis B., and John Brooke, eds. *The History of Parliament: The House of Commons, 1754–1790*. 3 vols. London: HMSO, 1964.

Owen, John B. *The Rise of the Pelhams*. London: Methuen, 1957.

Parsons, Usher. *The Life of Sir William Pepperrell, Bart*. Boston: Little, Brown, 1855.

Pool, Bernard. *Navy Board Contracts 1660–1832: Contract Administration under the Navy Board*. London: Longmans, Green, 1966.

Pothier, Bernard. "François-Nicolas de Chassin de Thierry, d. 1755." *Dictionary of Canadian Biography* III. Toronto: University of Toronto Press, 1974, 115–16.

Pritchard, James. *Anatomy of a Naval Disaster. The 1746 French Expedition to North America*. Montréal: McGill-Queen's University Press, 1995.

Rawlyk, George A. *Yankees at Louisbourg*. Orono: University of Maine Press, 1967.

Richmond, Sir Herbert W. *The Navy in the War of 1739–1748*. 3 vols. Cambridge: Cambridge University Press, 1920.

Rogers, L. Harding. "Vice-Admiral Peter Warren, 1703–52." *Dictionary of American Biography*. 22 vols. New York: Scribner's Sons, 1927–58, vol. 19, 485–87.

The Romance of English Harbour. Antigua: Friends of English Harbour, 1954.

Sampson, William R. "Peter Warren Dease, 1788–1863." *Dictionary of Canadian Biography* IX. Toronto: University of Toronto Press, 1976, 196–99.

Sedgwick, Romney, ed. *The History of Parliament: The House of Commons 1715–1754.* 2 vols. London: HMSO, 1970.

Simms, J. G., ed. "Irish Jacobite Lists from Trinity College Dublin MS, N.1.3." *Analecta Hibernica* 22 (1960): 104.

Sosin, Jack M. "Louisbourg and the Peace of Aix-la-Chapelle, 1748." *William and Mary Quarterly* 14 (1957): 516–35.

Sutherland, Maxwell. "Paul Mascarene, c. 1684–1760." *Dictionary of Canadian Biography* III. Toronto: University of Toronto Press, 1974, 435–40.

Taillemite, Etienne. "Constantin-Louis d'Estourmel, 1691–1765." *Dictionary of Canadian Biography* III. Toronto: University of Toronto Press, 1974, 213–14.

———. "Jacques-Pierre de Taffanel de la Jonquière. Marquis de la Jonquière, 1685–1752." *Dictionary of Canadian Biography* III. Toronto: University of Toronto Press, 1974, 609–12.

Thomas, David A. *Battles and Honours of the Royal Navy.* Barnsley, U.K.: Lee Cooper, 1998.

Thompson, Edgar K. "George Anson in the Province of South Carolina." *Mariner's Mirror* 53 (1967): 279–80.

Trafton, Burton W. F. "Louisbourg and the Pepperrell Silver." *Antiques* 89 (March 1966): 366–67.

Tully, Alan. *Forming American Politics. Ideals, Interests, and Institutions in Colonial New York and Pennsylvania.* Baltimore, Md.: Johns Hopkins University Press, 1994.

Varga, Nicholas. "Robert Charles: New York Agent, 1748–1770." *William and Mary Quarterly* 19 (1961): 211–35.

Warren, Rev. Thomas. *A History and Genealogy of the Warren Family in Normandy, Great Britain and Ireland, France, Holland, Tuscany, United States of America, etc. (A.D. 912–1902): with numerous pedigrees.* London: R. Clay and Sons, Ltd., 1902.

Williams, Basil. *The Whig Supremacy, 1714–1760.* 2nd edition, revised by C. H. Stuart. Oxford: Clarendon Press, 1962.

Wilson, Kathleen. "Empire, Trade, and Popular Politics in Mid-Hanoverian Britain: The Case of Admiral Vernon." *Past and Present* 121 (November 1988): 74–109.

Wood, Peter. *Black Majority: Negroes in Colonial South Carolina from 1670 through the Stono Rebellion.* New York: Knopf, 1974.

Woodfine, Philip. *Britannia's Glories: The Walpole Ministry and the 1739 War with Spain.* Woodbridge, U.K.: Boydell Press, 1998.

Index

48, 171; as Louisbourg governor, 111–12, 114, 122, 127, 150, 190n.44; and ship-building, 157–58, 201n.48

La Guaira, 48
La Have (Bridgewater), 28
Lake Champlain, 117, 118
Lake Ontario, 127
La Maisonfort du Boisdecourt, Alexandre de la Maisonfort, Marquis de, 87, 92, 187n.49, 188n.74
La Rochelle, 100, 129, 137, 148
lash, 42
Law, Jonathan, 131
Lawes, Nicholas, 9
Laws, William, 31, 34
Lee, Fitzroy Henry, 153
Leeward Islands, 10, 16, 43, 46, 56, 167; squadron, 46–47, 48–51, 55–63, 159
Le Havre, 50, 134
Leicester House, 155–56
Le Prévost, Jean-Baptiste-Louis Duquesnel, 53, 79, 80
Lestock, Richard, 119, 121, 122, 170
Levant Company, 20, 157
Leveson Gower, Granville, 151, 153, 199n.7
Lighthouse battery, 91
Lisbon, 5, 24, 135, 144, 145, 146, 198nn.130, 132
Lisle, William, 49, 61
London, 16, 58, 88, 98, 139, 151, 162, 165, 178n.55
L'Orient, 135, 136
Loring, Joshua, 88
Louisbourg, 52, 55, 126, 127, 165, 169, 173, 190n.44; British garrison, 100–101, 107–8, 114; careening yard, 110; fortress, 41, 78–79, 149; as free port, 99, 111; French garrison, 79–80, 185n.13; harbor, 27; recapture planned, 119–21; reconstruction project, xi, xiii; siege of, xi, xii, xiii, 60–61, 75–99; surrender demanded, 82; trade with New England, 28; Vice Admiralty Court, 111. See also Grand battery; Island battery; Lighthouse battery; militia

Macdonald, James, 88, 89, 90–91, 96
Madeira, 7, 24, 135, 148
Manhattan Island, xiii, 8, 162
Marblehead, 27, 76, 121
marines, 80, 82, 88, 96, 109, 134; from New York, 48
Martin, William, 93, 118–19, 120, 163
Martinique, 47, 50, 55–56, 58, 134, 145, 146, 147, 183n.66
Maryland, 172
Mascarene, Paul, 53, 121, 122
Massachusetts, 26, 60, 122, 131, 156, 157; agent for, 127; aids Annapolis Royal, 53; gifts to, 163; and Louisbourg, 76. See also Boston
mastships, 41, 42, 102
Mathew, William, 50
Mathews, Thomas, 50, 141, 170, 204n.14
Maurepas, Comte de. See Phélypeaux, Jean-Frédéric
Mayne, Perry, 190n.25
Meath, County, 1, 162
Mi'kmaq, 27, 54, 109, 114, 121, 122, 179n.21; as French allies, 53; at siege of Louisbourg, 84, 89, 92, 95
militia, 78, 81, 83
Minorca, 49
missionaries, French, 95
Mississippi River, 127
Mitchell, Cornelius, 140
Mohawk tribe, 26, 54, 118, 164
Mohawk valley, xiii, 25, 29, 41, 162, 168; war frontier, 53, 114, 118
Molasses Act, 51
Montagu, John, Earl of Sandwich, 42, 105, 107, 122, 131, 135, 150–51, 153–55, 158, 165, 169, 171
Montagu, Hon. William, 42, 87, 92, 98, 105, 131, 135, 152, 158–59, 165, 187n.48, 201n.56
Montgomery, John, 22, 24
Montréal, 117, 126
Montserrat, 60, 184n.84
Morris, Lewis, Jr., 51
Morris, Lewis, Sr., 24–25, 105, 122
Mostyn, Savage, 138, 146, 155
mutiny, 79–80, 107

Julian Gwyn, emeritus professor of history at the University of Ottawa, Canada, is the author of *The Enterprising Admiral: The Personal Fortune of Admiral Sir Peter Warren*. His most recent book, *Excessive Expectations: Maritime Commerce and the Economic Development of Nova Scotia, 1740–1870*, received the Canadian Historical Association's 1999 Clio Award.